MEDICAL PROGRESS AND THE LAW

MEDICAL PROGRESS
AND THE LAW

CLARK C. HAVIGHURST
Editor

OCEANA PUBLICATIONS, INC.
Dobbs Ferry, New York
1969

© Copyright 1967, 1968, 1969 by Duke University

Library of Congress Catalog Card Number 69-19794

Oceana Book No. 10-10

Originally published Autumn 1967

by

LAW AND CONTEMPORARY PROBLEMS

DUKE UNIVERSITY SCHOOL OF LAW

PRINTED IN THE UNITED STATES OF AMERICA

Titles Published in
The Library of Law and Contemporary Problems

POPULATION CONTROL, The Imminent World Crisis
MELVIN G. SHIMM, *Editor*

EUROPEAN REGIONAL COMMUNITIES,
A New Era on the Old Continent
MELVIN G. SHIMM, *Editor*

AFRICAN LAW, New Law for New Nations
HANS W. BAADE, *Editor*

ACADEMIC FREEDOM, The Scholar's Place
in Modern Society
HANS W. BAADE, *Editor*

THE SOVIET IMPACT ON INTERNATIONAL LAW
HANS W. BAADE, *Editor*

URBAN PROBLEMS AND PROSPECTS
ROBINSON O. EVERETT and RICHARD H. LEACH, *Editors*

ANTIPOVERTY PROGRAMS
ROBINSON O. EVERETT, *Editor*

INTERNATIONAL CONTROL OF PROPAGANDA
CLARK C. HAVIGHURST, *Editor*

HOUSING
ROBINSON O. EVERETT and JOHN D. JOHNSTON, JR., *Editors*

MEDICAL PROGRESS AND THE LAW
CLARK C. HAVIGHURST, *Editor*

THE MIDDLE EAST CRISIS: TEST OF INTERNATIONAL LAW
JOHN W. HALDERMAN, *Editor*

CONTENTS

FOREWORD 1
   Clark C. Havighurst

THE ROLE OF LAW IN MEDICAL PROGRESS 3
   E. Blythe Stason

ORGAN TRANSPLANTATION IN MEDICAL AND
   LEGAL PERSPECTIVES 37
   Delford L. Stickel

HUMAN EXPERIMENTATION: ETHICS IN THE
   CONSENT SITUATION 60
   John Fletcher

REGULATION OF PRESCRIPTION DRUG ADVERTISING:
   MEDICAL PROGRESS AND PRIVATE ENTERPRISE 90
   Richard B. Ruge

LEGAL ASPECTS OF COMPUTER USE IN MEDICINE 114
   Roy N. Freed

THE CHANGING STRUCTURE OF MEDICAL PRACTICE 147
   David Mechanic

INNOVATIONS AND EXPERIMENTS IN USES OF HEALTH
   MANPOWER — THE EFFECT OF LICENSURE LAWS 171
   Edward H. Forgotson and John L. Cook

FOREWORD

Medical progress proceeds in a constant flow from clinical investigation to implementation of new techniques in medical practice. At every stage of this continuous process the law seeks to guide, stimulate, or restrain the efforts of the medical profession, and in this way medical science is made more particularly responsive to society's needs and values. This symposium first reviews some of the ways in which the law bears on each stage in the flow of medical progress and then seeks to show how law and modern medicine confront social as well as scientific frontiers. The following introductory paragraphs may help to establish a framework for appraising the law's role in helping to deliver to the public the benefits of modern science.

The critical legal influences at the investigational stage in the flow of medical progress include, of course, all of the governmental policies and mechanisms that provide and direct the application of funds for medical research. The experimentation process itself is more directly affected, however, by legal rules and professional codes governing the conduct of experiments in which human subjects are employed, a step essential in perfecting practically any means of medical treatment; Professor Fletcher and Dean Stason explore these matters in their articles herein. Dr. Stickel's article on organ transplants illustrates how experimentation often cannot be separated from medical practice and calls appropriate attention in passing to what the author senses may be a failure of the law fully to respect medicine's investigative function.

Introducing new developments into medical practice presents a number of special problems for the law, which must seek to guard patients against dangerous methods not yet generally accepted without unduly inhibiting the introduction of valuable new techniques. Direct regulation accomplishes the necessary balancing in the area of prescription drugs, permitting their interstate sale only after efficacy and relative safety are established. On the other hand, in areas not subject to direct regulation, legal standards of care developed in malpractice cases are sometimes alleged to impede implementation of medical progress by deterring departures from current practices; this is said to result from the law's practice of comparing the physician's actions with the custom and practice of his peers in the community. While one may doubt that fear of malpractice claims often causes a doctor to resist employing a new procedure or drug in which he has well-founded confidence, it is probably true that doctors do not at present feel impelled by legal considerations to discover and evaluate the newest developments and to adopt the treatment that is best in light of the very latest learning. Of course, malpractice law would be an unwieldy device for assuring that medical breakthroughs are promptly implemented. Compulsory postgraduate education or periodic testing would perhaps be a more fitting response to a need that can only become greater as progress continues.

Several other articles herein deal with specific problems of implementing progress in health care. Mr. Freed's piece speculates on the possible confrontations between established legal doctrines and the computer as it is being adapted for uses in medicine, and Mr. Ruge deals with the special problem of how advertising of drug products can be and is being made to perform an educational rather than a purely promotional function. In both of these areas, problems of dealing with the private-industry adjuncts of the health care professions are considered. Finally, in Dean Stason's and Dr. Stickel's reviews of the legal problems involved in securing human organs for transplantation and other purposes, we have another useful case study of the law's need to accommodate itself to particular medical breakthroughs.

Once newly developed techniques have become routine in medical practice, the problems encountered would seem to fall outside the compass we have set for the symposium. Yet the perennial legal requirement of obtaining the patient's "informed" consent to treatment, delineated in up-to-date form by Dean Stason, seems to become more and more complex as medical advances accumulate: the more the doctor knows or should know the more he will almost necessarily be required to tell the patient, thereby heightening the doctor's problems of patient management and the demands on his time and powers of exposition. Likewise, however, the patient's ultimate dependence on the physician must also increase with added complexity, and, as this dependency is recognized, the consent required by law may come to be valued more as a ritual in recognition of the patient's humanity than because of any real enhancement of his control of his own fate. If, as Professor Fletcher's article suggests in a related context, the ritualistic element is indeed paramount in the consent situation, courts would be warranted in evaluating the doctor's method of obtaining consent solely on the basis of whether, under all the circumstances, he accorded the patient his full due as a human being (unless, as may sometimes be the case, what is really being tested is the physician's *own* awareness of the risks). Interestingly, Professor Fletcher's ethical point, introduced in this context, may link up with Professor Mechanic's discussion of the doctor's "sustaining" role and with the impression of many doctors that "bedside manner" is the most important factor in avoiding malpractice claims.

In the symposium's final two articles we have important appraisals of the structure of medical practice in the light of higher costs and a public commitment to wider availability of health care. Professor Mechanic surveys the inevitable trend toward increasing incidence of bureaucracy as an organizing and depersonalizing force in medical practice, and Dr. Forgotson reviews the anachronisms in occupational licensure laws governing the health professions. These articles convey a useful view of the institutional environment in which quality health care will be extended to the disadvantaged persons in American society, and, together with Dean Stason's discussions of gifts of human tissues and abortion laws, they highlight some of the larger questions about how the law and legislatures should govern the medical profession.

CLARK C. HAVIGHURST.

THE ROLE OF LAW IN MEDICAL PROGRESS

E. BLYTHE STASON*

Medical science expands at an ever accelerating rate. Kidney transplants are now almost commonplace; over 1000 of them have been performed in the last dozen years. Liver and heart transplants are making current headlines; the lung may be next. Radioisotopes are used for both diagnosis and therapy. The mechanism of human heredity is increasingly an open book. Cardiac catheterization is everyday business, and management of malignancy is constantly on the upgrade. Medical research has opened these and other new vistas, and better things are doubtless just around the corner. Modern medicine is indeed frontier business.

At the same time legal science—or should it be called an "art"?—is also constantly encountering new frontiers created by the continuing scientific and technological revolution. Nuclear substances are giving rise to new legal problems. Supersonic transports will soon carry us from New York to Tel Aviv in three hours, and their sonic booms are certain to have impact on the law. Electronic devices are leaving us with diminishing privacy and ultimately may penetrate the inmost thoughts of man. Modern medicine gives birth to new legal problems. The law and lawyers will be forced to play a significant role as the new order continues to unfold.

In this article we propose to examine one of these frontiers—medicine and law—to attempt an evaluation of the possibilities of law-medicine cooperation in finding helpful solutions for the future. Such interprofessional cooperation, while seemingly an obvious prerequisite of progress, cannot be taken for granted, for much disharmony and mutual mistrust exists between the professions. Medical malpractice suits in courts of law, the agonies of the expert medical witness on the stand, the federal restrictions on the use of investigational drugs, and various other encounters with the law have created in the minds of many doctors an image of law and lawyers that is far from complimentary. On the other hand, members of the legal profession are well aware of some of the medical profession's less appealing aspects—for example, some doctors' violent antipathy to "Medicare" and the problem sometimes characterized as the "conspiracy of silence" which makes it so difficult to get professional expert testimony in a malpractice suit against a defendant doctor. As a consequence of these and other abrasive contacts between the two professions, and notwithstanding the many thousands of fine personal friendships and much

---

* A.B. 1913, University of Wisconsin; B.S. 1916, Massachusetts Institute of Technology; J.D. 1922, University of Michigan. Professor of Law, Vanderbilt University. Dean Emeritus and Professor Emeritus, University of Michigan Law School.

The author acknowledges with appreciation the assistance of the editors, who have added to this article, written in the late summer 1967, the many more recent decisions and other developments in the fast moving field of medico-legal relations.

mutual admiration, there is found in each profession an unfortunately high degree of disrespect for the other calling, which seriously handicaps the necessary processes whereby the law impinges on medical practice.[1]

In the course of a recent lecture, Dr. Charles G. Child III, Professor of Surgery and Chairman of the Department of Surgery in the Medical School of the University of Michigan, approached this problem of professional dichotomy with candor and perspicacity.[2] After psychoanalyzing the two professions and identifying their differences, Dr. Child pointed out basic disparities in the personality and education of members of the two professions. Then he observed:

> In my opinion, the adversary method of administering justice may very well be the single most important deterrent to cooperation between law and medicine in the conduct of malpractice actions. This procedure is so ill-suited to any reasonable medical ends that its use engenders not only hostility but also reflects as well a conscious withdrawal amongst the medical profession. Few indeed have been the important issues in medicine that have been resolved by controversy and dispute.[3]

Dr. Child further contrasted medicine, with its scientific method and objective inquiry into facts, and the law, with its Socratic method which etches clearly things supposed to be derived from the past by rational beings. The thought processes of the two professions, he said, are so different that they do not readily merge in attack upon specific problems. Finally, Dr. Child noted that the slow pace and the delays in legal proceedings keep the doctor, whether a party or a witness, away from his patients and that even life itself may be adversely affected. In short, Dr. Child offers much food for thought for one seeking to explore "the role of law in medical progress," as we are doing in this article.

Notwithstanding the difficulties that Dr. Child suggests, we now proceed to look more closely at the various facets of the law-medicine relationship. Law and medicine meet in many areas. The role of law will, we safely predict, be one of increasing significance in the future of medicine.

I

POSSIBLE AREAS OF CONTACT BETWEEN LAW AND MEDICINE
OF THE FUTURE

To approach our task of considering the role of law in the medical future we will help orient ourselves by first surveying the larger scene. This will give an

---

[1] The American Medical Association has taken a constructive interest in medical professional liability. Since 1954 the Law Department of the Association has made a continuing study of the subject. In 1957 a series of twenty-one articles was published in the *Journal of the American Medical Association*, dealing with nearly all aspects of the matter. A bi-weekly publication, *The Citation*, is currently issued by the Law Department. Now in its fourteenth volume, this publication acquaints the medical profession with the many pitfalls of the law.

[2] Child, *Lawyers, Doctors and Medical Malpractice: A Surgeon Reacts*, in MEDICAL MALPRACTICE 43 (Institute of Continuing Legal Education, Ann Arbor, Mich., 1965).

[3] *Id.* at 47.

impression of the wide dimensions of the matter before we get down to the task of more careful examination of the role of law in dealing with a few subjects we have chosen for closer inspection.

Areas of interaction between law and medicine in the future will include at least the areas delineated in the fourteen ensuing paragraphs:

(1) *Psychiatry and the law.* The understanding of psychiatrists concerning mental illness and its treatment do not mesh satisfactorily with the rather more primitive precepts of the criminal law. The debate goes on not only over the various possible definitions of criminal responsibility, but also over the procedures whereby mental incompetents are committed for treatment and the sufficiency of the treatment given such persons to justify deprivation of their liberty in the absence of due process of law. The future holds the potential for unlimited development in this field as psychiatric techniques improve, as more funds are channeled into this needy area, and as law adapts its rather clumsy institutions to the subtle problems of coping with mental illness in an increasingly anxiety-inducing society.

(2) *Alcoholism.* Alcoholism has been called the nation's fourth most serious health problem, affecting some 6,000,000 persons, many of whom are potentially highly productive but are handicapped by compulsive drinking. Courts are beginning to hold that chronic alcoholism is not a crime but a disease.[4] Doctors must participate in working out changes in the laws and in setting up centers for the treatment of alcoholism.[5]

(3) *Narcotics offenders.* A "pusher" is a criminal; a user of narcotics may not be a criminal but a person needing medical aid whom the medical profession should be free to treat.[6] The law and medicine must cooperate to provide the opportunity and the means for effective treatment.[7]

(4) *Population control.* This is a controversial matter. The Supreme Court has provided protection from legislative intrusion for families wishing to practice birth control.[8] The more difficult and pressing problem is how the population explosion is to be kept within bounds. Family planning and birth control advice and equipment are a small step, it would seem, though religious pressures still inhibit full efforts in these areas. Economic disincentives to reproduce may be utilized in the future as well.

---

[4] *Compare* Driver v. Hinnant, 356 F.2d 761 (4th Cir. 1966) and Easter v. District of Columbia, 361 F.2d 50 (D.C. Cir. 1966) *with* Application of Spinks, 61 Cal. Rptr. 745 (Ct. App. 1967).

[5] *See generally* Kupferman, *Treatment of Alcoholism Must Change With Times*, TRIAL, Aug.-Sept. 1966, at 49-50.

[6] A statute punishing the "status" of drug addiction is cruel and unusual punishment in violation of the eighth and fourteenth amendments. Robinson v. California, 370 U.S. 660 (1962). California courts have found involuntary commitment imposed on the addict for purposes of treatment, as opposed to punishment, to not constitute cruel and unusual punishment. *In re* Trummer, 60 Cal. 2d 658, 381 P.2d 177, 36 Cal. Rptr. 281 (1964).

[7] *See generally* W. ELDRIDGE, NARCOTICS AND THE LAW 118-25 (1962).

[8] Griswold v. Connecticut, 381 U.S. 479 (1965).

(5) *Genetics.* A gradual movement toward premarital genetic testing and counselling may be expected as a means of minimizing birth defects and other hereditary maladies. Presumably the day is much farther off when law will attempt in any direct way to control the eugenic development of the population.

(6) *Artificial insemination.* Changes in the law will be necessary to assure legitimacy of births resulting from such procedures. Also, damage suit possibilities are present in the absence of informed consent, as well as in instances of breach of secrecy. Finally there are innumerable questions raised concerning relations in the family, such as grounds for divorce, child support, and inheritance rights.[9]

(7) *"Medicare."* This was one of the most controversial pieces of legislation of the decade because of the alleged trend toward "socialized" medicine, but seemingly the bureaucratic machinery is in fair working order today and is increasingly approved by laymen and by doctors. The influence of this law on the practice of medicine and quality of medical care is as yet incalculable. The guidance of the new administrative influences in the right directions is one of the paramount challenges in medical-legal affairs today.

(8) *"Medicaid."* This is the important extension of Medicare to low-income families under Title XIX of the Social Security Amendments of 1965.[10] It has disturbed many doctors and the budget makers in many states, but it is likely to be with us for a long time and to influence greatly the over-all quality of medical care provided in this country, where, incidentally, high infant mortality among the poor is a national disgrace.

(9) *"Good Samaritan" laws.* These are widely sought by the medical profession and are already on the books in thirty-two states. They limit malpractice actions against physicians who offer to help injured persons under emergency conditions, especially on the highways. Carefully collected statistics indicate that seldom does a good Samaritan action succeed and that there is not too much for doctors to fear.[11] But apprehension persists, and legal protection may be justified to prevent needed assistance from being withheld. The argument for legislation might be even stronger if the law were construed to create an affirmative duty to render such assistance.

(10) *Computers.* It may happen a decade hence, but someday diagnosis and treatment that does not include retrieval of relevant data from the memory of a computer will be deemed to fall short of the familiar standard, the practice of reputable physicians in the community.[12] Other uses of computers will likewise speed medical progress and improve the quality of medical care.

---

[9] *See generally* Verkauf, *Artificial Insemination: Progress, Polemics, and Confusion—An Appraisal of Current Medico-Legal Status,* 3 HOUSTON L. REV. 277 (1966).

[10] §§ 121-22, 79 Stat. 343 (codified in scattered sections of 42 U.S.C.).

[11] Plant, *"Good Samaritan" Laws in Legal Dilemma,* TRIAL, Oct.-Nov. 1966, at 34.

[12] *See generally* McGraw & McGraw, *Automating Medicine,* SATURDAY REVIEW, Oct. 7, 1967, at 66-69. *See also* Freed, *Legal Aspects of Computer Use in Medicine,* in this symposium, p. 674.

(11) *Homotransplantation*. The process of removing a part from one human body and implanting it in another is among the most dramatic of medical feats. Blood, skin, bone, and kidneys have been transferred from one living person to another, and corneas, kidneys, the liver, and, most dramatically, the heart have been salvaged from the dead. The legal questions are many.

(12) *Abortion*. Most abortion laws date from the nineteenth century. They contain prohibitions that conflict with the twentieth century's demands and with the judgment of most members of the medical profession.

(13) *Patient consent to therapy*. Informed consent is a new facet of malpractice and assault and battery now emerging in legal actions to add to the medical profession's exasperation with the law.

(14) *Subject consent to human experimentation*. The vast increase of medical research is assuredly for the benefit of mankind, but the necessarily increasing use of human research subjects is creating special problems with respect to which improved cooperation and understanding between law and medicine are clearly needed.

In the remainder of this article we shall direct more detailed attention to only the last four of the topics named, namely homotransplantation, abortion, patient consent to therapy, and subject consent to experimentation. From these we will try to draw some conclusions concerning the role of law in medical progress.

II

TRANSPLANTATION OF HUMAN TISSUES[13]

A. Technical Aspects

What will be the role of law in homotransplantations? Human bodies and human tissues are used in many aspects of medical science, and the use increases year by year, especially as knowledge advances with respect to immunology and rejection of foreign tissues. Human bodies and parts thereof are used in teaching, research, and transplantation. Whole bodies or their parts are dissected in teaching and research laboratories. Transplantation of parts under existing surgical procedures frequently involves skin, bone, blood, corneas, arteries, kidneys, and in recent months even the human heart. The pituitary glands are removed to recover hormones for medical uses. Even the liver has been transplanted, and in the future the lung and other vital parts may be subject to transfer from one body to another. Both living and nonliving donors are used.

These procedures are becoming increasingly numerous and important as medical science progresses from year to year. It is reported, for example, that there have been over 1000 kidney transplants performed in the world in the last thirteen years, with seventy-five per cent of them in the last five years. Transplants from living

---

[13] For a wider ranging treatment of legal and medical issues involved in organ transplants, see Stickel, *Organ Transplantation in Medical and Legal Perspectives*, in this symposium, p. 597.

relatives have been sixty-five to seventy per cent successful. Cadaver transplants have been about forty per cent successful.[14] Unfortunately there is a shortage of available kidneys. It is said that renal transplants may, in due course, if sufficient supply becomes available, save from 6,000 to 10,000 lives per year in the United States alone.

The potential supply of transplantable parts would actually exceed the demand if full utilization could be made of nonliving donors, but there are problems to be solved. There is the matter of logistics, which is indeed formidable. With a living donor in the next room, there is no great problem, but with a nonliving donor, time is of the essence. For a few minutes after death cellular metabolism continues throughout the majority of the body cell mass. Certain tissues are suitable for removal only during this brief interval, although improvements in storage and preservation may permit a short delay in actual implantation in the recipient. Cadaver tissues are divided into two groups according to the speed with which they must be salvaged. First, there are "critical" tissues, such as the kidney and liver, which must be removed from the deceased within a matter of thirty to forty-five minutes after death.[15] On the other hand, certain "noncritical" tissues may be removed more at leisure. Skin may be removed within twelve hours from time of death. The cornea may be taken at any time within six hours. The fact is, however, that in all cases action must be taken promptly to make use in a living recipient of the parts of a nonliving donor, and this gives rise to legal problems. There is but little time to negotiate with surviving relatives, and waiting for the probate of the will is out of the question.

B. Legal Aspects

As previously noted, transplantation may take place either from one living person to another living person or from a dead person to the living. In the former case, all that is required is the appropriate written and witnessed "informed consent," which will be discussed later in this article, authorizing the surgical removal from the donor and the implantation in the recipient. If utilization of all or any part of the body after death is intended, the matter becomes more complicated both in fact and in law.

The complications arise from the variety of interests in the dead body. The deceased naturally had an interest in his body during his lifetime, and any expression of his wishes as to its post-mortem disposition may or may not be effective, depending upon the local law. After death, the surviving spouse or, if none, the surviving

---

[14] Murray, Barnes & Atkinson, *Fifth Report of the Human Kidney Transplant Registry*, 5 TRANSPLANTATION 752, 774 (1967).

[15] After removal, the tissues can be preserved for six hours or so when stored at 5°C., and for even longer periods if continuously perfused with a proper blood and salt solution. This and other technical aspects of transplantation are discussed in Couch, Curran & Moore, *The Use of Cadaver Tissues in Transplantation*, 271 NEW ENG. J. MED. 691 (1964).

child or parent or other relative has an interest that must be recognized and dealt with. Primarily this is an emotional interest connected with the dignity of the disposition of the body. Finally, the public has an interest, as, for example, in finding the cause of death by autopsy when suspicious circumstances are involved.[16] Also, the public interest includes having available a sufficient number of bodies and parts of bodies to satisfy the needs of teaching, research, and therapy.[17]

These various interests in the body, some of which conflict with others to a greater or lesser extent, give rise to a number of troublesome points of law. The first revolves around the possession of rights in the dead body. Who possess such rights and what are they? Common law principles, originated in the seventeenth century in the English ecclesiastical courts, announced the concept that there are no "property rights" in the ordinary sense in the dead human body. This principle was carried into the common law courts in the latter part of the seventeenth century.[18] In general, the private rights, such as they are, that exist respecting a dead body involve the assurance of a dignified treatment of the body and a decent burial. The rights belong first to the surviving spouse, then to the children, and finally to the next of kin, in that order, unless the statutes specifically provide otherwise.[19] Moreover, the person who has the right to possession is entitled to receive the body in the same condition as when death occurred, unless this right is modified in some manner as provided by law. He can recover damages from anyone who performs an unauthorized autopsy on the body, or who mutilates it, or dissects it, or removes or keeps parts without his consent.[20] In view of the foregoing it is clear that any interest possessed by the survivors must be reckoned with. Before the surgeon undertakes a transplant, he must, unless the deceased has made a valid ante-mortem gift, negotiate with them to obtain consent. Moreover, time for so doing is limited.

A second legal question of significance in connection with human transplants is whether or not a person during his lifetime can make a legally effective gift of his body or a portion thereof to be carried out after his death, either by giving it to a named donee or to a specified hospital or to any person in need. Will such gift be

---

[16] Statutes in all states provide for autopsies by the coroner or medical examiner, who is given authority to proceed even against the wishes of the relatives.

[17] This interest of the public has been manifested by the adoption of statutes in about 80% of the states providing for the delivery of unclaimed bodies to medical schools for dissection in the teaching of anatomy and physiology and for medical research. There is always an inadequate supply of such bodies, especially at the present time with the generous burial provisions available through public bounty. In any event, since these bodies are usually embalmed and are normally released long after death, they are of no value for organ transplantation purposes.

[18] *See generally* Vestal, Taber & Shoemaker, *Medico-Legal Aspects of Tissue Homotransplantation*, 18 U. DET. L.J. 271, 273 (1954). The authors have set forth an extensively documented statement of the legal background.

[19] Larson v. Chase, 47 Minn. 307, 310, 50 N.W. 238, 239 (1891).

[20] The monetary damages may not be great. $3,000-5,000 seems to be about enough to assuage the usual plaintiff's grief, although some verdicts are larger. *See* Patrick v. Employers Mut. Liab. Ins. Co., 233 Mo. App. 251, 118 S.W.2d 116 (1938); Phillips v. Newport, 28 Tenn. App. 187, 187 S.W.2d 965 (1945). The principal damage often takes the form of injury to the public repute of the defendant surgeon. This can be serious.

a nullity if survivors object, or will it take precedence over the wishes and burial rights of the survivors? According to the common law any such attempted ante-mortem gift could be repudiated by the next of kin, and this is still the law in at least a dozen states.[21] In certain other states there is at least uncertainty with respect to the application of the common law. Therefore it is clear that if transplants are to be facilitated on any reasonably satisfactory and universal basis, there must be specific statutory authorization of such ante-mortem donations, which must prevail over contrary desires of survivors. The doubt must be eliminated, and those who act in good faith in reliance upon an antemortem authorization must be protected.

Because of the desirability of removing all doubt with regard to the effectiveness of ante-mortem consents, upwards of thirty states have in recent years, especially since about 1950, adopted statutes dealing with the subject in some manner, the majority of these laws being to some extent inadequate; several states have adopted statutes authorizing donation of corneas or eyes alone.[22] Because of this lack of uniformity in the statutes, there is a choice of law problem which may arise when the domiciliary of one state dies in another state, having made a gift of his organs in one or the other or even in a third state prior to his death.[23] Few of the statutes cover the details of execution, delivery, and possible revocation of agreements of gift, and some of them fail to include specific exculpatory provisions protecting surgeons, hospitals, and others from embarrassing complications if some of the survivors are dissatisfied.[24]

---

[21] Couch, Curran & Moore, *supra* note 15, at 693.

[22] The Law Revision Commission of New York has recently presented a report to the New York State Legislature recommending a comprehensive statute to replace the present statute which authorizes only gifts of eyes. The report includes an analysis of the laws of all the states. *See* N.Y. LEGIS. DOC. (1964) No. 65D.

[23] If the donor dies outside his state of domicile, a conflict in the choice of state law may arise when the law of the state of death is contrary to the law of the donor's domicile. One example would be where the law of the state of death authorized the donation, and the law of the state of domicile did not. Practically speaking, the question would be whether the next of kin could sue the doctor removing the donated organ contrary to their wishes, and thus effectively prevent the removal in the state of death.

Traditional application of the law of conflicts on testamentary disposition might result in application of the law of the domiciliary state. If, however, the interests served by the respective statutes in this problem are analyzed, the law of the state of death should prevail. Recipients benefited by such donations will reside in that state, and by enacting an authorization statute, the legislature has expressed a concern for their benefit and a desire to encourage progress in medical science. The state of domicile, on the other hand, is concerned with the interests of next of kin and wants to prevent the practice of organ removal by the medical profession through the prospect of a civil action being filed by the next of kin against the physician.

As a practical factor, physicians should not be responsible for compliance with the law of innumerable jurisdictions and for the resolution of conflicts with the law of their own state. A standard which consistently applies the law of the state in which death occurs will enable the doctor to act with the necessary promptness, provided, of course, that the state has enacted the requisite authorization statute.

[24] Gift of human tissue statutes are found on the books of the following states: Alabama, Alaska (eyes only), Arizona, Arkansas, California, Colorado, Connecticut, District of Columbia, Florida, Georgia, Hawaii, Illinois, Indiana, Iowa, Kentucky, Louisiana, Maine (eyes only), Maryland, Massachusetts, Michigan, Minnesota, Mississippi, Missouri, Montana, Nebraska, Nevada, New Jersey (eyes only),

From the foregoing discussion it becomes apparent that the proper shape of a state statute authorizing and effectuating ante-mortem gifts of human tissue should, among other things, make provision for the following:

1. Who may execute a valid ante-mortem gift of his own body or a portion thereof? Many statutes provide that anyone "competent to make a will" may do so.

2. Who among the survivors may make a gift, either post-mortem or just prior to death? The statute should set up the authorized order of priority among survivors.

3. To whom may human tissues be donated? Black-market tissue banks are not to be desired, and therefore potential donees must be carefully identified.

4. What is to be the manner of execution of gifts? Is it to be by will or by some other document? And what are to be the formalities of execution? Provision should be made for a simple form of document, with preference for a small card to be carried on the donor's person evidencing the gift.

5. Gifts should be permitted either to a specific donee or to a specific hospital or, in general terms, to anyone in need for an authorized purpose.

6. Since time is of the essence, probate should be expressly eliminated. If a specific donee is named and is not reasonably available, the attending physician at death or immediately thereafter should be authorized to act in reliance upon the card evidencing the gift. He should act as the agent of the donee with all of the powers of the donee to use the gift for any authorized purpose as he deems best.

7. Revocation of the gift should be permitted in case the donor changes his mind at the last minute.

8. Liability for damages should be negatived in every case of good faith reliance upon a gift without notice of revocation.

The National Conference of Commissioners on Uniform State Laws is currently engaged in drafting a Uniform Anatomical Gift Act that will meet the foregoing specifications. It will, when approved in final form, probably during 1968, be promulgated as a uniform act and recommended for adoption by all of the states. The act is currently being drafted with the cooperation and assistance of many doctors and their organizations as well as the lawyer members of the National Conference. The cooperative review by both professions should assure a satisfactory solution.

The uniform act should meet with ready acceptance by state legislatures, and, when adopted, it will certainly clarify many of the doubtful legal aspects with

---

New Mexico, New York, North Carolina, North Dakota, Oklahoma, Oregon, Pennsylvania, Rhode Island, South Carolina, Tennessee, Texas, Virginia, Washington, West Virginia (eyes only), and Wisconsin. For purposes of comparison the following are interesting: Ontario, Stats. 1962-63, ch. 59; Italy, Presidential Decree of June 26, 1967, [1967] Gaz. Uff. 3478; France, Decree No. 472057 of Oct. 20, 1947; and Regulations of United Kingdom, Human Tissues Act 1961.

respect to transplantation. It will facilitate taking advantage of modern medical and surgical developments for the benefit of those in need of corneas, kidneys, or other spare parts. Finally, the act will illustrate one aspect of the role of law in medical progress: an influential national legal organization will have undertaken to adjust the statutory law of the fifty states to accommodate a significant medical frontier—homotransplantation.[25]

III

ABORTION

A. State Statutes Dealing with Abortion[26]

Abortion is another area of medical concern where the law plays an important role. Most state abortion laws are highly restrictive. They were enacted in the nineteenth century and have been largely unchanged even in those states that have recently enacted new criminal codes. Although the statutory language differs slightly from state to state, the practical effect in most states is that abortion is a felony except when necessary to save the life of the mother. There are many detailed variations in the laws. For example, some states permit only a physician or surgeon to terminate a pregnancy; others permit anyone to do it if under legally justified circumstances. Many statutes purport to require that the abortion be absolutely necessary to save the life of the pregnant woman, while others, such as New York's,[27] are satisfied if the surgeon has a reasonable belief that such a necessity exists; other states, including Massachusetts, New Jersey, and Pennsylvania,[28] simply prohibit performing an abortion in broad terms qualified by language like "unlawfully" or "without lawful justification." Some states require consultation with one or more other physicians before operating. The statutes of Alabama, Maryland, New Mexico, and the District of Columbia[29] legalize abortions if necessary to protect the health, as well as to save the life, of the mother. In short, the statutes in the several states purport to set up an almost nationwide barrier to abortion. However, as in other areas, the law encounters the frailties of human nature, and the intentions of the framers of the statutes are not fulfilled.

---

[25] The first draft of the proposed Uniform Anatomical Gift Act was given a careful review at the 1967 Annual Meeting of the National Conference held in Honolulu, July 30-August 5. After revision, the measure will be reconsidered and possibly adopted at the 1968 Annual Meeting to be held in Philadelphia in August 1968. The Chairman of the National Conference committee who is the principal draftsman of the uniform act is the author of this article.

[26] *See generally* George, *Current Abortion Laws: Proposals and Movements for Reform*, 17 W. RES. L. REV. 371 (1965). In this article Professor George analyzes all of the state statutes in detail and with extensive citations.

[27] N.Y. REVISED PENAL LAW §§ 125.05, .40, .45 (McKinney Supp. 1965).

[28] MASS. GEN. LAWS ANN. ch. 272, § 19 (1956); N.J. STAT. ANN. § 2A:87-1 (1953); PA. STAT. ANN. tit. 18, § 4718 (1963).

[29] ALA. CODE tit. 14, § 9 (1958); MD. ANN. CODE art. 27, § 3 (1957); N.M. STAT. ANN. §§ 40A-5-1, -3 (1953); D.C. CODE ENCYCL. ANN. § 22.201 (1967).

Notwithstanding the generally uncompromising prohibitions of the law, there are estimated to be up to 1,000,000 abortions performed each year in this country,[30] most of them being illegal and carried out under hazardous conditions. There are, of course, no available sources for accurate statistical count. Some say that the total falls substantially short of the number stated though it is obvious that the activity is widespread. It is also frequently claimed that as many as 10,000 deaths occur each year from illegal abortions, although again some say that this figure is probably far too high and that the actual number may be as low as 500. Again accurate statistical information is not available.

It is known, however, that about 10,000 abortions are performed each year in ostensible accordance with the law. These abortions are carried out in hospitals with proper surgical supervision and for more or less proper medical reasons. There is no record of a criminal conviction as a result of an abortion carried out under these conditions even though there are reasons to believe that physicians have not strictly observed the statutory tests of legality.[31]

Professor B. James George, Jr., a codraftsman of the proposed revised criminal code in Michigan, has conducted a comprehensive survey of all of the state statutes on the subject.[32] He takes note of the fact that the present statutory restrictions force many women to turn to unqualified operators with all of the hazards inherent in their procedures. He comments on the over-all effect of the present laws in the following manner:

> To continue the present restrictive laws on abortion is to purchase the illusion of security at considerable human loss. Enforcement of criminal statutes in their present form may accomplish about all the protection possible against untrained abortionists, but with corresponding disadvantages which perhaps more than offset the gains. These disadvantages are the harassment of the medical profession by zealous prosecutors, and the creation of intolerable tension in the doctor who is torn between his desire to perform an abortion, which he believes to be necessary on humanitarian grounds, and his fear of performing it because it is illegal.[33]

The doctor's dilemma noted here is the central factor in the tentative reforms that have been accomplished in recent months.

---

[30] Sands, *The Therapeutic Abortion Act: An Answer to the Opposition*, 13 U.C.L.A.L. Rev. 285 (1966). *But cf. Rewriting the Law on Abortion*, Medical World News, Sept. 29, 1967, at 46, 52.

[31] *See generally* Sands, *supra* note 30; *The Law of Therapeutic Abortion: A Social Commentary on Proposed Reform*, 15 J. Pub. L. 386, 393-95 (1966). For a critical discussion of therapeutic abortions performed for "psychiatric reasons," see White, *Induced Abortions: A Survey of Their Psychiatric Implications, Complications, and Indications*, 24 Tex. Reports of Biology and Medicine 531 (1966). The California Board of Medical Examiners reprimanded one physician and placed a second on professional probation for violations of the state's law, which, even after a recent liberalizing amendment, does not legalize an abortion performed because of probable fetal deformity. N.Y. Times, Feb. 15, 1968, at 32, col. 8.

[32] George, *supra* note 26.

[33] *Id.* at 402.

B. Views of the Medical Profession

The medical profession is divided on abortion, but the great majority of doctors currently favor liberalization of the laws. In February and March of 1967, *Modern Medicine* conducted a survey of the profession in which 40,089 questionnaires were returned. Liberalization was favored by 94.6 per cent of the psychiatrists, by 83.7 per cent of the obstetricians and gynecologists, and by 86.9 per cent of all categories.[34] The Roman Catholic Church has been consistently opposed to liberalization, but 49.1 per cent of the doctors responding who identified themselves as Catholics answered that they were in favor of broadening the grounds for abortion.

All doctors subscribe to the Hippocratic oath, the relevant section of which appears to frown upon tampering with the processes of nature: "I will use treatment to help the sick according to my ability and judgment, but never with a view to injury and wrong doing. . . . I will not give to a woman a pessary to cause abortion. . . ." Notwithstanding the oath and the legal limitations in the statutes, members of the medical profession, who necessarily come into close contact with the tragic side of pregnancy as well as the happy side, are strongly committed to liberalizing the existing restrictions of the law.

C. Philosophical and Legal Views on Abortion

Mention has been made of the opposition of the Roman Catholic Church. It is widely believed that abortion has always been forbidden by the Church, but this is not borne out by history. Down to the reign of Pope Sixtus V (1585-90) termination of pregnancy was permitted within the first eighty days of pregnancy. Sixtus banned all abortions, but was reversed following his death by Pope Gregory XIV, who declared abortion illegal only after the fetus quickens. Not until 1869 did the Church, through Pope Pius IX, revive the strict doctrines of Sixtus, and these doctrines remain in effect to the present day. The Church is currently the most effective opponent of liberalization, though many Protestants take equivalent positions. Curiously, public opinion surveys indicate that lay Catholics and non-Catholics are not far apart in their views on abortion.[35]

As of the present time views concerning liberalization of abortion laws range throughout a wide spectrum. There are at least three widely divergent views, with many minor variations of each. The three views are these:

1. *Abortion is a form of murder.* First, there are those who line up with the Catholic Church and regard any interruption of a pregnancy as a crime, as murder. This position is grounded upon the view that the fetus is a human life from the

---

[34] 29.1% favored abortion for illegitimacy, and 26.6% favored abortion for socioeconomic reasons. *Abortion: The Doctor's Dilemma*, MODERN MEDICINE, April 24, 1967, at 12, 13.

[35] Brody, *Abortion, Once a Whispered Problem, Now a Public Debate*, N.Y. Times, Jan. 8, 1968, at 28, col. 5.

moment of conception and that to destroy it wilfully cannot be justified except when the mother's life is clearly jeopardized.[36]

2. *Abortion should be a matter of free choice.* At the opposite extreme are those who believe that the doctor should be given freedom to act subject only to the usual professional restraints; such a position would, of course, license the would-be mother as well, since she would have no difficulty locating a willing doctor. An especially radical position is that of the American Civil Liberties Union of Southern California, which contends that under the constitutional right of privacy established by the Supreme Court in *Griswold v. Connecticut*,[37] the birth control case, it is for each individual to determine when and whether to produce offspring.[38] Thus they would argue that the present laws outlawing abortion are unconstitutional.

3. *The Model Penal Code provision on abortion.* In between the foregoing extremes are those who take an intermediate position along the lines of the provisions of the Model Penal Code, which was drafted by the American Law Institute after ten years of study and is now ready for consideration by state legislatures. The Code penalizes as a felony an unjustified termination of pregnancy and defines the occasions for justification as belief that

> there is substantial risk that continuance of the pregnancy would gravely impair the physical or mental health of the mother or that the child would be born with grave physical or mental defect, or that the pregnancy resulted from rape, incest or other felonious intercourse. All illicit intercourse with a girl below the age of 16 shall be deemed felonious.[39]

Under the Code the operation must be performed by a licensed physician in a licensed hospital, and at least one other physician must join in a written certificate setting forth the justifying circumstances.

This proposed liberalization of the abortion laws is a rather conservative compromise position that would, in fact, have but little effect on changing the present status of illegitimate pregnancies or those of married couples who merely wish relief for social or economic reasons. It is possible that it would do little more than codify current practices of legitimate medical practitioners.

D. Impact of the Model Penal Code

The Code is already having substantial effect on current thinking in regard to abortion laws. First, we note that the American Medical Association House of Delegates, on June 21, 1967, voted to approve an official Association position allowing abortions substantially in accord with the recommendations in the Model Penal

---

[36] *See, e.g.,* Harrington, *Is Abortion a Crime?*, TRIAL, June-July 1967, at 42.

[37] 381 U.S. 479 (1965).

[38] This conclusion was reached by the Southern California A.C.L.U. after a year of study by a special committee of lawyers, sociologists, and doctors. *See* TRIAL, June-July 1967, at 40. The constitutional argument is derived by extension of *Griswold*, which held that a state could not constitutionally prohibit married couples from using, or obtaining advice on the use of, contraceptive devices.

[39] MODEL PENAL CODE § 230.8 (Proposed Official Draft 1962).

Code.⁴⁰ This was the first policy change on the subject by the AMA in ninety-six years. In 1871, the Association had issued a policy statement to the effect that it would be deemed unethical for a physician to induce abortion "without the concurrent opinion of at least one other physician, and then always with a view to the safety of the child if that be possible." The AMA House of Delegates now calls this announcement "antiquated and inadequate" for the purposes of 1967.

Until 1967, however, there had been no noticeable impact in legislative halls. The draftsmen of the proposed Illinois Criminal Code advocated abortion provisions paralleling the Model Code,⁴¹ but the legislature would have none of it. The draftsmen of the proposed Minnesota Criminal Code included a somewhat similar provision in its revision, but the legislature rejected it.⁴² During 1967 similar legislation died or was pigeonholed in a number of states, including Connecticut, Nevada, Michigan, Iowa, Maryland, New Mexico, New York, and Tennessee, largely because of vigorous opposition from the churches. In Indiana, the legislature passed a liberalization bill, but the governor vetoed it.

The year 1967 was, however, the year of change. Three states adopted abortion laws in substantial accord with the American Law Institute proposal. In April, after stormy consideration, the Colorado legislature adopted, and on April 25 Governor John A. Love signed, an act substantially similar to the Model Penal Code,⁴³ allowing abortions where a three-member doctor board in an accredited hospital agrees unanimously that (1) the pregnancy would result in the death of the mother or serious, permanent impairment of her physical or mental health, or (2) the child would likely be born with grave and permanent physical deformity or mental retardation, or (3) the pregnancy resulted from forcible rape or incest or statutory rape of a girl under sixteen years of age.⁴⁴ The law contains no residency requirement. If the request is made by a married woman, the husband must concur.

---

⁴⁰ J.A.M.A., July 10, 1967, at 27, 38.
⁴¹ Proposed ILL. REV. CRIM. CODE § 32-1 (Burdette-Smith ed. 1961).
⁴² Proposed MINN. STAT. ANN. § 609.345 (West ed. 1963), and MINN. STAT. ANN. § 617.18 (1964).
⁴³ COLO. REV. STAT. ANN. ch. 40, art. 2, § 50 (1967). *See* N.Y. Times, April 26, 1967, at 48, col. 8.

⁴⁴ The question may be raised as to whether a statute legalizing abortion because of the likelihood that the child may be born with physical defect, may create a duty in the physician to warn the expectant mother of the defect, and if she so desires, to abort her. In Gleitman v. Cosgrove, 49 N.J. 22, 227 A.2d 689 (1967), an expectant mother had German measles during her pregnancy, and her child was born blind, deaf, and mute. The mother alleged that her physicians had failed to warn her of the 20% chance that her child would be physically defective, and the court assumed for purposes of discussion that had she known of this risk she could and would have obtained a lawful abortion. The mother sought damages because an abortion would have freed her from the emotional problems caused by raising a child with birth defects, and the father sought damages because it would have been less expensive to abort rather than raise the child. The court denied recovery because "[t]he right of their child to live is greater than and precludes their right not to endure emotional and financial injury." *Id.* at 31, 227 A.2d at 693. *But cf.* Custodio v. Bauer, 59 Cal. Rptr. 463 (Ct. App. 1967), where the court would allow recovery in an action showing a negligent failure to sterilize which resulted in pregnancy, even when the mother would suffer no harm, if there was a measurable economic loss to the family resulting from the necessity of supporting and raising an additional child. *Id.* at 476.

In *Gleitman*, a claim brought on behalf of the child against the physician for damages resulting

Some of the reactions to the Colorado law were violent. "It's a law against motherhood," said one state legislator. "It's legalized state murder," said a minister. "The whole world now finds Colorado available," said a doctor. "My fear is that Colorado will become the abortion Mecca of America," said a state senator. The pathway to liberalization is a thorny one.

The Colorado action was followed by the North Carolina legislature, which disposed of the possibility of an "abortion Mecca" by adopting a four-month residency requirement "except in the case of emergency where the life of the said woman is in danger."[45] California has recently changed its statute to legalize an abortion when the pregnancy threatens the physical or mental health of the mother, or when the pregnancy resulted from forcible rape, incest, or statutory rape of a girl under fifteen years of age.[46] Unlike the statutes of Colorado and North Carolina, the California act does not legalize an abortion performed because of probable fetal deformity. The California Supreme Court may soon determine whether a pregnancy terminated because of fetal deformity is to be considered violative of the existing law.[47]

In New Jersey, action was taken not by the legislature, but by an organization of county prosecutors. In a policy declaration with reference to the 118-year-old statute which penalizes abortions performed "without lawful justification,"[48] the prosecutors stated that an abortion should be considered legally justified when performed by a physician "in good faith" and in accord with "accepted medical standards."[49] Further, the New Jersey Supreme Court has recently stated "it may well be that when a physician performs an abortion because of a good faith determination in accordance with accepted medical standards that an abortion is medically indicated, the physician has acted with lawful justification within the meaning of our statute and has not committed a crime."[50] Thus, reform may begin in some states whose legislatures have remained silent, through more liberal administrative and judicial construction of existing laws.

---

from his physical defects was reduced to a claim "[t]hat he should not have been born at all." 49 N.J. at 28, 227 A.2d at 692. No recovery was allowed because the privilege to live was thought to outweigh the harm suffered by the child because of his defects. Presumably the same policy considerations could govern a tort claim filed by a party raped, and upon whom an abortion is not performed, as well as any claim filed by the resulting illegitimate child. *See* Williams v. State, 46 Misc. 2d 824, 260 N.Y.S.2d 953 (Ct. Cl. 1965), *rev'd*, 18 N.Y.2d 481, 223 N.E.2d 343, 276 N.Y.S.2d 885, *aff'd*, 25 App. Div. 2d 906, 221 N.E.2d 181, 269 N.Y.S.2d 786 (1966).

[45] N.C. GEN. STAT. § 14-45.1 (Advance Legislative Service 1967).

[46] CAL. BUS. & PROF. CODE § 2377 (West Supp. 1967); CAL. HEALTH & SAFETY CODE §§ 25950-54 (West Supp. 1967); CAL. PENAL CODE §§ 274-76 (West Supp. 1967). The California act is discussed in Leavy & Charles, *California's New Therapeutic Abortion Act: An Analysis and Guide to Medical and Legal Procedure*, 15 U.C.L.A.L. REV. 1 (1967).

[47] *See* Leavy & Charles, *supra* note 46, at 25-27. For a favorable commentary on the California statute, *see generally* Giannella, *The Difficult Quest for a Truly Humane Abortion Law*, 13 VILL. L. REV. 257 (1968).

[48] N.J. STAT. ANN. § 21A:87-1 (1953).

[49] N.Y. Times, June 24, 1967, at 31, col. 3.

[50] Gleitman v. Cosgrove, 49 N.J. 22, 31, 227 A.2d 689, 694 (1967).

Preliminary reports from Colorado indicate that the new legislation did not significantly increase the number of legal abortions performed in the state,[51] and the view has been expressed that nationwide liberalization of the law would result in only perhaps 1,000 more legal abortions per year, roughly a ten per cent increase.[52] If experience bears out these indications, several important conclusions would have to be drawn: first, that physicians had been allowing their medical judgments to override the old legal inhibitions to a most surprising degree; second, that the benefits of adopting the Model Penal Code approach will accrue not so much to patients in need of abortions as to the law itself, by improving physician's respect for it; and, third, that the Model Penal Code approach would have practically no impact on the large number of illegal abortions now being performed.

This final conclusion means that it is possible that the current abortion reform movement will not be enough. One should not minimize the importance of relieving physicians of the conflict between their sensed professional responsibility and the law's proscription, but abortion will remain an important social problem. The proposed reform is desirable in bringing the law into accord with medical practice and medical ethics, but the law has an additional responsibility to accord with societal mores. It may be that this additional responsibility will come to be more and more felt.

Abortion reform is not confined to the United States. Of particular interest is the English abortion law, approved by the House of Commons on October 26, 1967.[53] An abortion will be legal if any two doctors agree that (1) the life of the mother is threatened, (2) the mother's physical or mental health might be injured, (3) any existing children might be mentally or physically injured, or (4) the child born might suffer from such physical or mental abnormalities as to be seriously handicapped. It is said that a major purpose served by the new law will be to sanction abortion in cases where the family is large and over-crowded, or where the strain on the mother which would be caused by raising an additional child would be too great.[54] As can be seen, the English reform legislation is more liberal than its counterparts in the United States.

---

[51] Brody, *supra* note 35, col. 2.

[52] Helleger, *Abortion, the Law and the Common Good*, MEDICAL OPINION & REVIEW, May 1967, at 76.

[53] N.Y. Times, Oct. 26, 1967, at 1, col. 2.

[54] *Id.* at 17, col. 1. Other countries have encountered the abortion problem and have taken action of a more or less liberal nature. In Sweden and Denmark, where abortion is much more easily obtained than in most places in this country, the operation must still meet certain standards. The limits of permissible abortion are about the same as those of the Model Penal Code, with the added stipulations that in cases of "weakness" of the mother or when economic hardship could cause disintegration of the family unit, the authorities would permit abortion. Contrary to common belief in the United States, abortions are not obtained merely for the asking by the pregnant female.

In Japan, Hungary, and the U.S.S.R., there is even greater liberality, the primary function of abortion in Japan being birth control. There it is deemed in the national interest to control the birth rate and therefore legal abortions are performed upon the request of the mother, often at state expense. There is no legal, medical, religious, or social pressure upon her decision. In Japan it is said that one out of every two pregnancies is interrupted by abortion.

At any rate, the corner toward liberalization in the United States has been turned. Some thirty states are currently reconsidering their abortion laws, and, despite opposition, many of them will soon adopt liberalizing measures.[55] Even though the moderate liberalization proposed by the Model Penal Code and now adopted by Colorado, California, and North Carolina does not solve all problems presented by the widespread demand for pregnancy termination, it does open the door to rationalizing the performance of abortions in a manner consistent with a certain measure of domestic contentment. Moreover, it resolves for the conscientious doctor the dilemma created by his normal desire to render medical assistance in case of need, on the one hand, and his countervailing concern over violation of state criminal laws. The process of modernizing the law in an area of vital concern to doctors has thus begun. It is notable that it was an organization of lawyers, the American Law Institute, that provided the impetus for this long-needed reform. Completing the process of reform requires the efforts of both professions.

E. The Legislature's Role in Controlling Abortion

The existing gap between the legal standard on abortion and actual medical practice demonstrates the severe limitations placed on the medical profession by legislation which inhibits the doctor in exercising his medical judgment. Serious questions can be raised about the extent to which legislatures should, as doctors often put it, "come between" the physician and his patient, prescribing the type of medical care that should or should not be given. Recently, for example, the New York legislature heard conflicting medical testimony on the therapeutic values and dangers of abortion in the process of deciding whether to amend the state's abortion law,[56] and it seems fair to question the competence of a legislature to weigh these matters. Similar problems of delineating the proper legislative function exist in other areas, such as euthanasia, sterilization, and the administration of drugs.

Interestingly, the Supreme Court, in *Griswold v. Connecticut*,[57] has created a constitutional limit on legislative interference in the dispensing of medical advice. While this case turned on the specially private interests of the recipients of the birth control information, one can envision extensions of the principle to other areas where a professionally qualified physician's relationship with the patient is encroached upon.

---

[55] The change will not come easily, for the opposition is potent and determined. The principal arguments are that modern science regards the moment of conception as the beginning of a new life; that the law owes a duty to protect this life; that its destruction should be prevented; that abortion constitutes a condemnation to death without a trial; that the possibility of deformed babies is negligible; and that the real solution lies in eliminating the causes of illegitimate pregnancies. *See* Harrington, *supra* note 36. The Georgia legislature has recently passed a liberalized law legalizing abortion if the mother's health is threatened, when probable fetal deformity would result, and in cases of rape. The bill was waiting for the approval of the governor at the date this issue went to press. N.Y. Times, Feb. 27, 1968, at 32, col. 8.
[56] *See, e.g.,* N.Y. Times, Feb. 4, 1967, at 24, col. 2; N.Y. Times, Feb. 11, 1967, at 18, col. 1.
[57] 381 U.S. 479 (1965).

We have already noted that the case has been cited by some as establishing the unconstitutionality of abortion legislation.[58]

There are recent indications that legislatures might elect repeal rather than amendment of existing abortion laws as the most desirable means of accomplishing the needed reform. For example, an official of the Minnesota Council for the Legal Termination of Pregnancy was recently quoted as saying, "I wouldn't be surprised if several states including Minnesota soon repealed their abortion laws and left the matter to physicians and their patients."[59] And a leading Catholic authority, the Reverend Robert F. Drinan, dean of the Boston College Law School, has recently argued that repeal is morally preferable to amendment, since the latter course puts the state in the position of deciding "who shall live and who shall die."[60] Repeal would at least leave the moral question in private hands. The case for repeal of all laws affecting the performance of abortions by licensed physicians is just beginning to be made, but it is becoming increasingly clear that the Model Penal Code is not the final answer.

Abortion laws thus bring sharply into focus the problem of the role of law in medical progress. A strong argument can be made that legislatures should confine their efforts to (1) setting minimum standards for admission to medical practice, (2) freeing doctors from unwarranted legal risks in providing for their patients (as is the object of the Model Penal Code's provisions on abortion), while maintaining standards of care and the legal remedies needed to protect the public, and (3) providing money to guarantee sound medical training and the best facilities and to extend care to more citizens. It may be unrealistic, given the public's intense interest in medical care, to expect legislatures to curb their own involvement, although hope for repeal of abortion laws is rising, or to rely on the courts to restrict the law's role in this way. Still, in any given legislative or judicial determination, the demonstrated integrity of the medical profession will militate against extending legal interference. Any demonstrated lack of integrity will, by the same token, be likely to produce a legal response.

IV

Patient Consent to Therapy: The Problem of Informed Consent

Over fifty years ago in *Schloendorff v. Society of New York Hospital*,[61] Judge Benjamin Cardozo commented, "Every human being of adult years and sound mind has a right to determine what shall be done with his own body; and a surgeon who performs an operation without his patient's consent commits an assault for which he is liable in damages."[62] These words, written by a distinguished jurist, reveal

---

[58] See text accompanying notes 37 & 38 *supra*.
[59] Brody, *supra* note 35, col. 2.
[60] *Id.*, col. 6.
[61] 211 N.Y. 125, 105 N.E. 92 (1914).
[62] *Id.* at 129-30, 105 N.E. at 93 (1914).

one side of a coin, the possibility of the legal action for assault and battery; if the case had called for it, Judge Cardozo probably would also have said that, if the patient were a minor, or of unsound mind, any purported consent by him would have been ineffective, and again there would have been an assault and battery. A recent court, citing the *Schloendorff* opinion, stated that "If the consent given to the operation in question was ineffectual, every phase of the operation . . . was a continuing battery for which recovery should be allowed, *even if the operation had been successful.*"[63]

On the other side of the legal coin there is something else, namely liability in damages for negligence. We know that if a physician, having undertaken to render medical service for a patient, in the course of treatment fails to utilize the degree of skill and care that would be exercised by reputable practitioners of the same school of practice in the community under similar circumstances, and injury follows, he is liable in damages for breach of the prescribed standard of care—in short, for negligence. This is the familiar action for medical malpractice.

Recent judicial decisions, utilizing language on both sides of the legal coin, have brought forth the doctrine of "informed consent." Even if the physician has obtained the patient's expressed consent to an operation or similar procedure, yet he may have failed to furnish sufficient information about hazards, or alternative forms of treatment, to enable the patient to give a meaningful reasoned or "informed" consent. Because of this omission, the physician may become exposed to liability. Under the traditional doctrine of assault and battery, the consent may be held ineffective and the physician is liable to the patient for any damage incurred by the unpermitted operation.[64] Under the more recently evolved standard of malpractice, or negligence, the physician is said to have a duty to disclose the risks inherent in the operation or treatment. This duty is presupposed by the standard of what other reasonable medical practitioners in the community would have disclosed under similar circumstances. Liability will follow if the patient can show that the harm resulted from the breach.[65]

---

[63] Shetter v. Rochelle, 2 Ariz. App. 358, 366, 409 P.2d 74, 82 (1965), *modified on other grounds*, 2 Ariz. App. 607, 411 P.2d 45 (1966). However, if the operation is beneficial or harmless, only nominal or very limited damages can be recovered. Lacey v. Laird, 166 Ohio Rep. 12, 139 N.E.2d 25 (1956); Keister v. O'Neil, 59 Cal. App. 2d 428, 138 P.2d 723 (1943).

[64] Conceptually it could be argued that failure to disclose a particular risk invalidates the patient's consent for all purposes and that the operation is therefore an assault and battery, regardless of whether the undisclosed risk actually materialized. Nevertheless, lack of informed consent seems to result in liability only for injuries resulting from risks which should have been but were not disclosed.

[65] In applying these two theories, the courts appear to be either confused or little concerned with distinguishing the grounds of recovery. Thus in one leading case, Natanson v. Kline, 186 Kan. 393, 350 P.2d 1093 (1960), *rehearing denied but opinion explained*, 187 Kan. 186, 354 P.2d 670 (1960), it was charged that the court in its first opinion had confused malpractice with assault and battery, "giving rise to a hybrid action which is neither one of negligence nor of assault and battery, but may be a combination of the two." 187 Kan. at 187, 354 P.2d at 671. It has been stated, "Unfortunately, the leading cases dealing with the failure of a surgeon to warn of inherent risks do not always make it clear as to what theory supports recovery, when recovery is permitted." Shetter v. Rochelle, 2 Ariz. App. 358, 363, 409 P.2d 74, 79 (1965), *modified on other grounds*, 2 Ariz. App. 607, 411 P.2d 45 (1966).

From the foregoing it is clear that a proper informed consent is an important defense—an insulation from legal liability—available to physicians and surgeons, but that, in the absence of such consent, any invasion of the body or mind of another person, even though accompanied by the utmost in medical skill, may become an actionable wrong. This doctrine relating to consent is important to the medical profession in two principal contexts: (1) in professional therapy for sick patients and (2) in clinical research involving the use of human subjects in seeking new medical knowledge. Many volumes of case law have been written through the years involving malpractice for failure to exercise the required skill and care in rendering medical services, but there are comparatively few cases involving liability for failure to inform and obtain the required consent from the patient receiving medical treatment, and none at all concerned with the human subject in medical research.

We shall develop further the requirement of informed consent—which, when it is met, will serve to insulate doctors from the hardships of the courtroom. Possibly we can see how the concept can be sharpened and its use facilitated for the benefit of both lawyers and doctors. In the remainder of this section we shall be considering only those aspects of informed consent that apply to cases of therapy for sick patients. In the following section, we shall turn to its use in connection with experimentation on human subjects.

As already indicated, the law on consent to treatment is of recent vintage and is not fully developed. An ill person who calls upon a doctor for treatment is entitled, except in certain emergencies, to a diagnosis, a prognosis, and a statement of the proposed therapy, together with a statement of the hazards, if any, and the expected results or effect upon health or person to be anticipated from the treatment of his medical problem.[66] The patient's request for medical services carries with it implied consent to all conventional, nonoperative procedures indicated for his diseased condition.[67] But if the physician finds that such procedures will not effect a cure, he may in the exercise of his own professional judgment decide that an operation is needed, or he may wish to try some new and unconventional treatment or drug in which he has confidence. Before doing either of these things he

---

A cause of action asserting an assault and battery does not preclude recovery based upon malpractice for failure to disclose risks. *See* Woods v. Brumlop, 71 N.M. 221, 377 P.2d 520 (1962) (plaintiff's claim was based upon two theories: failure to inform of danger in electroshock treatment, and lack of consent because of not being informed of the danger); Mayor v. Dowsett, 240 Ore. 196, 400 P.2d 234 (1965) (when an action for assault and battery was barred because the statute of limitations had run, the court treated the action as one for malpractice: "[T]he operation might constitute a technical battery, but it would still be a violation of the established standard of care and actionable as malpractice." *Id.* at 233, 400 P.2d at 251); Wilson v. Scott, 412 S.W.2d 299 (Tex. 1967) ("Regardless of what some earlier informed consent cases suggest, such an action need not be pleaded as one for assault and battery." *Id.* at 302.) *See also* Gravis v. Physicians & Surgeons Hosp., 415 S.W.2d 678 (Tex. Civ. App. 1967).

[66] Morse, *Legal Implications of Clinical Investigations*, 20 VAND. L. REV. 747, 749 (1967) (especially the cases cited in nn.8-10).

[67] B. SHARTEL & M. PLANT, THE LAW OF MEDICAL PRACTICE § 1-06 (1959).

must, unless the circumstances are exceptional, obtain the patient's expressed and informed consent to the operation or to the use of an experimental drug or treatment.

There are certain exceptions. Occasionally, the doctor may deem it desirable to withhold distressing information, as from a critically ill cancer patient. This may be justifiable, and in such cases informed consent may be omitted. The same is true if full explanation of the material facts is impossible because of emergency conditions, or if the facts are deemed emotionally so upsetting under the circumstances as to prejudice the treatment. Otherwise, before the doctor tries either ordinary operative measures or some unconventional treatment or procedure, the law requires that the consent be obtained and that it be preceded by informing the patient of the essential material facts, including in reasonable detail the means and methods of the proposed treatment, the inconveniences and risks involved, and the possible effects upon his health or person. Sometimes the doctor goes ahead without requesting a consent to the procedure involved, creating a potential lawsuit.[68]

Judicial decisions are attempting to fill in the foregoing general outline of the law on informed consent. One important question is whether the information furnished the patient must, in order to make the consent valid, include *all* of the facts and risks which the patient contends that he should have known, or whether it will suffice to give him *only* those that would be supplied by other reputable and reasonable physicians in the community under the same or similar circumstances. Is the latter a necessary standard against which to judge the physician's disclosure?

The Kansas Supreme Court in *Natanson v. Kline*[69] threw light on this matter. The court was confronted with an action for damages against a radiologist and the hospital in which he was giving radioactive cobalt treatments. The plaintiff received such treatments in connection with a mastectomy operation and damage ensued. The doctor was not chargeable with failure to exercise proper professional skill in the treatments, but negligence was claimed because of his failure to inform her of the hazards. The court in its two opinions charted some new ground. It held that the duty to disclose existed but qualified it by saying:

---

[68] On occasion, absent express consent, an implied consent may be derived from the peculiar facts. See Haywood v. Allen, 406 S.W.2d 721 (Ky. Ct. App. March 25, 1966, as modified on denial of rehearing, Oct. 14, 1966), where suit was brought against a physician for damages for the allegedly unauthorized tying off of the patient's Fallopian tubes in the course of a Caesarean section. The patient did not expressly consent to the tubal ligation, but there was discussion of its possibility as a "package deal" and there was a tacit understanding that the ligation should be done unless the patient should affirmatively tell the surgeon that she did not want it done. It was held that the surgeon was entitled to act on the basis of implied consent. *Compare* Carroll v. Chapman, 139 So. 2d 61 (La. Ct. App. 1962) *and* Shulman v. Lerner, 2 Mich. App. 705, 141 N.E.2d 348 (1966) *with* Bang v. Charles T. Miller Hosp., 251 Minn. 427, 88 N.W.2d 186 (1958).

[69] 186 Kan. 393, 350 P.2d 1093 (1960), *rehearing denied but opinion explained*, 187 Kan. 186, 354 P.2d 670 (1960).

The duty of the physician to disclose, however, is limited to those disclosures which a reasonable medical practitioner would make under the same or similar circumstances. How the physician may best discharge his obligation to the patient in this difficult situation involves primarily a question of medical judgment.[70]

A subsequent Kansas case involved a claim of malpractice by the parents of a minor who had undergone cardiac catheterization. In response to the allegation by plaintiffs that they had been told that in previous cardiac catheterizations there had not been any trouble, the court again held that the standard of the reasonable medical practitioner governed disclosure.[71]

It is clear that in an action for negligence or malpractice, the standard of disclosure elaborated upon by the Kansas court is the prevailing view,[72] and is substantially the same standard as that applied in a case of failure to exercise the proper degree of professional skill. On the other hand, the question may be raised as to whether this standard should be utilized in the action alleging lack of valid consent to an assault and battery. In this legal area there is less of a theoretical basis for looking to what other doctors similarly situated might have done.

Strictly speaking, an action for assault and battery raises only the issue of the patient's awareness, yet we do not expect the physician to suggest every risk factor nor do we demand a complete explanation of his medical decision, based as it is on various alternative modes of treatment and their relative probabilities of success. The courts have attempted to solve the problem in at least three ways: (1) by requiring only a general awareness of the risks on the part of the plaintiff,[73] (2) by simply submitting the question of consent as a fact issue to the jury without formulating any express standard,[74] or (3) by applying the negligence or malpractice standard of the reasonable practitioner.[75] It would seem that there must be some standard of reasonableness applied to determine the risks of which the patient must be informed and that questions of medical judgment are intimately involved in determining the fact of risk itself. The courts ought not to insist too rigidly on following the assault and battery rationale[76] and should apply the standard of the reasonable medical practitioner in all cases involving consent issues.

---

[70] 186 Kan. at 409, 350 P.2d at 1106.

[71] Williams v. Menihan, 191 Kan. 6, 379 P.2d 292 (1963); *accord*, Collins v. Meeker, 198 Kan. 390, 424 P.2d 488 (1967).

[72] *See, e.g.*, Wilson v. Scott, 412 S.W.2d 299 (Tex. 1967); Shetter v. Rochelle, 2 Ariz. App. 358, 409 P.2d 74 (1965), *modified on other grounds*, 2 Ariz. App. 607, 411 P.2d 45 (1966); Aiken v. Clary, 396 S.W.2d 668 (Mo. 1965); Roberts v. Young, 369 Mich. 133, 119 N.W.2d 627 (1963); Govin v. Hunter, 374 P.2d 421 (Wyo. 1962).

[73] "[A] consent to a surgical procedure is effectual if the consentor understands substantially the nature of the surgical procedure attempted and the probable results of the operation . . . ." Shetter v. Rochelle, 2 Ariz. App. 358, 369, 409 P.2d 74, 86 (1965), *modified on other grounds*, 2 Ariz. App. 607, 411 P.2d 45 (1966).

[74] Woods v. Brumlop, 71 N.M. 221, 377 P.2d 520 (1962).

[75] Di Filippio v. Preston, 53 Del. 539, 173 A.2d 333 (1961).

[76] *See, e.g.*, Ditlow v. Kaplan, 181 So. 2d 226 (Fla. Ct. App. 1965); Aikin v. Clary, 396 S.W.2d 668 (Mo. 1965); Govin v. Hunter, 374 P.2d 421 (Wyo. 1962).

No doubt this same principle should also be applied to the statements of the other essential elements of "informed consent"—for example, the sufficiency of the statements with respect to the method and means of procedure to be used and the inconveniences as well as the risks involved and, in particular, the amount of detail which the doctor must give to the patient. How much detail would reputable and reasonable practitioners give under similar circumstances? Would they speculate about remote possibilities or picture the most distressing possible effects? The information imparted must certainly include the more prominent features, those most likely to affect the decision of the patient to proceed or not to proceed.[77] However, the reasonable practitioner probably would not detail the one-in-10,000 possibilities or go into the more frightening aspects that, though remote, might deter the patient unnecessarily.[78] Unfortunately no iron-clad rule can be formulated; each case must be determined according to its own facts.

There are certain other elements to be considered. There is the question of capacity to consent, but that we shall discuss in the next section of this article. There is also the question of the manner of making proof. If the action is given the label of an assault and battery based upon complete absence of effective consent, lay testimony could be used to prove the deficiency, but if the action is based upon inadequacy of information furnished, *i.e.*, on negligence, then the medical standards of the community come into the case, and the plaintiff will have to offer expert testimony in proof.[79] If, as has been suggested, the standard of the reasonable physician is to be applied in all cases, then the plaintiff will always be required to introduce expert testimony to determine that standard. Because of the "conspiracy of silence" this may cause the plaintiff greater difficulty than the defendant, who will doubtless be able to get other doctors to testify in his defense. As a mitigating factor, the courts have ruled as a matter of law that the standard has been violated when the physician either is silent as to the possibility of risk,[80] or assures the patient that no danger could result, if in fact this is known by the physician to be an untrue statement.[81] In these situations, the plaintiff will not be required to offer expert testimony to prove his case, and the burden may be upon the defendant physician

---

[77] The standard was found violated by a failure to inform a patient of the 3% risk of death, paralysis, or other injury in an arteriogram procedure, Bowers v. Talmadge, 159 So. 2d 888 (Fla. Ct. App. 1963), and by a failure to disclose the 1% chance of loss of hearing in a stapedectomy with a vein graft (ear operation). Wilson v. Scott, 412 S.W.2d 299 (Tex. 1967).

[78] The reasonable medical practitioner would not inform the parents of a child of the remote possibility that the child might revive from the anesthesia and, in the course of his ensuing struggle, cause a catheter to puncture his heart. Williams v. Menihan, 191 Kan. 6, 379 P.2d 292 (1963).

[79] *See, e.g.*, Williams v. Menihan, 191 Kan. 6, 379 P.2d 292 (1963); Aiken v. Clary, 396 S.W.2d 668 (Mo. 1965).

[80] Collins v. Meeker, 198 Kan. 390, 424 P.2d 488 (1967); Natanson v. Kline, 187 Kan. 186, 354 P.2d 670 (1960); Mitchell v. Robinson, 334 S.W.2d 11 (Mo. 1960), *distinguished in* Aiken v. Clary, 396 S.W.2d 668, 673 (Mo. 1965).

[81] Woods v. Brumlop, 71 N.M. 221, 377 P.2d 520 (1962).

to prove that his failure to disclose did, in fact, conform to accepted professional standards.[82]

As a final element, a mere showing of negligence will not suffice to establish liability. The plaintiff must also show proximate cause, and in this context this means that he must prove that he would not have undergone the operation or procedure if he had been fully informed of the risk.[83] The subjective element is large, and it may simply be a jury question as to the credibility of plaintiff's testimony to this effect.[84]

We are discussing in general "the role of law in medical progress." In our consideration of the subjects of homotransplants and abortion, the law was seen as the benefactor of medicine by clearing the way. Candor compels the observation that the legally evolved doctrine of informed consent may well operate otherwise. It may add to the frustrations felt by doctors toward the law, lawyers, and the courts by seeming to create a disguised and dangerous pitfall into which a relatively innocent practitioner may inadvertently tumble. Possibly more extensive nonlitigious and objective intellectual cooperation between the professions, in institutes, conferences, joint publishing efforts, or otherwise, could hammer out the standards in terms of specifics and thus smooth the path toward better mutual understanding than that pictured by Dr. Child.[85]

V
THE SUBJECT'S CONSENT TO HUMAN EXPERIMENTATION

We have already noted the importance of informed consent in the situation where the doctor elects to employ an experimental drug or treatment.[86] In these instances the physician's goal and the patient's hopes coincide, and consent only serves the purpose of alerting the patient to the unusual risks that may be involved. In this section we will be concerned with the possibility of unhappy results where the experiment in which the patient or other volunteer participates holds out little or no hope of benefit to him. Such nontherapeutic experiments may involve healthy persons who volunteer to become guinea pigs for the sake of making contributions to medical science or persons who are paid for their participation. If injury results from such experimentation, the possibility of a damage suit again rears its head.

---

[82] Collins v. Meeker, 198 Kan. 390, 424 P.2d 488 (1967). *But see* Comment, *Informed Consent in Medical Malpractice*, 55 CALIF. L. REV. 1396 (1967), in which it is argued that the physician should always have the initial burden of proof when he makes less than a full disclosure of all known material risks.

[83] *Compare* Natanson v. Kline, 187 Kan. 186, 354 P.2d 670 (1960) *and* Shetter v. Rochelle, 2 Ariz. App. 607, 411 P.2d 45 (1966) *with* Aiken v. Clary, 396 S.W.2d 668 (Mo. 1965), where the court held that, while the plaintiff did not have to show that he would not have consented had he been fully informed, "this does not mean, however, that plaintiff is not required to establish a causal connection between the doctor's failure sufficiently to inform and the injury for which recovery is sought." *Id.* at 676.

[84] *See* Russell v. Hardwick, 166 So. 2d 904 (Fla. Ct. App. 1964).

[85] Note 3 *supra* and accompanying text.

[86] *See* p. 582 *supra*.

For the paid subjects, the primary benefit is the monetary reward. For the others, there is generally no benefit other than satisfaction of a possible desire to promote the general welfare. Not many persons are willing to put up with personal injury or even serious inconvenience either for the typically meager compensation provided or for the sake of the advancement of medical science. In such cases, moreover, in obtaining informed consent there can be no special considerations, such as emergency conditions or patient apprehension, warranting the investigator in withholding information or not obtaining consent. Accordingly the law should not and does not provide these excuses for failing to do so. So far as can be ascertained, there are no decided cases on the subject, but it seems practically certain that there will be such in the future. We must assume that the medical investigator will be held liable in damages if he does not make a proper disclosure and obtain an effective consent. Otherwise his action exposes him to liability, and if something goes wrong he must be held responsible. It has been said that he experiments at his peril, and this is certainly true unless consent has been obtained. We must ask, however, what is the necessary disclosure and what is an effective consent.[87]

At the outset we should note again that experimentation on a human subject without first obtaining an informed consent has especially pronounced moral aspects, as well as those of a strictly legal nature.[88] This moral aspect is even more important when the experimentation involves, as it often does, children, mental incompetents, students, prisoners, nurses, employees, and others who may be handicapped or subject to pressure in consenting to the experimentation. In such cases the moral aspects will have a direct bearing upon development of legal conclusions.[89]

A. Existing Codes, Standards, and Rules

We should first look at some of the ideas on the subject that have emerged in recent years in the form of specific codes and rules. Ever since the Nuremberg trials brought to light the wretched practices of the Nazis in Germany, the concern of interested persons and organizations has brought forth a variety of stated principles and rules to govern the use of human subjects in nontherapeutic medical investigation.[90] Most of these have come from the medical profession itself. In the ensuing paragraphs we review the several principal efforts briefly and chronologically. A gradual evolution of ideas and refinement of principles have taken place.

---

[87] Although the courts have not spoken, there is an impressive body of medical and legal literature on the subject. See, e.g., I. LADIMER & R. NEWMAN, CLINICAL INVESTIGATION IN MEDICINE (1963), which collects numerous materials and provides an extensive bibliography; and later references cited in Fletcher, *Human Experimentation: Ethics in the Consent Situation*, in this symposium, p. 620, n.2.

[88] See generally Fletcher, supra note 87.

[89] Professor Paul A. Freund, of Harvard Law School, discussing the moral aspects, has suggested, "In the end we may have to accept the fact that some limits do exist to the search for knowledge." Freund, *Is the Law Ready for Human Experimentation?*, TRIAL, Oct.-Nov. 1966, at 46, 49.

[90] Many of the codes and stated principles are collected in I. LADIMER & R. NEWMAN, supra note 87. See also Fletcher, supra note 87, at 628-31.

The Nuremberg Articles (1946).[91] These Articles, drafted by a committee of the American Medical Association, comprise ten points, set up in the form of accepted and established principles to deal with nontherapeutic research. They were prepared as a guide for the Nuremberg tribunals in trying the Nazi criminals. The Articles call for voluntary consent by each subject of experimentation; they demand that human subjects be used only when fruitful results for the good of society unprocurable by other means may be promoted; experiments must be based upon prior animal experimentation and upon knowledge of the natural history of the problem; unnecessary physical and mental suffering must be avoided; there must be no experiments involving the likelihood of death or disabling injury; the risk must be set off against and must not exceed the humanitarian importance of the project; proper preparation and facilities must be provided; scientifically qualified investigators must be used; the subject of investigation must be free to withdraw at any time; and assurance must be given that the investigators will terminate the project at any time if it seems to be getting out of hand. This code was excellently framed for its purpose, to deal with the Nuremberg criminals. It did not, however, purport to settle all questions or even to be a guide for future experimental practices.

American Medical Association, Principles of Medical Ethics (1946).[92] The Association adopted some but by no means all of the principles of the Nuremberg Code. A report prepared by its Judicial Council was approved by the House of Delegates in December 1946. The report sets up the following requirements for clinical investigations on human beings: "(1) the voluntary consent of the person on whom the experiment is to be performed must be obtained; (2) the danger of each experiment must have been investigated previously by means of animal experimentation; and (3) the experiment must be performed under proper medical protection and management."

National Institutes of Health, Guiding Principles in Medical Research Involving Humans (1953).[93] A clearance procedure required for projects deviating from accepted medical practice incorporated the idea of group review of the scientific and ethical propriety of each project. The desirability of group review of nontherapeutic experiments is now generally recognized and is uniformly utilized in greater or lesser degree in all reputable centers.[94]

Public Health Council of the Netherlands, Report on Human Experimentation (1955).[95] In a published summary of a report submitted by the Council to the Nether-

---

[91] *Trials of War Criminals Before the Nuremburg Military Tribunals Under Control Council Law No. 10*, 2 THE MEDICAL CASE 181 (1949), reprinted in Beecher, *Experimentation in Man*, 169 J.A.M.A. 461, 472-74 (1959).

[92] 132 J.A.M.A. 1090 (1946).

[93] Ladimer, *Ethical and Legal Aspects of Medical Research on Human Beings*, 3 J. PUB. L. 467, 496 (1954).

[94] *See* Sessoms, *What Hospitals Should Know About Investigational Drugs: Guiding Principles in Medical Research Involving Humans*, 32 J. AM. HOSP. ASS'N 44, 62, 64 (1958).

[95] Reprinted in I. LADIMER & R. NEWMAN, *supra* note 87, at 156-58.

lands Minister on Social Affairs and Health, the following principle was included in a listing of "standards."

> Experiments on children; in institutions for children, old people, etc.; on the insane; or on prisoners, which involve dangerous risks, inconvenience or pain are not approved. All experiments on the dying under any circumstances are disapproved.

American Psychological Association, Ethical Standards of Psychologists (1959).[96] The eighteen "principles" in this formulation brought out, among other points, the need for confidentiality of information about individual subjects of experimentation. The following was included as a limitation on research to be conducted:

> Principle 16. Harmful Aftereffects. Only when a problem is significant and can be investigated in no other way is the psychologist justified in giving misinformation to research subjects or exposing research subjects to physical or emotional stress.
> a. When the possibility of serious aftereffects exists, research is conducted only when the subjects or their responsible agents are fully informed of this possibility and and volunteer nevertheless.

Medical Research Council (Great Britain), Responsibility in Investigations on Human Subjects (1962-63).[97] This statement is intended to serve as a guide for medical men engaged in research. With procedures not of direct benefit to the individual, it acknowledges the possibility of "undue influence," particularly when the investigator stands in a special relationship to the subject, such as a physician-patient relationship. It suggests that the investigator should obtain the consent while in the presence of another person to protect himself, and for the protection of the subject. The statement concludes as follows:

> Owing to the special relationship of trust that exists between a patient and his doctor, most patients will consent to any proposal that is made. Further, the considerations involved in a novel procedure are nearly always so technical as to prevent their being adequately understood by one who is not himself an expert. It must therefore be frankly recognized that, for practical purposes, an inescapable moral responsibility rests with the doctor concerned for determining what investigations are, or are not, proposed to a particular patient or volunteer . . . .
> In the opinion of the Council, the head of a department where investigations on human subjects take place has an inescapable responsibility for ensuring that practice by those under his direction is irreproachable.

World Medical Association, Code of Ethics (Declaration of Helsinki, 1964).[98] This is an important document, second only to the Nuremberg Articles in worldwide influence. It constitutes a fairly complete ethical code to guide medical experi-

---

[96] 14 AM. PSYCHOLOGIST 279 (1959).
[97] 2 BRIT. MED. J. 178 (1964).
[98] Reprinted in 2 BRIT. MED. J. 177 (1964); Morse, *Legal Implications of Clinical Investigations*, 20 VAND. L. REV. 747, 768-69 (1967). The Declaration has been approved by the American Medical Association, the American Federation for Clinical Research, the American College of Physicians, the American College of Surgeons, the Society for Pediatric Research, and the American Academy of Pediatrics.

menters in conducting clinical research. The Declaration draws the important distinction between purely scientific experimentation, presumably on normal persons, and experimentation for therapeutic purposes carried out on patients under the doctor's care, patients whose illness does not yield to conventional treatments. More exacting standards are imposed for the former than for the latter. The provisions concerning nontherapeutic research are as follows:

(1) In the purely scientific application of clinical research carried out on a human being it is the duty of the doctor to remain the protector of the life and health of that person on whom clinical research is being carried out.

(2) The nature, the purpose and the risk of clinical research must be explained to the subject by the doctor.

(3a) Clinical research on a human being cannot be undertaken without his free consent after he has been informed; if he is legally incompetent, the consent of the legal guardian should be procured.

(3b) The subject of clinical research should be in such a mental, physical and legal state as to be able to exercise fully his power of choice.

(3c) The consent should as a rule be obtained in writing. However, the responsibility for clinical research always remains with the research worker; it never falls on the subject even after consent is obtained.

(4a) The investigator must respect the right of each individual to safeguard his personal integrity, especially if the subject is in a dependent relationship to the investigator.

(4b) At any time during the course of clinical research the subject or his guardian should be free to withdraw permission for the research to be continued. The investigator or the investigating team should discontinue the research if in his or their judgment it may, if continued, be harmful to the individual.

This formulation contains a number of novel expressions of the interests and duties involved in human experimentation.

The Kefauver-Harris Amendments to the Food, Drug and Cosmetic Act (1962).[99] These amendments, which were precipitated largely by the thalidomide tragedies, and the Food and Drug Administration regulations implementing them, established detailed "informed consent" requirements applicable to the testing of investigational drugs that are to be shipped across state lines. Although the provisions apply only to new drugs, they are nevertheless persuasive with respect to and in connection with fixing standards for experimental processes that do not involve such drugs. FDA regulations specifically require consent in all cases of scientific investigation and in all but "exceptional cases" (emergency, apprehension, etc.) in therapy situations. Consent is carefully defined as follows:

"Consent" or "informed consent" means that the person involved has legal capacity to give consent, is so situated as to be able to exercise free power of choice, and is provided with a fair explanation of all material information concerning the

---
[99] Pub. L. No. 87-781, 76 Stat. 780 (codified in scattered sections of 21 U.S.C.).

administration of the investigational drug, or his possible use as a control, as to enable him to make an understanding decision as to his willingness to receive said investigational drug. This latter element requires that before the acceptance of any affirmative decision by such person the investigator should make known to him the nature, duration, and purpose of the administration of said investigational drug; the method and means by which it is to be administered; all inconveniences and hazards reasonably to be expected, including the fact, where applicable, that the person may be used as a control; the existence of alternative forms of therapy, if any; and the effect upon his health or person that may possibly come from the administration of the investigational drug. Said patient's consent shall be obtained in writing by the investigator.[100]

Notable new elements here are the requirement that consent be in writing and that the subject's possible use as a control be revealed to him.

U.S. Public Health Service, Policy and Procedure Order No. 129 (1966).[101] This is a directive, a "guideline," prescribing procedures for experimentation under Public Health Service grants-in-aid of research. It requires institutional group review of all projects to assure the protection of the "rights and welfare" of individuals involved, the appropriateness of the methods used to obtain informed consent, and the objective appraisal of the risks as balanced against the potential medical benefits of the investigation. The institutions reviewing the research must also assure continuing surveillance of projects and must provide continuing advice for investigators especially with respect to the safeguarding of the rights and welfare of human subjects. The possibility of withholding grants-in-aid is a powerful sanction. The stated standards apply literally only to projects carried on under the PHS grants, but they will doubtless be applied more broadly. This directive emphasizes strongly both the legal and the ethical obligations connected with nontherapeutic experimentation on normal humans.

American Medical Association, House of Delegates, Ethical Guidelines for Clinical Investigation (1966).[102] This document, referring to previous action endorsing the Declaration of Helsinki, enlarges upon the fundamental concepts by setting up some important "guidelines." It is a significant document with especially thoughtful differentiation between therapeutic and nontherapeutic experimentation.[103] It includes some original handling of the problem of experimentation on minors and incompetents.

---

[100] 21 C.F.R. § 130.37 (1967).
[101] Surgeon General, Public Health Service, Dep't of Health, Education, and Welfare, Investigations Involving Human Subjects, Including Clinical Research: Requirements for Review to Insure the Rights and Welfare of Individuals, PPO 129, Revised Policy July 1, 1966.
[102] American Medical Association, Declaration of Helsinki and AMA Ethical Guidelines for Clinical Investigation (undated pamphlet printed by the AMA).
[103] The provisions on these subjects are quoted in Fletcher, *supra* note 87, at 629. The experimenter's role vis-à-vis the patient was defined thus:

> 2. In conducting clinical investigation, the investigator should demonstrate the same concern and caution for the welfare, safety and comfort of the person involved as is required of a physician who is furnishing medical care to a patient independent of any clinical investigation.

B. Comments on Existing Codes, Standards, and Rules

The foregoing are the principal existing codes and rules. They represent much professional soul-searching, and when viewed historically serve to illustrate how the medical profession has come to grips with the problems. Many of the essential rules and standards can be distilled from them; yet they still do not fully serve to meet some of the most troublesome problems encountered in the course of medical experimentation. Large gaps remain, and important questions are unanswered. Let us list some of the questions and, where possible, undertake to suggest some tentative answers.

1. *Identifying Risks and Duties With Greater Precision*

Should not some kind of line be drawn between procedures that consist only of observation of natural functions of the subject, with no attendant risks or negligible risks, and those that involve affirmative invasion of mind or body to modify the functions for the purposes of the experiment, with something more than negligible risk? Comparatively unrestricted authority might be in order as to the former, but careful laying out of the ground rules would be indicated for the latter. The former could include all manner of superficial measurements and tests, even including X-rays, electrocardiograms, electroencephalograms, simple blood tests, and so forth. The latter would include the administration of many drugs, certain biopsies, and material alterations of bodily or mental functions in some manner. The former generally involve no significant risk, the latter otherwise in varying degrees.

But can a line necessarily be drawn between the two? Is a skin biopsy "observational" and a kidney biopsy "invasional"? Is violent exercise to observe heart function just observational? And what about the varying degrees of risk? Can meaningful lines be drawn? Or is each case dependent upon its own facts? Doctors must tell us whether meaningful lines can be drawn and whether the spectrum of degree of risk can be usefully illustrated by common examples. If the existing general principles can be made more specific in this manner, this would be a valuable guide for use in the design of research projects, in selecting human subjects, in duly informing them of risks, and eventually, if need should arise, in the courts.

2. *Defining Disclosure Requirements*

The American Medical Association "Ethical Guidelines" call for a "reasonable explanation" of the "nature" of the procedure to be used and of the "risks to be expected." This raises several questions. We might ask: reasonable to whom, the investigator, the human subject, or some hypothetical "reasonable man"? Does "nature of the procedure" include duration and purpose of the project as required in the Food and Drug Administration regulations? Do "risks" include "inconveniences"? Do they include the one-in-10,000 possibility of injury? What about risks that are not reasonably to be expected to occur?

The expressed standard, "reasonable explanation," is perhaps as satisfactory as any that can be devised, but it badly needs embellishment.[104] Since nontherapeutic experimentation by definition does not benefit the subject affected, the standard of the reasonable medical practitioner that is applied when a doctor is caring for a sick patient will doubtless not be available, and the informed consent will be judged on recognized contract principles. This means that failure of the experimenter to disclose facts that the "reasonable man" *would want to know* before serving as the subject of experimentation will vitiate the consent. This standard may differ greatly from what a "reasonable investigator" would have revealed under the circumstances. For one thing, the jury's role would be ostensibly greater under the "reasonable man" standard and expert testimony would be largely dispensed with in establishing whether a duty had been breached.

3. *Evaluating the Voluntariness of Consent Obtained*

We find that the consent must be "voluntary"; the person involved must be "so situated as to be able to exercise free power of choice"—so say the Nuremberg Articles, the American Medical Association "Guidelines," and the FDA Regulations. But when is consent truly voluntary? When is it the result of a free power of choice? Even with a normal adult the question may be raised by opening up a great range of psychoanalytic possibilities with which the law probably ought not to concern itself. But even setting these matters aside, consider the following possibilities:

Children. What about the use of children as subjects of experimentation? If the child has reached the age of understanding so that he can appreciate the inconveniences and risks, his consent together with that of his parents should suffice, or perhaps at some age short of majority his own consent becomes sufficient, as it would be in case of needed therapy.[105] But what about children who are too young,

---

[104] Under the present formulation shocking action can be taken even in seemingly good causes. In Hyman v. Jewish Chronic Disease Hosp., 42 Misc. 2d 427, 248 N.Y.S.2d 245 (Sup. Ct. 1964), *rev'd per curiam*, 21 App. Div. 495, 251 N.Y.S.2d 818, *rev'd*, 15 N.Y.2d 317, 258 N.Y.S.2d 397, 206 N.E.2d 338 (1965), a substance derived from cancer cells was injected into chronically ill patients, who were told only that they would receive a harmless substance which might cause some discomfort. In a separate proceeding the doctors were disciplined on the ground that this was not enough information to satisfy the informed consent requirement. *See* Langer, *Human Experimentation: New York Verdict Affirms Patients' Rights*, 151 Sci. 663 (1966).

[105] RESTATEMENT OF TORTS § 59, comment *a* at 111 (1939), dealing with therapy situations, states as follows:

"If a child or person of deficient mental condition, though under guardianship, is capable of appreciating the nature, extent and consequences of the invasion, his assent prevents the invasion from creating liability, though assent of the parent, guardian or other person is not obtained or is expressly refused. If the invasion is one the nature, extent and consequences of which the child or person of deficient mental condition is incapable of appreciating, the invasion creates a liability unless the parent, guardian or other person [standing in like relation] has consented, in which case the consent of the parent, guardian or other person, if it be within his power to give it, is effective though the child objects to the invasion."

Although this comment is addressed to therapy situations, it is possible that the same principle might apply to experimentation.

who cannot understand the material facts—the infants just born, the eight-year-olds? Obviously they cannot give "informed" consent. May the parents consent for them? In case of needed treatment for illness the parents can, of course, consent. There is less justification for validating the parental consent in the case of nontherapeutic investigation for the benefit of medical science. But because of the public's interest in the advance of medical science, the door to the use of infants should not be completely closed so that research in diseases and conditions of infants cannot be conducted. New guidelines and possibly special safeguards are called for. Observational procedures would be unobjectionable, but procedures that involve significant dangers to the mind or body should certainly be controlled if not prohibited.[106]

Prisoners. Can a "voluntary" consent be obtained from prisoners? Or are institutional pressures inevitable and such as to preclude freedom of choice. Federal prisoners are used in considerable numbers by federal investigators. In Iowa, prisoners may be used, but they must volunteer in writing and may withdraw consent at any time.[107] In Virginia, prisoners are permitted to participate in medical research under regulations prescribed by the State Board of Prisons.[108] Prisoners have time on their hands, and many of them might welcome medical experimentation as a means of gaining a little variety in their daily routines and some self-respect. If no pressures are exerted, if no special parole favors are held out as bait (although serving as a subject can constitute favorable evidence on the parole record), and if freedom to withdraw at any time is preserved, there would seem to be good justification for use of adult prisoners who consent after being reasonably informed.

Mental incompetents. Much the same questions arise with mental incompetents as in connection with children except that the possibilities are somewhat more favorable for using them in the process of needed therapy. They certainly should not be used without consent of a parent or guardian. Consent of the institutional authorities is, of course, necessary, but not sufficient. Again some carefully drawn guidelines would be helpful.

Students, nurses, or employees. If these subjects are adults the only question is that introduced by possible pressures. Can they really exert freedom of choice? Or will the hope of better grades or job preferment exert undue influence? If pressures cannot be eliminated these persons should not be used. Guidelines would help, but the matter defies precise definition.

Paid subjects. A financial reward prompts further concern that consent is not voluntary, that economic need may have overcome the patient's judgment. The problem seems closely akin to the case of prisoners, students, nurses, and employees, but it has not been spelled out in any of the published principles. This would seem to be an area where guidelines could be used to point out the potential for abuse.

---

[106] *See* Freund, *supra* note 89, at 46-49; Morse, *supra* note 98, at 757.
[107] IOWA CODE ANN. § 246.47 (Supp. 1966).
[108] VA. CODE ANN. § 53-57.1 (Supp. 1966).

4. *The Future.*

With the vast increase in medical experimentation on human beings and the likelihood of personal damage to subjects of experimental procedures, we may be sure that some type of regulation is inevitable. One or two unfortunate occurrences will precipitate it. What form will this regulation take? Statutes adopted by state legislatures are not likely to prove satisfactory. They are not adopted in a scientific atmosphere. Moreover, they are usually too rigid, and they cannot possibly meet all of the variants of the many problems involved. Likewise, administrative regulations are likely to be rigid, bureaucratic, and not too satisfactory. Administrative "guidelines" issued by government officials are something fairly new on the scene, but they can be one-sided and can even be dangerous in an essentially scientific area. Yet in some way law is certain to take a hand.

Doubtless the optimum approach is through carefully drawn and objectively considered codes or guidelines drafted by the professions for themselves such as those above sketched. Yet these may be hard to come by, for views diverge and a consensus may be difficult to obtain. The expressions of principle to date have been characterized by progress but also by generality that is not easily applied in practice. More efforts of this kind are needed, however, until the gap between published principles and practical application is eliminated or greatly narrowed. The medical profession's good record to date is to be noted with favor, but vigilance to avoid the equivalent of the thalidomide tragedies is called for.

VI
Evaluation of the Role of Law in Medical Progress

The foregoing discussion should make it apparent that the law is going to play a large role in the future of at least the four medical areas explored in this article, and the same is true of other areas in which law and medicine interact. No longer will the doctor be the free agent responsible only to his conscience, his Hippocratic oath, and some rather general ethical principles. The law will be a part of his life. The sources of law are many. Legislatures fill the statute books; courts fill volumes of case reports; administrators issue reams of regulations. Neither legislators nor judges nor administrators are omniscient, especially in the scientific world of which medicine is a part. They need all the help they can get.

In the statutory field the American Law Institute's Model Penal Code has made a significant contribution to improvement in the statute law on abortion; the National Conference of Commissioners on Uniform State Laws will do the same for homotransplantation. These important deliberative bodies are made up of objective, legally trained persons who work *pro bono publico.* Perhaps law and medicine could learn to work effectively together through a prestigious interprofessional group possessing a similar dedication to the public interest. Certain it is that in the years to come the advance of medical science will create a host of new problems of concern to the law, and lawyers will be constantly seeking to readjust the legal order to meet changing social needs. The two professions can benefit society as well as themselves by working harmoniously side by side in seeking the solutions that best accord with the public interest.

ORGAN TRANSPLANTATION IN MEDICAL AND LEGAL PERSPECTIVES*

DELFORD L. STICKEL[†]

INTRODUCTION

The interests of law and medicine interrelate at many points. It is not surprising, therefore, that a number of medical-legal questions have arisen in the wake of recent rapid advances in medical science. Several of these questions have arisen in the field of tissue and organ transplantation. The purpose of this paper is to draw attention to some of these questions; to describe the medical situations out of which they arise; and to suggest, from the medical point of view, the considerations which seem of importance in seeking solutions to the legal problems that exist.

I

MEDICAL BACKGROUND

A. Transplantation: Treatment by Replacement

The main principle upon which transplantation as a form of treatment is based is quite simply the principle of replacement. In situations wherein disease is confined to one part of the body, and that part of the body is damaged beyond repair, restoration of health depends upon some form of replacement of that part. There are three general categories of replacement. First, the replacement may be only a functional replacement, such as, for instance, injections of insulin for the patient with diabetes due to disease of the pancreas, or of thyroid extract for the patient with inadequacy of the thyroid gland. Second, replacement may be in the form of artificial devices: false teeth; artificial limbs; pacemakers of the heart; artificial heart valves; artificial bones; artificial blood vessels; and artificial entire vital organs: artificial kidneys and temporary artificial hearts and lungs. Transplantation of tissues and organs is the third category. The choice of which category of replacement to employ will vary with different tissues and organs depending upon the relative cost and effectiveness of the available types of replacement.

B. Transplantable Tissues and Organs

Either in animals or in man the following tissues and organs have been removed from the body and transplanted into another individual with a good functional

---

* Preparation of this paper was supported in part by U.S. Public Health Service Grants GM 12535 and MO 1 FR 30.

† A.B. 1949, M.D. 1953, Duke University. Fellow, American College of Surgeons; Diplomate, American Board of Surgery; Diplomate, Board of Thoracic Surgery. Associate Professor of Surgery, Duke University Medical Center. Chief, Surgical Service, Veterans Administration Hospital (Durham). Contributor of articles to medical and surgical journals.

result: blood (if blood may be considered a tissue), cornea of the eye, kidney, skin, bone marrow, liver, lung, heart, intestine, pancreas, endocrine glands, ovary, lymph nodes, spleen, bone, cartilage, arteries, and veins. Thus, the list is long, and it includes most of the vital organs.[1] In the treatment of human disease, success thus far has been confined for the most part to blood, the cornea of the eye, and (to a limited extent) the kidney. Blood vessels, bone, and cartilage may be added to the list, but their function does not depend upon their staying alive in the recipient. From experience with animals, however, there is every reason to believe that all of the other tissues listed eventually will be transplantable in man. Quite a few experimental animals, particularly dogs, are frisking around in good health, living and depending entirely on hearts or livers transplanted from other dogs;[2] and it would seem now almost to be a rule: if accomplished in dogs it soon will be done in man. Indeed, as this was being written, the press prominently reported the initial success of a homotransplantation of a human heart in South Africa.[3] Multiorgan transplants also appear imminent, as for example one combination which already has been attempted a time or two in patients with some success: the combination of transplanting kidney and pancreas for the patient with both severe kidney disease and severe diabetes.[4] It would appear that there will be further advances, and undoubtedly new questions which will be as numerous and as perplexing as those we confront today.

Nerves and any structure the function of which is dependent upon a nerve supply recover only a fraction of normal function when one attempts either transplantation or reimplantation back to the same individual. A measure of success has been achieved with the recovery and reattachment of extremities severed in accidents; but failure of complete restoration of function of the nerves (and therefore persistence of considerable numbness and paralysis of the tranplanted part) results in a rather limited degree of success.[5] The brain and the spinal cord may for all practical functional purposes be regarded as not transplantable in the foreseeable future.

C. Kidney Transplantation

Most of the medical-legal questions to be discussed are of importance with respect to kidney transplantation. Further, since the clinical transplant experience of the author has been entirely with the kidney, kidney transplants will be discussed in the greatest detail. Transplants of cornea, bone, cartilage, and blood vessels raise few if

---

[1] *See generally* M. WOODRUFF, THE TRANSPLANTATION OF TISSUES AND ORGANS 251-615 (1960); Shumway, Angell & Wuerflein, *Process in Transplantation of the Heart*, 5 TRANSPLANTATION 900 (1967); Starzl et al., *Homotransplantation of the Liver*, 5 TRANSPLANTATION 790 (1967).

[2] *See* Shumway, Angell & Wuerflein, *supra* note 1, at 901-02; Starzl et al., *supra* note 1.

[3] *See, e.g.*, N.Y. Times, Dec. 4, 1967, at 1, col. 2; *id.* at 57, col. 1.

[4] Kelly et al., *Allotransplantation of the Pancreas and Duodenum Along With the Kidney in Diabetic Nephropathy*, 61 SURGERY 827 (1967).

[5] *See generally* Inoue et al., *Factors Necessary for Successful Replantation of Upper Extremities*, 165 ANNALS OF SURG. 225 (1967).

any additional medical-legal questions. Transplantation of liver, lungs, heart, skin, gonads, endocrine glands, and other tissues no doubt will create new medical-legal questions; but clinical experience with these thus far has been scant.

1. *Kidney Transplantation and the Artificial Kidney*

For the patient who has lost all kidney function of his own, these forms of treatment provide means—the only two means available at present—to maintain life. Both the artificial kidney and transplantation have shortcomings, and both fall short of being ideal forms of treatment; but with either, health can be restored to the point of return to gainful employment. The advantages and disadvantages of each of these forms of treatment are such that they complement each other; and in the course of treating a particular patient, treatment is likely to depend primarily upon the artificial kidney at times and primarily upon a transplant at other times. In most centers, therefore, these two forms of treatment are available in a combined program. Both are complex. Both require great financial outlays and place a heavy demand upon skilled and professional services which are in short supply. By using both forms of treatment in a combined program more patients can be treated than if all available resources were concentrated on one or the other.

2. *Judging the Success of Kidney Transplants*

Well over a thousand kidney transplants have been performed in patients throughout the world.[6] This experience has been almost entirely during the last thirteen years, and three-quarters of it has been in the last five years or so. In judging success or failure in an individual patient or in a series of patients, it is important to remember that kidney transplants can function well for a number of weeks or even months only to fail later on. The transplant can fail after the patient has returned home from the hospital and made what would appear to be a complete recovery. Most of such failures, however, occur during the first six months; the failure rate decreases thereafter. The one-year point in time is arbitrarily taken as a point at which to judge success or failure, partly because one year is a round number but more significantly because transplants that are functioning well at this time will function well for a number of additional years with but few exceptions. Because such a large proportion of our total experience has been in the last five years, it is not yet possible to predict the long-term success rate, that is, results as of five, ten, or more years after the transplant.

Results are steadily improving. The improvement appears to be partly the improvement that accompanies experience and partly improvement from new techniques of management. Particularly encouraging is the progress already made and in prospect with regard to avoiding or overcoming the problem of immunologic rejection of incompatible transplants. This problem, however, is still the main

---

[6] Murray, Barnes & Atkinson, *Fifth Report of the Human Kidney Transplant Registry*, 5 TRANSPLANTATION 752 (1967).

barrier which stands in the way of transplantation on a much larger scale and with a much greater success rate than is now possible.[7]

Failure of the transplant sometimes but not always results in death of the patient. The transplant that has failed can be removed; and in many cases treatment with the artificial kidney can be used until another donor is available.

3. *Living, Related Kidney Donors*

Kidney transplants can be divided into two main categories which can be considered separately: one in which the kidney is removed from a healthy close blood relative of the recipient, that is, a parent or a brother or sister; and the other in which the kidney is removed from the body of an unrelated person who has just died, the so-called "cadaveric" transplant.

With the use of living donors who are parents, brothers, or sisters of the recipient the success rate as of one year post-transplant is about sixty-five to seventy per cent.[8] In the successful cases health is restored either completely or almost completely with return to work in most instances. Because of the long-range uncertainties already discussed, transplant patients are not encouraged to have children; nevertheless, a small number of women have had children and have experienced little or no trouble in the process.[9]

A most important aspect of the use of a living donor is the risk to the healthy person who undergoes removal of one of his two normal kidneys. The risk can be described in two components: one, the immediate risk of operation; and the other, the long-range risk of living with one healthy kidney rather than with two. Both of these risks are small and hard to assess precisely; however, the following statements can be made. In the worldwide experience with over 650 such operations there have been no known fatalities or permanent disabilities.[10] The immediate risk of such ill effects therefore is low, but it is doubtful that the figure will remain zero forever. The risk of general anesthesia alone is about one in 2,000, and if one adds a comparable factor for the operative procedure itself one gets an over-all immediate risk of about one in 1,000 or some fraction of one per cent.

With regard to the long-range risk of living with one healthy kidney rather than with two, the first point to understand is that one healthy kidney provides more than adequate function. In other words, one's health is entirely normal so long as the one kidney is healthy. The risk lies entirely with the small probability that, through disease or injury, the person might lose the remaining kidney and need the "spare" and not have it. The probability that such a situation might arise is

---

[7] *See generally id.*

[8] *Id.* at 774.

[9] *See* Hume et al., *Comparative Results of Cadaver and Related Donor Renal Homografts in Man, and Immunologic Implications of the Outcome of Second and Paired Transplants*, 164 ANNALS OF SURG. 352, 386-87 (1966).

[10] Murray, Barnes & Atkinson, *supra* note 6, at 756, table 3.

quite low—so low that insurance companies insure at standard rates if the patient has had a kidney removed and is healthy in all other respects.[11]

Although both the immediate risk and the long-range risk of undergoing removal of a kidney are small, these risks are not negligible. Although not great, these risks are significant, and they are risks to which a healthy person would not submit lightly.

In the experience with the use of living, related donors it is perfectly clear that the benefits gained by the recipients have exceeded by far the losses, in terms of pain and temporary disability, suffered by the donors. In this sense the experience has been very good and gratifying. Legal and moral questions are raised, however; and of course the reason is that the donors in themselves stand to gain nothing tangible for the risks which they take.

4. *Cadaveric, Unrelated Kidney Donors*

As already noted, in this transplant situation the kidney used is one which has been removed from the body of a person just after death. The first consideration in this situation is the obvious fact that there is no risk to a healthy donor.

The second consideration is that patients who receive a cadaveric transplant usually wait many weeks or months before a suitable kidney becomes available. All this time the patient must be maintained on an artificial kidney, and treatment by artificial kidney is expensive and scarce. The number of cadaveric kidney transplants that can be performed therefore is limited partly by limited availability of artificial kidneys. In contrast, recipients of kidneys of living, related donors do not go through a long waiting period, require far fewer treatments on the artificial kidney, and therefore contribute relatively little to the shortage of the artificial kidney.

The third consideration is that kidneys that are to be transplanted ought to be removed not later than thirty minutes after the death of the donor and preferably sooner. If the kidneys are not removed within this time, post-mortem deterioration is excessive, and they cannot be used.[12]

The fourth consideration is that the success rate as of one year post-transplant is approximately thirty to forty per cent.[13] The results therefore are only slightly more than half as good as with the use of living, related donors. The difference in success between using a living, related donor and using a cadaveric, unrelated donor is due to the difference in *relationship* between donor and recipient and not due to the fact that the donor is living in one situation and dead in the other. In other words, the results are about the same with living unrelated donors as with cadaveric unrelated donors.[14]

---

[11] *See* Merrill, *Clinical Experience is Tempered by Genuine Human Concern*, 189 J.A.M.A. 626, 627 (1964).
[12] *See* Couch, Curran & Moore, *The Use of Cadaver Tissues in Transplantation*, 271 NEW ENG. J. MED. 691 (1964).
[13] Murray, Barnes & Atkinson, *supra* note 6, at 774.
[14] *See id.* at 771.

5. *Other Donors*

Healthy, living, unrelated donors constitute a minor category for reasons which already have been stated. Their use entails risk to a healthy person; and the anticipated success rate is as low as with the use of unrelated cadaveric donors. Nevertheless, a small number of such donors have been used, mostly spouses of recipients and prisoner volunteers.

In a biologically similar category is the use of a kidney removed from another patient as a surgical specimen. "Surgical specimen" is the term applied to the tissue or to an organ removed from a patient during a surgical operation. Such tissues and organs usually are diseased, deformed, or functionless prior to removal and therefore are rarely suitable for use as transplants. On occasion, however,—for instance, in an operation performed for the treatment of hydrocephalus, or in an operation for disease low in the ureter (the tube that transmits urine from kidney to bladder)—the necessary surgical procedure entails removal of a healthy kidney. With the use of such an organ as a transplant there is the advantage of being able to plan the procedure, as with other living donors. The anticipated success rate, however, is as low as with the use of cadaveric donors because donor and recipient are unrelated.

Rarely, the patient with kidney disease will have a healthy identical twin who is a suitable donor. Such a donor is uniquely suitable because the biologic problems of rejection are avoided. Tissues may be transplanted from an identical twin with anticipation of the same degree of acceptance as if the transplant were from one part of the body to another in the same individual.[15]

A small number of kidney transplants have been performed from chimpanzees and from baboons to man. There was no success with the use of baboons, which phylogenetically are not as closely related to man as are chimpanzees. The survival of one patient on a chimpanzee kidney for nine and one-half months[16] is a highly significant fact which alone justifies consideration of further use of chimpanzees for this purpose, especially if improved means of testing for tissue compatibility are developed or if methods to prevent rejection are developed which are much better than the methods presently available.

II

MEDICAL-LEGAL QUESTIONS

A. The Legality of Donation of Human Tissues

1. *Healthy Adult Donors*

In the worldwide experience with over 650 healthy adults who have donated a kidney remarkably few questions have arisen with regard to the legality of the

---

[15] *See* Murray & Harrison, *Surgical Management of Fifty Patients with Kidney Transplants Including Eighteen Pairs of Identical Twins*, 105 AM. J. SURG. 205, 214 (1963).

[16] Reemtsma *et al.*, *Renal Heterotransplantation in Man*, 160 ANNALS OF SURG. 384, 392-94 (1964).

donations, except for questions which pertain to informed consent of the donor. From the medical standpoint, therefore, there appears to be little need for laws to legalize such donation formally. The shifting emphasis from living to cadaveric donation may decrease still further the importance of considering enactment of such laws.

The law in Italy is an interesting exception. A law was enacted in 1940 which specifically forbade the removal of a part or an organ of the human body the loss of which permanently diminishes physical integrity.[17] Significantly, in the wake of advances in the field of kidney transplantation, a new law has been enacted which changes the 1940 statute at least with respect to kidney transplantation.[18] This law permits kidney transplantation from living donors who have given their consent, and establishes elaborate administrative mechanisms to control practice in this field. It is significant to note that judicial approval must be obtained before the removal and transplantation will be allowed.

Consent of the donor must be entirely *voluntary*, and the donor must be *informed* as to what the procedure entails. These qualities of consent have been discussed at great length as they pertain to this and to other consent situations; all this need not be reviewed in detail here.[19] One point, however, does deserve emphasis. The donor does not stand to derive physical benefit from the procedure to which he submits; therefore, the critical attention that has been given to the quality of the consent of the healthy living kidney donor is appropriate. Both with regard to donors who are closely related to the recipient, and with regard to unrelated healthy volunteers, prisoners, and others, the question frequently is raised whether the consent is properly informed and voluntary. Most difficult to deal with is the question whether subtle forms of coercion enter into family and other situations sufficiently to invalidate consent. Opinions vary on these questions of consent; and opinions vary with regard to the essential morality or immorality of the use of healthy, living donors. Accordingly, practice varies from, on the one hand, preponderant use of healthy, living donors[20] to, on the other hand, exclusion of healthy, living donors from consideration.[21]

The use of prisoner volunteers as kidney donors deserves a special note. Although no grounds have been established on which to declare the use of prisoners as absolutely wrong legally or morally, in Denver this practice was discontinued despite considerable experience which demonstrated unique medical and scientific advantages in their use. The reason given for the discontinuance of this practice was that the

---

[17] Cortesini, *Outlines of a Legislation on Transplantation*, in ETHICS IN MEDICAL PROGRESS 171, 172 (G. Wolstenholme & M. O'Connor eds. 1966).

[18] Presidential Decree of June 26, 1967, [1967] Gaz. Uff. 3478.

[19] *See* I. LADIMER & R. NEWMAN, CLINICAL INVESTIGATION IN MEDICINE (1963).

[20] *See* Starzl *et al.*, *Chronic Survival After Human Renal Transplantation*, 162 ANNALS OF SURG. 749 (1965).

[21] *See* Dossetor *et al.*, *Cadaver Kidney Transplants*, 5 TRANSPLANTATION 844 (1967).

use of prisoners, however properly handled in the local situation, was deemed inevitably to lead to abuse if accepted as a reasonable precedent and applied broadly.[22]

2. *Healthy Donors who are Minors*

Because the validity of their consent is subject to question, persons under twenty-one years of age generally are not considered as kidney donors. The issue is forced, however, in identical twin cases because the healthy identical twin is, biologically, uniquely suited to donate. In a discussion of several judicial cases,[23] one involving a set of identical twins nineteen years of age and two involving sets who were fourteen years of age, Curran observes that the action of the court in approving the renal transplant operation in each case was based (1) partly on the consideration that the donors understood the procedure and wished to donate and (2) partly on the consideration that, if approval had been denied, the donors would have suffered emotional trauma in being denied the opportunity to save their twins. While the actions of the courts in these cases may leave intact the principle that consent given solely by parent, guardian, or court on behalf of a minor is not valid except for procedures which benefit the minor, these cases do not constitute precedent for the general use of donors who are minors, even when the donor is an identical twin.[24]

3. *Surgical Specimens as Transplants*

As mentioned above, the opportunity for use of surgical specimens as transplants arises infrequently. Nevertheless, this situation raises two interesting medical-legal considerations. (1) If there is more than one method of treatment available for the patient who is the donor, the choice of treatment must not be influenced by the need to use the surgical specimen as a transplant to treat another patient; and the operation to remove the organ must not be modified at the risk of the donor to benefit the recipient, except by consent of the donor. (2) Such use of a surgical specimen may be regarded as extraordinary; it therefore might be wise to obtain the consent of the donor for such use of a specimen, even if disposition of the specimen is normally not the legal prerogative of the patient. Informing the patient generally

---

[22] Remarks of T. Starzl, in ETHICS IN MEDICAL PROGRESS 75-77 (G. Wolstenholme & M. O'Connor eds. 1966).

[23] Curran, *A Problem of Consent: Kidney Transplantation in Minors*, 34 N.Y.U.L. REV. 891 (1959), reprinted in I. LADIMER & R. NEWMAN, *supra* note 19, at 237. This article discusses Masden v. Harrison, No. 68651 Eq. (Mass. Sup. Jud. Ct., June 12, 1957); Husky v. Harrison, No. 68666 Eq. (Mass. Sup. Jud. Ct., Aug. 30, 1957); Foster v. Harrison, No. 68674 Eq. (Mass. Sup. Jud. Ct., Nov. 20, 1957).

[24] *See* Curran, *supra* note 23, at 893. In Bonner v. Moran, 126 F.2d 121 (D.C. Cir. 1941), the court was confronted with an analogous problem. A fifteen-year old boy consented to removal of his skin, in a graft operation, for the benefit of his cousin. He was taken to the operating physician by an aunt and there gave his consent, but his mother was never told of the operation. The physician was held liable, the court reasoning that "here we have a case of a surgical operation not for the benefit of the person operated on but for another, and also so involved in its technique as to require a mature mind to understand precisely what the donor was offering to give. . . . [T]he court below should, in the circumstances we have outlined, have instructed that the consent of the parent was necessary." *Id.* at 123. Implicit in this reasoning is the conclusion that, if consent had also been obtained from the parent, the court would have sanctioned the skin graft operation performed upon one minor for the benefit of another.

is advantageous, and there is the additional consideration that members of certain religious sects might oppose such use of a specimen on the same grounds that they oppose donation of blood for transfusion.

4. *Post-mortem Donation of Human Tissues*

With this topic it must be noted first of all that tissue and organ transplants are but one of several medical uses which are made of human bodies or parts thereof post-mortem. Whole bodies are dissected for teaching and research in human anatomy. Autopsies are performed to determine the cause of death either for medical purposes only or at the direction of the coroner or medical examiner in the public interest; and autopsies are useful in many aspects of medical research. Growth hormone extracted from human pituitary glands is an important therapeutic agent; and in some countries, particularly Russia, blood obtained freshly post-mortem has been an important source of blood for transfusions. Transplantation of the cornea of the eye is an established surgical practice which is completely dependent upon post-mortem donations. An increasing proportion of kidney transplants are procured from post-mortem sources. Limited use has been made of transplants of liver, lung, skin, heart valves, and other tissues obtained from dead bodies, and there is every reason to believe that progress in the field of transplantation will greatly increase the need for such transplants in the foreseeable future. In summary, human bodies and parts thereof are needed and used extensively in all three of the major subdivisions of medical science: diagnosis and treatment, education, and research.

Numerous legal considerations are encountered in fulfilling the needs listed in the preceding paragraph. Medical and legal technicalities intermesh so extensively on this subject that it is possible only through appropriate statutes to provide adequately for these medical needs and to provide at the same time due regard for the various rights and interests involved (some of which conflict with each other). Sound statutes require considerable joint medical and legal effort in the drafting and then considerable political effort and perhaps compromise to secure passage. A lag between the time a need is identified and the time it is provided for in statutory law is understandable, therefore, but disadvantageous nevertheless.

A special committee of the National Conference of Commissioners on Uniform State Laws is now, after a number of years of extensive medical and legal research, about ready to recommend a Uniform Anatomical Gift Act, which would provide for those uses of human tissues which are not provided for in autopsy laws.[25] Because not only the Uniform Anatomical Gift Act but also a summary of the underlying medical and legal considerations will be available shortly from the National Conference, there is no reason here to develop this topic in detail. To emphasize the scope and magnitude of this project, however, it is noteworthy that the proposed uniform act will take all of the following considerations into account:

---

[25] *See* Stason, *The Role of Law in Medical Progress*, in this symposium, pp. 563, 571-72.

(1) all of the medical uses of human tissues listed above, including the problem of securing organs within minutes of death for use as transplants; (2) the interests of the deceased in his own body; (3) the interests of the surviving spouse, relatives, or person assuming the duty of burial; (4) the public interest—for instance, in finding the cause of death when suspicious circumstances are involved and in medical education and research; (5) property rights in dead bodies; (6) existing autopsy laws; (7) the use of unclaimed bodies for medical education; (8) liability for mutilation of human bodies; (9) consent for the utilization of human tissues, either post-mortem by relatives or by will or other form of consent by the deceased; (10) determination immediately at the time of death that this consent is legally valid; and (11) conflict of laws between states. Although most states already have statutes that deal with some of the above considerations, in no state are the existing laws adequate to cope with all the problems raised. The Uniform Anatomical Gift Act will soon be available as a possible solution to these inadequacies. It is hoped that it will be promptly considered and enacted by the fifty state legislatures.

Opportunities for completing successful transplant operations would be increased at present by facilitating the transportation of human tissues and organs across state lines. The need for this transportation will become more acute in the future. Such transportation probably will involve federal as well as state laws. Interrelations between blood banks, the licensing of blood banks, and federal regulations regarding interstate shipments of blood apply to the transfusion of blood when it must be transported across state lines. As tissue and organ banks are developed and used more and more it will be necessary to coordinate medical and legal developments in considerable detail in order to arrive at workable arrangements for the transportation of parts of the human body.

B. Definition of the Time of Death

For reasons that will be given, it is not justified at present to deviate from the traditional medical and legal definition of time of death, which is that point in time when first it can be declared that heart, lungs, and brain all have irrevocably ceased to function. It generally is not difficult to identify this point in time with accuracy, and certainly death *has* occurred by this time; plausible arguments might be made for an earlier but probably not for a later time.

Until recently use of this definition had raised no serious questions. Now, however, questions regarding the management of patients during their last illness and definition of time of death are topics which are under considerable discussion.[26] Although the discussion has not arisen particularly with respect to transplantation, the subject is of obvious importance to transplantation because of the increased use that is being made of cadaveric donors. Patients now are resuscitated who

---

[26] *See, e.g.,* ETHICS IN MEDICAL PROGRESS *passim* (G. Wolstenholme & M. O'Connor eds. 1966); Williamson, *Life or Death, Whose Decision?*, 197 J.A.M.A. 793 (1966).

formerly might have been pronounced dead. Situations have been created wherein patients are kept alive by rather artificial means—so artificial, sometimes, that important questions are raised seriously. Is treatment being carried too far? Is the treatment really accomplishing any good? Should we re-examine the traditional medical and legal definition of time of death?

When the dying patient in question happens to be a prospective donor for another patient awaiting a transplant, another consideration is added which constitutes further reason to question, critically, practices which pertain to timing the pronouncement of death. In transplanting tissue from a cadaveric donor there is the need to remove the tissue from the body *after* the death of the donor but *before* the death of the tissue being removed. Tissues such as skin and the cornea of the eye remain viable up to twenty-four hours after death of the donor, and twenty-four hours is ample time to secure such tissues for use as transplants. As already mentioned, however, the time factor is more critical with tissues such as kidney, liver, lung, heart, and others which deteriorate rapidly after the death of the donor and which must be removed within a half hour or less of the time of death. If not removed within this critically short period of time, deterioration of the tissue is excessive, and the transplant does not function satisfactorily.

It of course would be medically, legally, and ethically wrong to do anything at the expense of the life or the comfort of the dying patient who is a prospective donor, just to secure a healthy transplant. On the other hand, it would seem one also has the obligation not to delay pronouncement of death unnecessarily when such a delay would reduce the likelihood of successful treatment of the recipient. The needs of the recipient constitute a new factor to be weighed in the situation which surrounds the death of a donor. No longer is an unnecessary delay inconsequential. Such a delay now could conceivably make the difference of life and death to the prospective recipient who awaits transplantation, but the possibility of this occurring or of a transplant's being rendered impossible by an unnecessary delay in fixing the time of death is quite remote.

The suggestion has been made that time of death be defined in new terms. Couch[27] has suggested that pronouncement of death not be delayed until *all* the vital organs cease to function but that death be pronounced as soon as it is certain that the function of any *one* irreplaceable vital organ has ceased irrevocably. By definition any biologic organism depends for its existence upon all its vital organs; and when the organism loses any one of its vital organs it no longer exists as a whole organism but only as a disintegrated collection of organs. After one vital organ is lost, signs of life in the other organs will persist for a time and, if artificially supported, for quite some time, varying considerably with the particular organ

---

[27] Couch, *The Legal Aspects of Human Organ Transplantation*, in PROCEEDINGS OF FIRST INTERNATIONAL CONGRESS [1967] OF THE TRANSPLANTATION SOCIETY (forthcoming).

in question; but such life is quite different and distinguishable from the life of the integrated organism.

These considerations can be applied to any biologic organism, especially to man. In man the question arises particularly in situations of irreversible loss of function of the brain and central nervous system. Indeed, certain practices already have been established which essentially regard human life as ceasing at that point in time when there is irreversible and complete loss of function of the brain. With regard to the decision whether or not to resuscitate or to restart a heart which has stopped, it now is generally accepted practice to base the decision not upon the likelihood of restoring function of the *heart* but upon the likelihood of restoring function of the *brain*. Restarting the heart is not attempted if function of the brain has been lost irrevocably.[28]

One must hasten to add there are many strictly *medical* questions to be answered before we can seriously consider defining time of death in terms of the central nervous system alone rather than in the traditional terms of cessation of all vital functions. How does one define, for instance, when loss of function of the brain is irreversible? The electroencephalogram (EEG) has been suggested as a useful tool with respect to this question, but a precise definition of time of death of the brain based on the EEG has not been established. How long must the EEG waves be absent before death is certain? And how much does this time vary with differing causes of death? For instance, will the time be the same for barbiturate poisoning as for brain tumor or for physical trauma to the brain?[29]

Arriving at a medical consensus on questions such as these and public acceptance of death defined in new terms undoubtedly will take some time. In the meantime, there seems to be no compelling necessity and no other justification (including a better alternative) for deviating from the traditional medical and legal definition of time of death.

C. Shortcomings of Available Insurance

1. *Professional Liability Insurance and Clinical Investigation*

Transplantation of tissues and organs engages physicians and surgeons with clinical investigation of two types. First, as a form of treatment of patients who are recipients, transplantation is still in the investigational phase in a number of respects. Second, healthy human volunteers are used as subjects in experiments, for instance, in test skin graft experiments, which are playing an important role in elucidating some of the biologic problems of transplantation in man.

Bergen[30] points out that most professional liability insurance policies are not explicit with regard to coverage of clinical investigation and therefore that interpre-

---

[28] *See* Jude, Kouwenhoven & Knickerbocker, *A New Approach to Cardiac Resuscitation*, 154 ANNALS OF SURG. 311, 316-17 (1961).

[29] ETHICS IN MEDICAL PROGRESS 69 (G. Wolstenholme & M. O'Connor eds. 1966).

[30] *See* Bergen, *Insurance Coverage for Clinical Investigation*, J.A.M.A., Aug. 7, 1967, at 305.

tation is subject to question. He states that there is no record of a court deciding whether the language of a professional liability policy covered liability associated with clinical investigation. He cites cases, however, wherein other questions of extent of coverage were raised. From such cases he observes that when insurance policies are tested in court the ruling tends to be in favor of the insured if the language is not clear. He suggests that only for activities which clearly are outside of the physician's professional practice would the courts be likely to deny coverage. In other words, most medical professional liability insurance policies probably cover clinical investigation though not explicitly and not beyond some question.[31]

Bergen then raises a question that is of interest with respect not only to professional liability insurance but also with respect to insurance coverage for experimental subjects and healthy living kidney donors, which is discussed in the following paragraphs. The question is, who should pay for the coverage? He suggests that the cost of underwriting any additional protection for the clinical investigator should be the responsibility of the organization which financially sponsors the research. The reasons he gives are (1) that the cost of such insurance is appropriately a part of the operational cost of the sponsoring organization, like any other cost; (2) that sponsoring organizations need protection themselves and could well provide personal insurance protection for the clinical investigators who work under their sponsorship; and (3) that the sponsoring organization could probably obtain the insurance coverage at lower cost than the combined cost of separate coverage for each of the investigators.

2. *Insurance for Healthy Volunteer Subjects of Human Experiments*

Insurance for healthy subjects of human experimentation generally is not available. Such insurance is needed to cover the financial risks to which subjects submit and for which there is no insurance coverage unless the physician in charge is found guilty of malpractice; insurance of this type, if widely used, would accomplish the same result as would the judicial evolution of a legal principle of "liability without fault" for harm resulting from experimentation.[32] The underwriting of such risks

---

[31] *See id.*

[32] Such strict liability might be accomplished by carrying out the implications of the widely stated but unfortunate principle that "the physician experiments at his peril." *See* notes 41-42 *infra* and accompanying text. But, while the object of shifting the burden of losses suffered by research subjects to those supporting the research is a valid one (*see generally* Comment, *Legal Implications of Psychological Research with Human Subjects*, 1960 DUKE L.J. 265, 274), the medical profession would have good reason to resent the achieving of this result by a process imputing blame to the experimenters in every case. Insurance of a nonmalpractice variety would seem to be the more desirable way of providing the needed protection for research subjects. Perhaps a legal doctrine imposing liability on the experimenter for failure to provide such insurance, enabling the injured subject to recover even in the absence of other negligence, would ultimately be appropriate; however, the availability and widespread use of such insurance would be prerequisites to such a legal rule, unless a duty to provide such insurance were created by legislation or regulatory action. In addition, the premiums on such insurance, which would presumably be set by negotiation between the insurer and the experimenter, would provide useful checks on overly dangerous research.

would accomplish two things: (1) It would relieve the subject of the financial risk associated with unanticipated but possibly serious untoward effects of the drug or procedure to which he submits. Admittedly, subjects in clinical investigation incur such expenses only rarely as a result of their participation; but when such expenses are incurred, it would seem that the subject ought not to be the one to pay. (2) In the event of such an unfortunate occurrence, insurance coverage of this nature would eliminate the motive of the subject to sue the physician for malpractice or to sue the hospital or the granting agency for negligence in order to recover his losses (in much the same way that workmen's compensation insurance protects employers from suits for negligence in connection with injury sustained by employees on the job). In short, such coverage would protect the subject, the physician, the institution, and the supporting agency. For the same reasons which Bergen expresses clearly with respect to professional liability insurance,[33] the supporting agency would appear to be in the best position to provide such coverage. In most instances this would be the National Institutes of Health.

3. *Insurance for Healthy Living Kidney Donors*

The kidney donor probably ought not to be forced to pay the expenses of his donation, whether the anticipated ordinary expenses of absence from work, travel, and medical care before and after the operation or the rare but possibly heavy expenses of treatment and disability resulting from unexpected complications. In practice, relatives, employers, and research grants usually assume the responsibility for the anticipated expenses, but there is no alternative but for the donor himself to take the risk of large unanticipated expenses. In this regard his position is quite comparable to the healthy volunteer in a human experiment. So long as kidney transplantation is carried out under the sponsorship of research grants, perhaps such insurance coverage could most appropriately be covered as suggested in the preceding section on healthy volunteer subjects. If the use of healthy living donors still is commonplace after kidney transplantation is established as a routine form of treatment, perhaps the recipient's health insurance carrier would be the one in the most appropriate position to underwrite this risk.

4. *Gaps in Health Insurance Coverage for Research Patients*

For a number of reasons patients who are the subjects of clinical investigation not infrequently have difficulty maintaining their health insurance in effect; and the organization which is sponsoring the research naturally limits its responsibility to paying only for treatment which is essential to the research. The resulting gaps can present problems to the patient, to the physician, and to the sponsoring organization; but these problems may dissipate as the trend to broader and broader coverage of the costs of health care continues.

---

[33] Bergen, *supra* note 30, at 306.

D. Self-Government Within the Medical Profession

Stason[34] has observed that professional codes constitute an important aspect of law. To what extent ought the legal questions raised by tissue and organ transplantation to be answered in the written and unwritten codes and standards of the medical profession?

A principle which has been established with respect to transplantation of cadaveric kidneys provides a good example of the resolution of a quasi-legal question within the medical profession. The principle is that there shall be a complete separation of authority and responsibility between the physician or group of physicians who are responsible for the care of the recipient and the physician or group of physicians who are responsible for the care of the patient who is a prospective donor. In other words, no one on the transplant team has any authority in the care of the donor before his death, and the determination of the time of death is exclusively the responsibility of the physician in charge of the patient who is the prospective donor.[35] The possibility of a physician's becoming involved in a potential conflict of interest between donor and recipient is thus recognized. Because of the pressures of time and the need to remove kidneys within a half hour of the time of death, and because the initial steps in preparing the recipient for the transplantation are undertaken before the death of the donor, this question can legitimately be raised: Will the care of the dying prospective donor tend to be any different because he *is* a prospective donor? In other words, can concern for the prospective recipient influence the care of the prospective donor? And, if so, is there any possibility that this will not be in the best interests of the prospective donor? Such a possibility, even though improbable, would be better excluded altogether; and to this end the principle noted above has been formulated and generally adopted in those transplant centers where cadaveric donors are used. This principle is included in the Uniform Anatomical Gift Act, and it probably is wise to give this principle the additional force of being incorporated into statutory law; but the significant point in the present context is that the principle initially was recognized and was adopted within the medical profession, as it should have been, and was not first imposed by external law.

Because of the investigative aspects of tissue and organ transplantation, the clinical practice of transplantation is subject to the codes of ethics for conducting clinical research, particularly the Nuremberg Code,[36] the Declaration of Helsinki,[37] and the statement of the Medical Research Council of Great Britain.[38] These professional

---

[34] Address by E. Blythe Stason at Lawyers and Physicians Conference, Lake Junaluska, N.C., Aug. 12, 1967.

[35] *See* Couch, Curran & Moore, *supra* note 12, at 693-94.

[36] *Trials of War Criminals Before the Nuremberg Military Tribunals Under Control Council Law No. 10*, 2 THE MEDICAL CASE 181 (1947), reprinted in Beecher, *Experimentation in Man*, 169 J.A.M.A. 461, 472-74 (1959).

[37] World Medical Association, *Code of Ethics of the World Medical Association* [Declaration of Helsinki], in 2 BRIT. MED. J. 177 (1964) (accepted at Helsinki in June 1964).

[38] Medical Research Council, *Responsibility in Investigations on Human Subjects*, 2 BRIT. MED. J. 178 (1964) (statement in Annual Report for 1962-63).

codes, judging from the extent to which they have been followed, appear to be good examples of effective self-government. In a legal analysis of the status of clinical investigation, Ladimer[39] observes that clinical investigation has been practiced extensively with remarkably little control by external law.

Some medical-legal questions, of course, practically insoluble except in the courts or by statutory law. Examples include questions discussed in two preceding sections: the questions pertaining to the identical twin donors who were minors and the questions that prompted the drafting of the Uniform Anatomical Gift Act.

Although professional codes may not be regarded generally as law, and although for the most part they are unwritten, they have some of the important attributes of law. Within the professional group to which they apply they constitute rules, principles, and standards of practice and conduct which generally are followed within the group, and violations are subject at least to the penalty of sacrifice of standing or reputation within the group and possibly to greater penalties. The greater penalties, rarely imposed, would include formal censure by, or suspension from membership in, the county medical society; suspension of hospital privileges (the privilege to treat patients in the hospital); and revocation of the doctor's license to practice. Professional codes of course apply only to a small segment of society; and compared to laws of local, state, and federal governments, professional codes generally are less formal and systematized in their creation, modification, and enforcement. The great advantages of simplicity and directness are strong arguments for self-government. There would appear, however, to be the proviso that self-government is satisfactory only insofar as it is effective and insofar as it is consonant, both in content and enforcement, with the expectations of society generally.

Self-government seems to relate to general law in two important respects. First, as already implied, enlightened self-government from within the profession obviates the need for government from without. Second, when a practitioner is called to task in a lawsuit he may be held liable if it be established that he failed to measure up to the standards and codes of practice within his professional community.

E. Transplantation, Clinical Investigation, and Medical Practice

Discussion in preceding sections has shown that legal problems raised in the area of transplantation are similar to legal problems in clinical investigation. One further point that is illustrated in experience with transplantation is that the investigative and the established components of medical practice may not be separable. A question that is often asked is whether kidney transplantation is of established value as a form of treatment or whether it is still an investigative form of treatment. The answer is that it is not one or the other but both. Kidney transplants

---

[39] *See* Ladimer, *Ethical and Legal Aspects of Medical Research on Human Beings*, 3 J. PUB. L. 467, 471, 497 (1954), reprinted in I. LADIMER & R. NEWMAN, *supra* note 19, at 179.

provide effective treatment which is obvious even to the untrained observer, but at the same time major unsolved problems limit the effectiveness of the treatment. There is no justification for undertaking this form of treatment without simultaneously conducting studies aimed at improving the treatment.

The investigative component of medical practice, characterized by the acquisition of new knowledge, coexists in practice with the established component, characterized by the utilization of existing knowledge. In a legal analysis of clinical investigation in relation to medical practice, Ladimer[40] emphasizes with a number of points the closeness of the relationship between the investigative and the established components: (1) Both the profession and society generally regard the advancement of scientific medical knowledge as one of the duties of the profession. (2) Between two extremes is a spectrum of types of practice which can be regarded as investigational in varying degrees. On the one hand there are highly formal and controlled clinical studies with either patients or healthy human volunteers. On the other hand there are trial and error searches among several established forms of treatment for the thing which works best in a given patient, which may or may not result in addition to general knowledge and which therefore may or may not be regarded as research. (3) With few exceptions all physicians engage at one time or another in practices which in some degree are investigational.

Considering that clinical investigation and established medical practice are so closely intertwined, it is remarkable that there has been so little formal recognition of the legitimacy of clinical investigation. As already noted, this may reflect a healthy degree of self-government within the profession. One is troubled, however, by the negativism of the legal maxim to which reference is usually made whenever the legality of clinical research is discussed—"the physician experiments at his peril."[41] It is reassuring to note that historically this admonition arose out of cases of irresponsible experimentation with new treatments without making full use of established forms of treatment.[42] Nevertheless, one is left with the feeling that laws that

---

[40] Ladimer, *supra* note 39, at 469-70, 482-83.

[41] "In 1767 the first malpractice case involving alleged experimentation, Slater v. Baker, 95 Eng. Rep. 860 (K.B. 1767), established the rule that experimentation was at the physician's peril." *Id.* at 476.
One authority has emphasized the negativism implicit in the law's characterization of any surgical procedure as an assault and battery which is legitimized only by the patient's express or implied consent. With specific reference to transplantation, he says "[I] would advocate viewing the whole transaction, from the start with the living donor to the finish . . . as one composite curative transaction. Even where blood, kidneys or corneas are stored, their removal is not in the nature of assault and battery . . . but is to be considered part of an intricate, curative procedure." Daube, *Transplantation: Acceptability of Procedures and the Required Legal Sanctions*, in ETHICS AND MEDICAL PROGRESS 188, 194 (G. Wolstenholme & M. O'Connor eds. 1966).
The perverseness of the law's assault and battery analogy is paralleled by that of the maxim quoted in the text, and one might hope that the implicit bias or burden of proof might be reversed by courts willing to recognize and endorse the experimental as well as the curative aspect of medicine. Still, this should not mean that the doctor should be permitted to balance the conflicting claims of science and the patient in a particular case but only that adherence to prevailing professional standards concerning informed consent and due care will relieve the doctor of liability.

[42] *See* Ladimer, *supra* note 39, at 476-80.

pertain to medical practice and medical licensure ought to recognize explicitly the investigative component of medical practice; advancing medical knowledge has, after all, been a part of the duty of the physician since the beginning of the scientific revolution.

F. A Digression on Law and the Educative Aspect of Medicine

Having referred to the law's seeming undervaluation of medicine's investigational responsibilities, we may appropriately digress from the subject of transplantation to note briefly some aspects of the law's attitude concerning the third component of the classic triad of medical care, the educative component.

The teaching of medicine has been regarded as an important activity within the profession since Hippocrates gave it prominence in the Oath of the Physician. Like research, teaching, unless too narrowly defined, is to some extent a part of virtually all types of medical practice. Only in the practice of solitary physicians in remote areas could one possibly find examples of medical practice almost totally devoid of both teaching and research. The training of new doctors and other medical personnel and the continuing education of practitioners is an essential element of providing medical services on a continuous basis, and there will necessarily be occasions when the best interests of individual patients may seem to be in conflict with educational goals. The law and the makers of policy must be alert to the importance of the educational function in resolving these apparent conflicts.

The law's undervaluation or misconception of the teaching element in the rendering of medical services is most apparent in Medicare regulations requiring that all surgical procedures on Medicare patients be performed by or under the "personal and identifiable direction of"—interpreted in the case of surgery as meaning "supervision in person by"—a staff surgeon other than an intern or resident.[43] This requirement must be met if a "reasonable charge" is to be collected under the Medicare program for the professional services rendered. The alternative, if supervision is not provided, is to have only some small portion of the resident's salary and other costs associated with the surgery reimbursed to the hospital.[44] The effect is thus to deny the usual professional fee on the ground that the surgeon, while professionally competent to perform the particular procedure, was still only a resident. The economic impact will be such that hospitals will in most cases provide the required supervision, at a loss of efficiency in the use of medical manpower and, as indicated below, of important educational advantages. In many instances, it can be predicted, the additional supervision provided will be only perfunctory because of the senior surgeon's feeling that his presence is not necessary except to qualify under these regulations.

---

[43] Social Security Administration Reg. § 405.521(b), 32 Fed. Reg. 12,602 (1967).

[44] Social Security Administration Reg. § 405.521(d), 32 Fed. Reg. 12,602 (1967), quoted in note 46 *infra*. The principle seems to be that the hospital's economic costs are to be covered but nothing more.

The chief objection that has been raised to these regulations has been their failure to make allowance for the essential characteristics of surgical training whereby the young surgeon is gradually given greater and greater responsibility, performing procedures of increasing difficulty throughout his residency.[45] By arbitrarily dividing surgeons into two groups, the trained and the untrained, without regard to the particular procedure and the individual's competence to perform it, the regulations misconceive and undercut the training process by penalizing the process of gradual exposure of the young doctor to responsibility in the operating room.[46] Thus, the regulation accords the diagnostic and treatment aspect of medicine a place in policy formation without due regard for the educative aspect; surely the careful education and training of young surgeons should be given greater weight. The regulation's deficiencies may be seen as an attempt to secure for Medicare patients the services of fully trained surgeons, in reaction against the impression that public patients have in the past been made available to residents and interns for "practice." The assumption that care rendered by interns and residents is necessarily of less than the best quality is unwarranted. In properly conducted training programs the residents—trained in the particular procedures which they undertake, supervised and assisted by senior surgeons as needed, and backed by all of the hospital's resources—provide surgical care which is of the same quality as that rendered personally by senior surgeons. Training in even the most complex and difficult procedures can and should always be accomplished without sacrifice in the quality of the diagnostic and treatment services rendered to the patients involved. There can never be any justification for accepting the needs for education and training as an excuse for providing less than the best in this quality. Notions to the contrary are fostered in the minds of the public by present Medicare policy, to the detriment of training programs.

---

[45] See Russell, *Surgical Education and Social Change*, 62 SURGERY 561 (1967).

[46] Social Security Administration Reg. § 405.521(d), 32 Fed. Reg. 12,602 (1967), purports to recognize the educational considerations and indicates a belief that reimbursement of the resident's salary and other costs is sufficient compensation to the hospital:

"(d) It is recognized that there will necessarily be situations where a patient will receive medical services in the teaching setting for which payment on the basis of reasonable charges will not be applicable. For example, there will be instances where it will neither be necessary from the standpoint of the medical needs of the patient nor appropriate from the standpoint of the continuing development of the residents' competence for there to be an attending physician who carries out the responsibilities referred to in paragraph (b) of this section. Whether or not a physician makes a charge recognized under the supplementary medical insurance program for services to patients which involve the participation of residents or interns, the hopsital can receive reimbursement on a cost basis for an appropriate share of the compensation it pays its residents and interns. If the teaching program is an approved educational activity of the hospital, reimbursement will also be available on a cost basis to the hospital for an appropriate share of the compensation it pays to physicians for teaching services (as opposed to professional services which contribute to the diagnosis or treatment of the patient) and for other costs of educational programs conducted by the hospital. These costs are allowable in accordance with the principles of reimbursement for provider costs (see § 405.421 of Subpart D)."

The effect, nevertheless, is to deny recovery for the value of services rendered, and the economic impact, either of foregoing the fee or of providing the additional supervision, will be felt in the cost of the hospital's other services.

Another area where social objectives, coupled with a faulty perspective on the needs of medical education, may tempt the law to intrude is the matter of patient privacy in teaching hospitals. Traditionally, public patients are exposed to residents, interns, medical students, other hospital personnel, and other patients more than are private patients; and public patients for understandable reasons are provided in many instances with less comfortable waiting, examining, and treating facilities. Private patients often are given priority over public patients in the scheduling of diagnostic and treatment procedures such as x-rays and operations.[47] It is thus understandable, and perhaps proper, that social progress would dictate some legal protection of Medicare clients and public patients from undue and demeaning intrusions on their personal privacy; but there persists a danger that the teaching process will be impaired if the patient population easily available for teaching purposes is curtailed or eliminated. Primary reliance for dealing with this problem must ultimately be placed on doctors' professional responsibility and on teaching hospitals' ability to instill proper attitudes. Legal and regulatory involvement in this area, if ultimately required as the result of the inadequacy of voluntary efforts, should be limited, it would seem, to the establishment of advisory guidelines created to balance the needs of medical education against patients' legitimate expectations concerning their personal dignity.

G. Transplantation, Privacy, and the Free Press

The patient and his family generally seek privacy especially when experiencing a crisis. There is hardly a time when they are less prepared to interview a reporter than when a transplant operation in the family is about to be performed or has just been performed. Both donor and recipient may be relatively young and parents of several dependent children; and the outcome, at least for the recipient, is all too uncertain. Despite carefully considered decisions beforehand, the tension within the family may be heightened by anxieties as to whether the right decisions were made. These feelings persist for days and subside only as evidence accumulates that all is going well. Public curiosity and the persistence of reporters are apt to appear morbid and to be resented. Exceptions to these observations do occur—most recently and most notably in the case of the South African who received the first heart transplant—but most families would prefer to avoid the notoriety.

Two separate factors can be identified in support of respecting the right of the patient and his relatives to privacy during such a crisis. One is the natural desire and simple right to be left alone. The other factor relates to the consent of the donor as discussed in a preceding section. There is general agreement that the freedom of the kidney donor to revoke his consent at any time, even at the last minute, must be protected. Revelation of the identity of the prospective kidney

---

[47] Davis, *The Future of Medical Education and Its Relationship to the Teaching Hospital*, 31 THE PHAROS OF ALPHA OMEGA ALPHA 6 (1968).

donor to a reporter, with or without a promise to withhold publication until after the transplant, would be inimical to this freedom. Families therefore ought to be counseled to avoid involvement with reporters especially prior to the operation. Overtures to "do a complete documentary" on a family experiencing a kidney transplant, beginning with pre-transplant interviews, ought to be discouraged in the strongest possible terms.

On the other hand the public news media have a responsibility in events which are of public interest. The level of interest tends to be high with regard to the introduction of new forms of treatment and with regard to procedures which capture the public imagination, such as transplantation of a vital organ from one person (living or dead) into another. Pursuit of stories and information which the public either needs or enjoys is a duty of the newsman. A number of effective techniques are available and necessary at times to obtain information which is either inherently difficult to obtain or deliberately repressed. How intensively, however, ought these efforts be pursued when invasion of privacy becomes a question?

In coping with situations wherein intense public interest tends to invade privacy, one needs a reasonable guide for determining which interest shall take precedence. Perhaps it would be useful to draw a distinction between two categories of public interest: public *curiosity*, which has little bearing on public welfare, and public *concern*, upon which public welfare does depend. To illustrate the distinction, the health of a particular private citizen may be the subject of intense public curiosity but not be of legitimate public concern; whereas the health of a candidate for public office is of legitimate concern to the voting public. The public needs to be kept informed with regard to newly available forms of treatment; and indeed, new forms of treatment do not reach their full potential of usefulness if the public is not informed. With few exceptions, however, the public does not need to know the personal details of individual patients undergoing new forms of treatment. Public curiosity, however intense, does not justify the revelation of personal details without the freely given consent of the persons involved.

The physician's first concern should of course be for his patient, so that when public curiosity threatens the patient's privacy and peace of mind he instinctively reacts protectively in behalf of the patient, who physically and emotionally may not be in a good position to protect himself. Of course the physician who is a clinical investigator has an additional responsibility, namely to publish the results of his studies. These he publishes in the scientific literature, thereby subjecting his findings to the critical review of the scientific community. Premature accounts in lay publications typically are overly enthusiastic about significance of success and discovery and, therefore, are more misleading than informational. As Moore[48] has emphasized, however, articles in the public news media are important sources of public education,

---

[48] F. MOORE, GIVE AND TAKE 169 (1964).

and the professional scientist can enhance the value of such articles by providing background information to science writers. Because the educational value of such writings depends little if at all on the identity and personal circumstances of patients, exclusion of information which tends to invade privacy generally does not reduce the value of articles. Moreover, it is through the use of personal information that articles not infrequently are given an emotional pitch which misleads readers. As judged from misimpressions which readers receive as a result of emotional slant, they sometimes misinterpret factually accurate articles. Personal information, then, is nonessential to educational content and actually can be detrimental.

News writers and science writers take the position that inclusion of personal information is important on occasion to increase interest, to increase the number of readers, and therefore to increase the total educational effect of an article. No exception is taken to this position. The patient is free to release personal information if he wishes to, and in order to enhance readership and to satisfy public curiosity, the writer is free to use personal information with the consent of the patient. The only constraints suggested are (1) that personal information be obtained without pressure (which invalidates consent and which is itself an invasion) and at a time which is suitable to the patient; and (2) that, when used, personal information be used in a manner to enhance and not to detract from educational effect.

Conclusion

Transplantation of tissues and organs accounts for many of the medical-legal questions that have arisen during the last decade or two in the wake of rapid advances in medical science.[49] In the foregoing discussion of some of these questions one can distinguish two means through which these questions can be approached and through which associated problems can be prevented or resolved.

First, there is the means of self-government and self-regulation within the medical profession. Numerous examples can be cited wherein general adherence to written or unwritten codes and standards of medical practice either have not left opportunity for problems to arise or have satisfactorily solved those problems that did arise. This approach, where applicable, has the great advantages of directness and simplicity. But to be applicable this approach must be effective and must be attuned to the expectations of the public.

Second, there is the means of answering questions and preventing or resolving medical-legal problems through the mechanisms of the courts, the legislatures, and the administrative offices having jurisdiction. Examples can be cited for which this is the only feasible approach. Perhaps the best current example of this approach is the drafting of the Uniform Anatomical Gift Act, a piece of recommended legis-

---

[49] Stickel, *Ethical and Moral Aspects of Transplantation*, 3 MONOGRAPHS IN THE SURGICAL SCIENCES 267 (1966).

lation which will bring together logically a complex of interrelated medical and legal considerations. This approach, too, must be responsive to the feelings and the needs of the public, and if it is to be effective in producing workable principles it must have the benefit of considerable joint medical and legal effort in the preparation and argument of cases, in the drafting of and lobbying for new legislation, and in the presentation of viewpoints and evidence to the responsible administrators.

HUMAN EXPERIMENTATION: ETHICS IN THE CONSENT SITUATION

JOHN FLETCHER*

I

BACKGROUND FOR AN ETHICAL APPRAISAL OF THE CONSENT SITUATION

The coupling of the art of healing with the method of scientific investigation for medical research in human beings causes many profound questions to leap into the minds of those whose consciences have been shaped within democratic and religious institutions. Many medical investigators who have carried out research in human subjects have attempted to describe the professional-ethical conditions under which these questions must be resolved.[1] A survey of the medical-legal literature and popularly written commentaries on experimental medicine likewise reveals a large number of essays attempting to supply the legal, political, medical, and moral dimensions of the several ways in which humans are presently utilized for research.[2] The overriding legal and moral importance of the subject's informed con-

---

* B.A. 1953, University of the South; B.D. 1956, Virginia Theological Seminary; Fulbright Scholar, University of Heidelberg, 1956-57. Assistant Professor of Church and Society, Virginia Theological Seminary. Th.D. Candidate, Union Theological Seminary. Contributor to theological publications.

I wish to express my thanks to Roger L. Shinn and Charles Gozonsky for a critical reading of the first draft of this essay and for several helpful suggestions. Dr. Robert Farrier and the Reverend LeRoy Kerney of the Clinical Center, National Institutes of Health, Bethesda, Maryland, made it possible for the author to work in the ideal setting for study of the question of human experimentation. The essay does not necessarily represent the views of the National Institutes of Health.

[1] For the most extensive anthology and bibliography on the subject of human experimentation, *see generally* I. LADIMER & R. NEWMAN, CLINICAL INVESTIGATION IN MEDICINE (1963). The beginning inquirer will perhaps be aided in following the writing of Dr. Henry K. Beecher, a scientist who has earned the right to speak authoritatively on human experimentation. Beecher's writings prior to 1963 are cited in *id.* at 496. Later writings are *Consent in Clinical Experimentation: Myth and Reality*, 195 J.A.M.A. 34 (1966); *Some Guiding Principles for Clinical Investigation*, 195 J.A.M.A. 1135 (1966); *Ethics and Clinical Research*, 274 NEW ENG. J. MED. 1354 (1966).

[2] Some 500 articles and books are collated in I. LADIMER & R. NEWMAN, *supra* note 1, at 494-516. Since 1963 some of the most informative writings are the following: ETHICS IN MEDICAL PROGRESS (G. Wolstenholme & M. O'Connor eds. 1966) [hereinafter cited as ETHICS IN MEDICAL PROGRESS] (with special reference to transplantation); NATIONAL ACADEMY OF SCIENCES, NATIONAL RESEARCH COUNCIL, USE OF HUMAN SUBJECTS IN SAFETY EVALUATION OF FOOD CHEMICALS (Proceedings of a Conference, 1967); Alexander, *Limitations of Experimentation on Human Beings with Special Reference to Psychiatric Patients*, 27 DISEASES NERV. SYST. 61 (Monograph, July 1966); Freund, *Ethical Problems in Human Experimentation*, 273 NEW ENG. J. MED. 687 (1965); Langer, *Human Experimentation: Cancer Studies at Sloan-Kettering Stir Public Debate on Medical Ethics*, 143 SCI. 551 (1964); Langer, *Human Experimentation: New York Verdict Affirms Patients' Rights*, 151 SCI. 663 (1966); Morse, *Legal Implications of Clinical Investigations*, 20 VAND. L. REV. 747 (1967); Ruebhausen & Brim, *Privacy and Behavioral Research*, 21 AM. PSYCHOLOGIST 423 (1966); Scribner, *Ethical Problems of Using Artificial Organs to Sustain Life*, 10 TRANSACTIONS AM. SOC'Y ARTIFICIAL INTERNAL ORGANS 209 (1964); Stumpf, *Some Moral Dimensions of Medicine*, 64 ANNALS INTERNAL MED. 460 (1966); Wolfensberger, *Ethical Issues in Research with Human Subjects*, 155 SCI. 47 (1967); Comment, *Experimentation on Human Beings*, 20 STAN. L. REV. 99 (1967); Editorial, *Moral Problems in the Use of Borrowed Organs, Artificial and Transplanted*, 60 ANNALS INTERNAL MED. 309 (1964); Editorial, *The Experimental Use of Human Beings*, 65 ANNALS INTERNAL MED. 371 (1966).

sent to the experiment is widely noted, but nowhere in the broad and varied literature is there an empirically based study of the interactions of those who give and those who obtain this consent. The consent situation has been treated heavily from the vantage point of principle but lightly from the ground of practice.

This article attempts to assess the potential in the existing legal and professional-ethical environment for continuing legal and moral conflict over the validity of a subject's consent to experimentation. The approach adopted, however, is that of a student of ethics, and the study proceeds to explore the conditions of consent-giving in this light and to formulate, from this same ethical perspective, some untested but promising hypotheses for the improvement of the consent situation itself. The reader may be interested to see how the law and professional ethics of human experimentation, and current practices, coincide with or diverge from the conclusions ventured here.

A. The Legal and Professional-Ethical Context

Since the formulation of the Nuremberg Code in 1947,[3] there have been a number of other codifications by international and national professional medical bodies.[4] These formulations essentially embody the ten well-known criteria of the Nuremberg Code. In addition, and of special legal interest, there are several important regulations, directives, and policy memoranda spelling out procedures within research institutions themselves.

In this country the most influential of these quasi-legal mandates originate within the federal government and its health agencies. In July 1966, the Surgeon General issued a policy and procedure statement to all grantee institutions,[5] in which requirements for review to insure the rights of individuals involved in clinical research were set forth. In substance the directive stipulated that no grants in support of research were to be continued or awarded unless arrangements were made for consideration of proposals for research involving human subjects by the author's institutional associates in a committee organized along interdisciplinary lines. In brief, these institutional committees are charged with determining three things: (1) that the rights and welfare of those involved are protected, (2) that appropriate methods

---

[3] *Trials of War Criminals Before Nuremberg Military Tribunals Under Control Council Law No. 10*, 2 THE MEDICAL CASE 181 (1947), reprinted in Beecher, *Experimentation in Man*, 169 J.A.M.A. 461, 472-74 (1959).

[4] American Psychological Association, *Ethical Standards of Psychologists*, 14 AM. PSYCHOLOGIST 279 (1959); World Medical Association, *Code of Ethics of the World Medical Association [Declaration of Helsinki]*, 2 BRIT. MED. J. 177 (1964) (accepted at Helsinki in June 1964); Medical Research Council, *Responsibility in Investigations on Human Subjects*, 2 BRIT. MED. J. 178 (1964) (statement in Annual Report for 1962-63); American Medical Association, *Ethical Guidelines for Clinical Investigation* (approved by House of Delegates on Nov. 30, 1966), in Declaration of Helsinki and AMA Ethical Guidelines for Clinical Investigation (undated pamphlet printed by the AMA).

[5] Surgeon General, Public Health Service, Dep't of Health, Education, and Welfare, Investigations Involving Human Subjects, Including Clinical Research: Requirements for Review to Insure the Rights and Welfare of Individuals, PPO 129, Revised Policy July 1, 1966.

are used to obtain informed consent, and (3) that the risks of the procedure are proportionate to the potential medical benefits.[6]

A memorandum was issued on the same date from the Office of the Director of the National Institutes of Health (NIH) outlining the group consideration and informed consent practices which would obtain for each Institute.[7] An ascending system of review committees, beginning in each Institute, rising to a Clinical Research Committee of the Medical Board, and culminating in the Medical Board itself, was arranged to pass on (1) all research projects involving the participation of normal volunteers, (2) therapeutic or diagnostic studies with unusual hazard which might be referred for approval, and (3) nondiagnostic, nontherapeutic studies involving patients which might be referred. Expectations of voluntary and informed consent of patients and volunteers were outlined along with procedures for making records of such information. In the realm of principles, the statement underlined these as central to clinical research: (1) group consideration, (2) informed consent of the patient or volunteer, and (3) the freedom of the subjects to withdraw from a project at any time. As many research institutions model their practices after NIH, the effects of this memorandum, coupled with the significant changes brought about by the policy statements of the Surgeon General, extend far beyond their source. The Institutes, with a proposed budget for 1968 of $1.4 billion, now support some 65,000 senior researchers, over 2,000 research and training institutions, and 30,000 clinical and basic scientists who are undergoing additional training.[8]

In carrying out the requirements of the federal Food, Drug and Cosmetic Act[9] in the field of regulating the use of investigational drugs in interstate commerce, the Food and Drug Administration has recently required the written consent of the patient in all cases where investigational drugs are administered.[10] The regulation itself develops criteria to judge meaningful consent and furnishes examples of situations when exceptions to the written consent requirement may be made by the physician. In these latter respects the regulation is unprecedented, and the document could prove to be a significant collateral source of standards governing consent. The specific exceptions to the general rule of written consent will be discussed later in this paper.

Occasional statutes and formal codes of professional ethics may furnish other

---

[6] *Id.*

[7] Memorandum on Group Consideration and Informed Consent in Clinical Research at the National Institutes of Health, from Director, National Institutes of Health to Institute Directors *et al.*, July 1, 1966.

[8] Medical World News, July 7, 1967, at 61, col. 3.

[9] 52 Stat. 1040 (1938), *as amended*, 21 U.S.C. §§ 301-392 (1964, Supp. II, 1965-66).

[10] Food and Drug Reg. § 130.37, 32 Fed. Reg. 8753 (rev. June 20, 1967). For legal discussion the reader should note Morse, *supra* note 2, at 762, 763. For interpretation of FDA policy and history of the amendment, see Gottlieb, *Federal Legislation and Regulations*, in NATIONAL ACADEMY OF SCIENCES, *supra* note 2, at 175-81.

sources of standards for clinical investigation.[11] A further source, in the form of precedent which, while not binding, is persuasive in establishing professional practice, might be directives stating expectations or memoranda describing actual practices in outstanding institutions. Another source might be judicial precedent, but the legal situation with regard to judicial decisions on the appellate level concerned with human experimentation has not changed since Sessoms noted as follows in 1958:

> No reported court decision has considered research specifically in terms of the right and liability of a trained professional to use a living patient or a normal subject as a means of discovering new knowledge not necessarily of direct benefit to that patient or subject. None of the cases that have actually come before the appellate courts have involved a real scientist observing the proper precautions and giving primary consideration to the welfare of his patient.[12]

There is, however, one important decision by an official, quasi-public American body in regard to a specific case. This was the censure in 1966 by the Regents of the University of the State of New York of Drs. Southam and Mandel.[13] The Regents have jurisdiction in New York over all public and private education and all licensed professions except the practice of law. It is composed of fifteen members elected for fifteen-year terms by both houses of the New York legislature. After their examination of the charges that the two physicians had not obtained adequately

---

[11] Ladimer, *Ethical and Legal Aspects of Medical Research on Human Beings*, in I. LADIMER & R. NEWMAN, *supra* note 1, at 195.

[12] Sessoms, *Guiding Principles in Medical Research Involving Humans*, HOSP., Jan. 1, 1958, at 44, 60.

[13] For discussion of the decision of the Board of Regents of the State of New York, see Carley, *Patient Consent to Research: Rules Set*, Wall Street Journal, Jan. 21, 1966, at 12, col. 4; Lear, *Experiments on People—The Growing Debate*, SAT. REV., July 2, 1966, at 41; Langer, *Human Experimentation: New York Verdict Affirms Patients' Rights*, 151 SCI. 663, 664, 665 (1966). The Medical Grievance Committee of the Board of Regents of the State of New York initiated an investigation of the experiments following legal action by a member of the board of directors of the Jewish Hospital for Chronic Diseases, William A. Hyman, to inspect charts, records, death certificates, laboratory data, and so forth, pertaining to the patients participating in the experiments. Hyman v. Jewish Chronic Disease Hosp., 42 Misc. 2d 427, 248 N.Y.S.2d 245 (Sup. Ct. 1964), *rev'd per curiam*, 21 App. Div.2d 495, 251 N.Y.S.2d 818, *rev'd*, 15 N.Y.2d 317, 206 N.E.2d 338, 258 N.Y.S.2d 397 (1965). Hyman's motion was granted by the Supreme Court. On appeal by the hospital the Appellate Division of the Supreme Court reversed the previous decision on the basis of law and facts, but on grounds unrelated to standards for clinical investigation. This decision was appealed by Hyman, and the Court of Appeals reversed the second decision, holding that the director was entitled to an inspection of such records to investigate alleged improper experimentation on patients. The issue of confidentiality was to be solved by inserting an order that names of particular patients be kept confidential as the director inspected the records. Although the *Hyman* case was conducted on grounds of the rights of a member of a hospital board to inspect records when improper activities of the hospital were in question, the Appellate Division of the Supreme Court of New York did make the following observation as to standards for consent:
"The Hospital's future policy will be in accordance with petitioner's contention that experiments such as the one here involved should be done only with the patient's written consent after the patient has been properly informed. On September 7, 1963, the Hospital's Grievance Committee approved the experiment. On September 30, 1963, its board of directors approved its Grievance Committee's report. On January 27, 1964, the Hospital's Research Committee approved continuance of the cancer immunization studies, but only upon the written, informed consents of the patients."
21 App. Div. 2d at 499, 251 N.Y.S.2d at 822.

informed consent for the injection, in the course of an experiment, of cancer cells into twenty-two hospitalized and seriously ill patients, the Regents found the two guilty of obtaining consent fraudulently. The object of the procedure—to test the immune response in seriously ill persons—was not in question, but the method of obtaining consent was. Even though the cells were felt to be harmless to the patients, it was judged that because the investigators had not specifically stated what kind of cells were being injected, material information necessary to make an informed decision was withheld. The Regents suspended the licenses of the doctors for one year and then stayed this decision on condition of good behavior.

This decision is of legal significance because it was made by a legislatively appointed body and could possibly be persuasive to a court deciding a case involving similar circumstances. Of perhaps deeper significance is the vast effect that this widely publicized decision had in deepening public awareness of medical research in humans and of the central importance of informed consent.[14]

B. The Ascendency of Research

There are many indicators showing the increasingly rapid growth of medical research, as well as of research in the social sciences. Figures available through NIH show the following rise in appropriations for on-site and off-site research:[15]

	Off-site	*On-site*
1965	$545,000,000	$77,000,000
1966	604,000,000	82,700,000
1967	681,000,000	90,000,000

As an indicator of the financial commitment to research and its expansion through use of federal funds, the breakdown of figures in Table 1 confirms the general growth of research in all of the sciences. These figures indicate that behind such expenditures is a value commitment to a scientific foundation for the pursuit of sounder health and treatment of disease. The expanding system of research, however, multiplies the incidence of the utilization of human beings in its process, for there comes a point in the continuum of the experimental process when testing must be done in human subjects in order to complete the information necessary to application of new drugs or therapies. Moreover, the very magnitude of the funds available is a source of temptation to those who might find reasons to attach more importance and prestige to such funds than to the quality or necessity of research done. It is also sobering to reflect on the fact that this vast research "industry" cannot be maintained without human research subjects.

---

[14] *See generally* Lear, *supra* note 13; Goodman, *Doctors Must Experiment on Humans, But What are the Patient's Rights?*, N.Y. Times, July 2, 1967, § 6, at 12, col. 1.

[15] Figures available through the office of Dr. John Sherman, National Institutes of Health. These figures include appropriation for the National Institute of Mental Health which became a separate bureau in 1966. The figures for 1967 include appropriations to the Division of Environmental Health.

TABLE 1
(millions of dollars)
SUMMARY OF FEDERAL FUNDS FOR RESEARCH,
FISCAL YEARS 1965, 1966, 1967

Field of Science	1965 (actual)	1966 (estimated)	1967 (estimated)
Physical sciences, total	3,370.3	3,680.7	3,649.2
Life sciences, total	1,182.9	1,352.4	1,427.4
Medical sciences	819.4	953.1	1,015.9
Biological sciences	258.1	283.9	302.9
Social sciences	127.4	188.4	221.9
Psychological sciences	103.5	136.7	157.9
Agricultural sciences	105.3	115.4	108.7
Total	5,863.4	6,710.6	6,883.9

Source: National Science Foundation[16]

C. Values and Decision Making in Research

It may be observed that within the process of research activities there are several different occasions for decision making in which the socio-moral values of the decision-makers become more visible. Moving from the collective to the individual levels, at least three settings for decision making may be located.

1. *Social Policy Decisions*

Basic policy decisions as to which physical, social, or environmental conditions deserve attention, funding, and personnel are made against the background of a certain policy structure. The goals envisioned by policy makers have a crucial effect on how human beings will be involved in research.[17] Ethical questions can be fruitfully raised at this level, both as to the realism of goals and the ways in which policy makers intend and visualize the world. Imbedded in their decisions are images, drawn from many sources, which have a theological dimension insofar as commitment and loyalties are involved. Unfortunately, treatment of policy making at this level is beyond the scope of this paper.

2. *Institutional Decision Making*

Turning to the question of assessment of the scientific value and quality of design of each proposed experimental project, it would appear that effective schemes of interdisciplinary group consideration are a useful means of critique. However, a thorough study of the group consideration process in several research settings

---

[16] NATIONAL SCIENCE FOUNDATION, NSF 66-25, FEDERAL FUNDS FOR RESEARCH, DEVELOPMENT, AND OTHER SCIENTIFIC ACTIVITIES 77, 78 (1966).

[17] *See generally* Weinberg, *Criteria for Scientific Choice*, 1 MINERVA 159, 171 (1963); R. DUBOS, MAN ADAPTING 455 (1965); Simpson, *Biology and the Public Good*, 55 AM. SCI. 161 (1967); Gorovitz, *Ethics and the Allocation of Medical Resources*, 5 MED. RESEARCH ENGINEERING 5, 7 (1966).

remains to be done and would be an important addition to the literature on the social setting of human experimentation. The author's consultation with a number of investigators and officials[18] indicates that group consideration can be a reliable and just method of preventing the "thoughtless and careless" experiments which Beecher has criticized.[19]

The group consideration process is not infallible, for any process managed by human beings is subject to domination by the self-interest of an individual or clique. Enthusiasm for a particular project by a popular member or a desire for speed in decision could subdue challenges from other members. It is notable, however, that no legal challenges have arisen at this level of decision making. All of the rules of the Nuremberg Code can be effectively implemented through this method of regulation, depending upon the objectivity and freedom of members of the group to challenge proposals. The group review process would appear to be effective in estimating the significance of the experiment, its necessity, the calculated risks in proportion to the importance of the benefits, the conditions and protocol for the experiment, and the skills and training of the investigators. Rules regarding termination of the experiment by subject or investigator, and the rule regarding consent, are less amenable to implementation through group review since they presuppose a transaction between those persons, though in regard to each of these rules the advisory group may review methods of obtaining consent and effecting termination.

3. *Investigator-Subject Decision Making*

Experiments in medical research may be designed to study a general condition which the patient presents, but the conduct of the study may not aid the patient directly. This kind of study is for the purpose of enlarging the general knowledge of medicine and is referred to in this paper as "nonbeneficial." Other studies may be designed to test diagnostic or therapeutic procedures and thus may have a direct "beneficial" effect upon the patient. Experimental subjects for all studies may include patients as well as normal volunteers. The complexity of the issues that arise stems from the great variety in the types of research, the varying degrees of risk and potential benefit, and the variations possible in the prospective subject's personality and physical condition; when the categories of minors or persons too ill to give consent are added, new participants in the form of guardians, parents, or other representatives of the patient may appear, adding additional permutations to existing complexity.

Article 1 of the Nuremberg Code charges the principal scientific investigator with the responsibility of obtaining informed consent and with being the judge of

---

[18] Twenty interviews were conducted by the author, June-Aug. 1967, in the Clinical Center, National Institutes of Health, with senior investigators, administrators, and legal advisers.

[19] Beecher, *Ethics and Clinical Research*, 274 NEW ENG. J. MED. 1354, 1356-59 (1966).

the quality of that consent. Each of the possible combinations of investigator-subject relations deserves careful study from the legal and ethical points of view. Only the outlines of such studies can be suggested in this paper.

II

INTERESTS INVOLVED IN THE CONSENT SITUATION

A. Indications of the Critical Importance of Consent

Within the complex of problems associated with human experimentation, there are several reasons to conclude that the consent situation will be the focal point of the most serious legal difficulties and moral dilemmas.

First, in twenty interviews conducted by the author in the summer of 1967 among physicians, investigators, and legal officers in NIH's Medical Center, the most commonly mentioned "difficulty" in human experimentation was the problem of informed consent. Specifically, in fifteen of the twenty interviews informed consent for nontherapeutic procedures in ill persons was said to be the most intensely felt moral problem. Such perceptions by persons actively involved in experimentation with humans are both indicative of the importance of consent and reassuring as to the attitudes prevalent among researchers.

Second, the consent situation has come to represent the primary encounter of legal significance between investigator and subject. In discussing tort liability in relation to medical research, Ladimer notes, "the essence of tort liability, other than that arising out of some form of negligence—for which the general rules established in malpractice cases are applicable—would in large measure depend on the scope and validity of the consent obtained."[20] Pointing out the contractual aspect of the legal relation between investigator and subject, he concludes that

> The essence of the research contract lies in the complete understanding of the parties.
>
> . . . .
>
> Assuming there is complete understanding and no unequal bargaining, a research contract involving scientifically and morally acceptable research can stand against trespass and liability for unauthorized invasion.[21]

Third, in the research continuum the consent situation may occur as one of the last steps in preparation for the initiation of the experiment. The significance of the consent situation is, for this reason, open to being overshadowed by the expense, effort, and technicalities in which the investigator has been involved prior to this time. Subjects and patients may hear of the experiment, its risks, and its conditions only once. On the other hand, much preparation on the part of the investigators has preceded encounters for consent purposes. There is thus a built-in

---

[20] Ladimer, *supra* note 11, at 200.
[21] *Id.* at 207.

element of "incommensurate preparation" on the part of participants which is unavoidable in the experimental environment. This factor may influence the mode of interaction in the consent situation and calls for its special scrutiny.

Fourth, the outstanding public challenges to medical ethics in human experimentation have centered ultimately on the consent situation. The Mandel-Southam case is the leading American instance, while the two cases of greatest interest abroad have concerned consent questions in combination with the problem of the proper definition of death.[22] The public seems conditioned to human experimentation and to have recognized the central importance of consent in determining its legal and ethical propriety.

Fifth, a survey of the language of the formulated rules governing human experimentation, including their qualifications and exceptions, reveals that apprehensions of possible conflicts of interest in the consent situation manifest themselves repeatedly. The following section catalogues the published rules and documents the manner in which consent has become in Western society the key to the legitimacy of scientific experimentation on human subjects.

B. Legal and Ethical Formulations and the Issues They Raise

The law and professional ethics of consent to human experimentation reflect, in part at least, the concern of society that conflict of interest may disable a scientific investigator from exercising the independent, disinterested, and conscientious judgment that alone might legitimize employing a human subject for research purposes without his knowledge or against his will. Whether a broader ethical principle arising from theological concern is also at work is a question we reserve for treatment subsequently.

Conflicts of interest in human experimentation may originate either in the investigator's anticipation of the social benefits which are expected to result from the study or in the investigator's personal investment of his skill, prestige, and self-image. In either case, there results a conflict with the professional's responsibility for the welfare and protection of the subject, a responsibility that is only the more obvious where the subject for some reason lacks full control over his own capacity to give or withhold consent. The law and medical ethics wisely do not inquire as to the source of the conflict with the possible object of distinguishing the disinterested investigator from the man who might allow his personal involvement to

---

[22] The legal questions in *Hyman v. Jewish Hospital for Chronic Diseases* and the Regents' decision are discussed in note 13 *supra*. Two European cases of interest involve transplantation of a kidney from a person with severe brain damage to critically ill renal patients. In each case the donor was, in the view of the physicians, irreparably damaged; one died two days later, the second was found to be "legally" dead after the nephrectomy when the respirator was disconnected. Although the closest relative had given consent to the donation, in each case the physician was charged with manslaughter in contributing to the "death" of the donor. 14 CLEV.-MAR. L. REV. 467 (1963); 31 MED. LEGAL J. 195 (1963); *see* Louisell, *Transplantation: Existing Legal Constraints*, in ETHICS IN MEDICAL PROGRESS 92-93.

affect his judgment; the conflict is held to exist in every case, and the subject's free and informed consent is made an almost unvarying requirement.

The exceptions to the requirement that the individual subject's consent be obtained fall largely into three classes: (1) If the subject is legally unable to give consent due to mental incapacity or minority, his legal representative's consent may be held acceptable; (2) if complete disclosure might be harmful to the subject's mental or physical health, the physician may be allowed to dispense with a full explanation of risks; and (3) where the experiment depends in some material way on the subject's ignorance, consent may not be insisted upon. Exceptions of the class (1) variety were omitted from the Nuremberg Code but have been standard in subsequent formulations. The following extensive excerpts from some of the important formulations reveal various qualifications of the requirement of informed consent and furnish evidence of the continuing potentiality for conflicts of interest in the research situation:

World Medical Association, Code of Ethics
(Declaration of Helsinki)[23]

Clinical Research Combined with Professsional Care

. . . .

> If at all possible, consistent with patient psychology, the doctor should obtain the patient's freely given consent after the patient has been given a full explanation. In case of legal incapacity consent should also be procured from the legal guardian; in case of physical incapacity the permission of the legal guardian replaces that of the patient.

Non-therapeutic Clinical Research

. . . .

> 3a. Clinical research on a human being cannot be undertaken without his free consent, after he has been fully informed; if he is legally incompetent the consent of the legal guardian should be procured.
> 3b. The subject of clinical research should be in such a mental, physical, and legal state as to be able to exercise fully his power of choice.

Medical Research Council (Great Britain),
Responsibility in Investigations on Human Subjects[24]

Control Subjects in Investigations of Treatment or Prevention

> Such controlled trials may raise ethical points which may be of some difficulty. In general, the patients participating in them should be told frankly that two different procedures are being assessed and their co-operation invited. Occasionally, however, to do so is contraindicated. For example, to awaken patients with a possibly fatal illness to the existence of such doubts about effective treatment may not always be in their best interest; or suspicion may have arisen from suggestion, and it may be necessary to introduce a placebo into part of the trial to determine this. Because of these and similar difficulties it

---

[23] World Medical Association, *supra* note 4.
[24] Medical Research Council, *supra* note 4.

is the firm opinion of the Council that controlled clinical trials should always be planned and supervised by a group of investigators and never by an individual alone.

Federal Food, Drug and Cosmetic Act[25]

[E]xperts using such drugs for investigational purposes certify to such manufacturer or sponsor that they will inform any human beings to whom such drugs, or any controls used in connection therewith, are being administered, or their representatives, that such drugs are being used for investigational purposes and will obtain the consent of such human beings or their representatives, except where they deem it not feasible or, in their professional judgment, contrary to the best interests of such human beings.

Food and Drug Administration Regulation[26]

This means that the consent of such humans (or the consent of their representatives) to whom investigational drugs are administered primarily for the accumulation of scientific knowledge, for such purposes as studying drug behavior, body processes, or the course of a disease, must be obtained in all cases and, in all but exceptional cases, the consent of patients under treatment with investigational drugs or the consent of their representatives must be obtained.

. . . .

When consent is necessary under the rules set forth in this section, the consent of persons receiving an investigational new drug in Phase 1 and Phase 2 investigations (or their representatives) shall be in writing. When consent is necessary under such rules in Phase 3 investigations, it is the responsibility of investigators, taking into consideration the physical and mental state of the patient, to decide when it is necessary or preferable to obtain consent in other than written form. When such written consent is not obtained, the investigator must obtain oral consent and record that fact in the medical record of the person receiving the drug.

Board of Regents of State of New York, Decision in the Southam-Mandel Case[27]

No consent is valid unless it is made by a person with legal and mental capacity to make it, and is based on a disclosure of all material facts. Any fact which might influence the giving or withholding of consent is material . . . . We do not say that it is necessary in all cases of human experimentation to obtain consents from relatives or to obtain written consents.

American Medical Association, Ethical Guidelines for Clinical Investigation[28]

3. In clinical investigation *primarily for treatment*—

. . . .

In exceptional circumstances and to the extent that disclosure of information concerning the nature of the drug or experimental procedure or risks would

---

[25] 21 U.S.C. § 355i (1964).
[26] 32 Fed. Reg. 8753 (1967).
[27] Reprinted in Langer, *supra* note 13, at 664-65.
[28] American Medical Association, *supra* note 4.

be expected to materially affect the health of the patient and would be detrimental to his best interests, such information may be withheld from the patient. In such circumstances such information shall be disclosed to a responsible relative or friend of the patient where possible.

4. In clinical investigation *primarily for the accumulation of scientific knowledge—*
. . . .
  C. Minors or mentally incompetent persons may be used as subjects only if:
    i. The nature of the investigation is such that mentally competent adults would not be suitable subjects.
    ii. Consent, in writing, is given by a legally authorized representative of the subject under circumstances in which an informed and prudent adult would reasonably be expected to volunteer himself or his child as a subject.
  D. No person may be used as a subject against his will.

U.S. Public Health Service,
Clinical Investigations Using Human Beings as Subjects[29]

No subject may participate in an investigative procedure unless:

(a) He is mentally competent and has sufficient mental and communicative capacity to understand his choice to participate; and
(b) He is 21 years of age or more, except that if the individual be less than 21, he may participate in a procedure intended and designed to protect or improve his personal health or otherwise for his personal benefit or advantage if the informed written consent of his parents or legal guardian be obtained as well as the written consent of the subject himself if he be mature enough to appreciate the nature of the procedure and the risks involved.

The issues of law and interpretation raised by exceptions to the consent requirement formulated as above are discussed in connection with their ethical significance at a later point.

III
Obtaining Consent for Medical Research: Ethical Reflection

As indicated earlier, there is a spectrum of ethical issues associated with research in man; this spectrum includes (a) broad social policy goals, underlying which are fundamental images of man and society; (b) the scientific value, timing, and design of the experiment; (c) the informed consent of the subject; and (d) the conditions surrounding publication and application of the findings of the study to wider groups. Consent questions can be seen most clearly within the perspective of the "research continuum," and each consent situation must be judged within its own contextual setting and in terms of the specific participants.

Stumpf, a moral philosopher, in the context of grappling with the social and moral setting of human experimentation, has raised the question whether consent on the part of the patient is *the* decisive question in medical research.[30] Although

---
[29] U.S. Public Health Service, Dep't of Health, Education, and Welfare, Clinical Investigations Using Human Beings as Subjects, Bureau of Medical Services Circular No. 38, June 23, 1966.
[30] Stumpf, *supra* note 2, at 468.

he never answers his own query specifically, Stumpf does place a heavy emphasis, as others have, upon the significance of the "mood and basically internal control physicians possess when they engage in experiments."[31] After pinpointing what, to him, is the most significant control in experimentation—the professional and ethical sensitivity of the physician—Stumpf proceeds to recognize a general communal acceptance of medical experimentation. He then shifts his emphasis to distilling from the values of this consensus a set of moral principles to "delineate some acceptable boundaries and limits to the use of human beings in research."[32] The third of four principles he delineates—the necessity to treat men as persons—is the source of Stumpf's comments on consent. He observes,

> Indeed, the usual stress upon the element of consent in experiments is a recognition that the act of consent is what is entailed in being a person. A person can be used as a thing whenever his conscious capacity to respond to the truth is denied to him. Consent is not always feasible, nor is consent always decisive as we pointed out before.[33]

Stumpf's sense of the importance of relating the goals of research to acceptable limits well meets the aim of the search of modern science for relation to the communal conscience while engaging in startling innovation. If a moralist did try to draw the line of ethical seriousness across the activities in medical research only at the question of consent, he would distort the actual situation and fail to address other important questions. If there is no single issue in medical research which can realistically be treated as *the* decisive issue (including the internal control of physicians), there is value in asking in what sense consent may be decisive within the complex of the several kinds of moral issues previously mentioned. On the basis of a study of the literature, interviewing in the field, and observation of a number of consent situations,[34] it appears to this writer that the conduct of the consent situation is decisive for the patient's or volunteer's sense of being respected as a person, especially when the request is for a procedure which is nonbeneficial.

Obviously, the consent situation is decisive of the legal outcome. To the degree that the subject is furnished with facts and is capable of a response, he assumes risks of legal significance, or his representative assumes them for him. On this occasion the researcher also assumes legal responsibility for having complied with the existing rules and standards governing consent. The legal significance thus attached to this step results in its being given a degree of solemnity that might otherwise be lacking,

---

[31] *Id.* at 469.
[32] *Id.* at 468.
[33] *Id.* at 469.
[34] Five consent situations were observed by the author. The possible forms of consent were covered: ill person for therapeutic study, ill person for nontherapeutic study, parent of minor for consent to therapeutic study, normal volunteer for consent to nonbeneficial study. The one remaining possibility which was not observed was parent of minor or representative of an incapacitated patient for nontherapeutic study.

and this in turn promotes on both sides the sense of the transaction's ethical importance.

The consent situation in medical research is formally constituted when a request for participation is initiated by a scientist to another individual or group (who may be either ill or normal); participation would involve some alteration of the subject's mental, physical, or social functioning, with the scientist planning to observe and record the results. The subject is asked to surrender, temporarily, some personal rights with a possibility of risk or discomfort.[35]

The consent situation has a formal moral dimension insofar as the subject or patient is a "person," with all the rights, status, and symbolic significance that term implies. He is a being whose humanity calls for the respect of the scientist, since in their common humanity they are equals, and no amount of rationalization can erase the resistance to one man's being used by another strictly as a means to an end. Experimentation of the nonbeneficial variety involves the use of a man as a means to improving the welfare of the human species, but societal values provide no sanction for the experimenter based on the desirability of the goal in view. The last credential evidencing the legitimacy of the experiment must, as a general rule, be conferred by the subject himself. This principle is embodied in the law and in professional practice and provides the foundation for ethical reflection on the methods of its application and on the exceptions to it deemed expedient for the general good.

What is new and what is permanent here? In one sense, the consent situation is a uniquely modern social interaction, dramatizing an aspect of the difficulty of reconciling the ethic of the scientific mission with our society's other values. Experimentation is as old as medicine, but the routinization—through professional and governmental influences—of the practice of obtaining consent to experimentation is uniquely modern. Such structural arrangements to meet the requirements of the communal conscience can both insure the freedom of men to experiment and protect those who participate. Men could not conduct medical experiments if they did not enjoy that creativity of spirit which springs from self-transcendence. Yet these same men cannot afford to pursue experimentation without legal and moral arrangements to protect the individual against accumulations of power. Self-interest in its collective forms can destroy as effectively as self-transcendence can create.[36]

What is permanent in the consent situation is the encounter between selves when the limits of one self touch the limits of another. The underlying moral problem of the consent situation is the possibility of its depersonalization through excessive

---

[35] This definition is drawn from several places in medical literature where experienced investigators give definitions of the experimental process. Shimkin, *The Problem of Experimentation on Human Beings: The Research Worker's Point of View*, in I. LADIMER & R. NEWMAN, *supra* note 1, at 58: Ladimer, *supra* note 11, at 190; Wolfensberger, *supra* note 2, at 49.

[36] Guttentag, *The Problem of Experimentation on Human Beings: The Physician's Point of View*, 117 SCI. 207, 210 (1953); P. TILLICH, THE PROTESTANT ERA 115 (1960).

secrecy and the arrogation of the right to know and to choose, which right belongs, in principle if not in fact, to each man. Tillich has located the basic structure of moral interaction:

> Without this resistance of the "thou" to the "ego," without the unconditional demand embodied in every person to be acknowledged as a person in theory and practice, no personal life would be possible. A person becomes aware of his own character as a person only when he is confronted by another person.[37]

The discussion which now follows moves through three levels of examination: (a) the context of the consent situation; (b) constituted rules for consent; and (c) ethical principles.[38]

A. The Context of the Consent Situation

The intent of this part is to record, from the consent-giving settings in which interviews were held and observations were made, the ideas, sentiments, and attitudes of the parties to human experimentation. In particular, the consent-giving process is examined for forces interfering with the "free" exercise of the power to give or withhold consent.

Since the publication of the Nuremberg rule on consent, perhaps the main point of difference between those involved in public debate over its significance has been the stringency of the definition of informed consent. Reflecting on the strictness of language used to define consent, Welt comments:

> There are, no doubt, a small number of subjects, perhaps the investigators themselves, who may be properly qualified to grant consent in terms of the quality of consent which is demanded here. However, in many instances it is certainly impossible either to evaluate the risks this precisely or to communicate with the subject in such a fashion that he freely sees the problem in all the dimensions that are necessary for proper consent.[39]

Other investigators echo this reaction to the rule and plead that informed consent is "a goal toward which to strive"[40] or that there may be inherent limitations to what a patient can consent to.[41]

Investigators, in person and in their writings, participate in the public debate about consent with highly mixed sentiments. There is in no sense a uniform or standardized attitude prevalent in this field, but if there was a consensus on the

---

[37] P. TILLICH, *supra* note 36, at 125.

[38] It would require too lengthy a footnote to account for the many sources utilized in the discussion of rules and principles which follows. The principal recent works which figure in the author's point of view here are H.D. AIKEN, REASON AND CONDUCT (1962); JOSEPH FLETCHER, SITUATION ETHICS (1966); H.R. NIEBUHR, THE RESPONSIBLE SELF (1963); J. PIAGET, THE MORAL JUDGMENT OF THE CHILD (1932); P. TILLICH, SYSTEMATIC THEOLOGY III (1963); Gustafson, *Context Versus Principles—A Misplaced Debate in Christian Ethics*, 58 HARV. THEOL. REV. 171 (1965).

[39] Welt, *Reflections on the Problems of Human Experimentation*, 25 CONN. MED. 77 (1961).

[40] Beecher, *Consent in Clinical Experimentation: Myth and Reality*, 195 J.A.M.A. 34 (1966).

[41] Beeson et al., *Panel Discussion: Moral Issues in Clinical Research*, 36 YALE J. BIO. & MED. 455, 458 (1964).

part of those interviewed, it was this: that highly legalistic or idealistic images of what "ought to be"—*i.e.*, of freely given and informed consent—can probably be satisfied through the routinization of consent forms but that the outcome of the medical-research situation itself, as a result of personality factors and subtle pressures that may operate as restrictions on free choice, may often disappoint ideals. Researchers insisted that the decision about which patients to approach for inclusion in a study must be decided on an individual basis in terms of the fitness of a specific patient for a particular study. There was general acceptance of the norm of informed consent, since in its moral dimensions this norm accords with the general principles of the professional ethic of the trained scientist, but there was a strong sentiment among those interviewed that each case is different in terms of the make-up of the patient and of the design of the particular study. There was also evidenced a sentiment for the exceptional case when the rule about informed consent must be suspended. Thus, there appears to be no rejection of the purposes underlying the consent rule, but there is serious doubt as to the viability of formal legal definitions of consent. Thus, experimenters ask the legal proponent to pay close attention to the situation in which "free" consent is expected, and there would seem to be no doubt about the need for lawyers, judges, and administrators to take account of the charge that existing legal doctrine tends to be unrealistic and consequently not adapted to achieving its professed and generally accepted object.

Reviewing some possibilities for restriction on the exercise of free choice by patients and volunteers, one can become sensitized to situational aspects in which free consent giving is expected. Besides those inner compulsions and conflicts which psychology has shown interfere with the ideal of "free choice" in daily life, it is well known that illness drastically reduces the energy and conscious determination of the individual. It is also well known that ill and hospitalized persons show a marked tendency to be dependent. Several studies show that the process of hospitalization itself greatly increases anxiety;[42] hence if consent is requested during this period inherent restrictions on choice in the patient may be present. Patients who are being treated in an institution where research is also being done are apt to relate requests to do research to their own expectations about treatment. A patient might feel an inner reluctance to disappoint a doctor, even one other than his attending physician, fearing that interest might be lost in "his case." Park's interesting study of the subjective experience of research patients showed that they tended to relate obvious research instruments (questionnaires, one-way mirrors, tape recorders) to their treatment.[43] Patients tend not to distinguish between research

---

[42] *See, e.g.*, Goldman & Schwab, *Medical Illness and Patients' Attitudes: Somatopsychic Relationships*, 141 J. NERV. & MENT. DIS. 678 (1965); Vernon, Shulman & Foley, *Changes in Children's Behavior After Hospitalization*, 111 AM. J. DISEASES OF CHILDREN 581 (1966); Mason et al., *Corticosteroid Responses to Hospital Admission*, 13 ARCH. GEN. PSYCH. 1 (1965).

[43] Park et al., *The Subjective Experience of the Research Patient: An Investigation of Psychiatric Outpatients' Reaction to the Research Treatment Situation*, 143 J. NERV. & MENT. DIS. 199 (1966).

and treatment, and hence entertain an inner sentiment that the procedure, even when they are told it is nonbeneficial, holds out some hope for their improvement. Park's study was conducted with psychiatric outpatients, a majority of whom were in a lower socioeconomic status and who were generally uninformed as to what the psychiatric situation was. Therefore, it is possible that social and educational differences among patients affect in some measure the quality of consent they are able to give.

The psychological situation of "normal" volunteers has been studied in part. Available studies, published and unpublished, show that conflicts of a serious nature appear in a significant percentage of those volunteers examined.[44] The types of pressure to which prisoner and student volunteers might be subjected have also been reported elsewhere.[45] In general, the author agrees with those who would put the sharpest restrictions upon the use of prisoner populations in medical research, since by virtue of their imprisonment they cannot be truly said to possess an active capacity to consent. No argument based on prisoners' availability or on their presumed willingness to recompense for their social deviance relieves others of their responsibility to protect the liberties of all by being realistic as to the temporary loss of liberty of the prisoner. No general rule sanctioning the use of prisoners should be acceptable to the communal conscience; thus, any suggestion that prisoners be used in research must be treated as a rare exception which must be subjected to vigorous public scrutiny. One of the "checks and balances" which should be employed in selection of suitable populations for research is that those who have experienced the most severe form of social control, the loss of public liberty through imprisonment, should not then be made to go through the charade of seeming to possess what has been temporarily removed.[46]

Several physicians noted in interviews that consent from the patient has an "automatic" quality, due to the ready acceptance of the physician by the patient, and this response has also been amply noted in the literature.[47] Thus the very role perception of the physician by the patient tends to exaggerate his sense of the

---

[44] National Institutes of Health, Public Health Service, Dep't of Health, Education, and Welfare, How Normal is a Normal Control Patient?, Feb. 13, 1958 (unpublished manuscript, Combined Clinical Staff Meeting, Clinical Center); Esecover, Malitz & Wilkens, *Clinical Profiles of Paid Normal Subjects Volunteering for Hallucinogen Drug Studies*, 117 AM. J. PSYCH. 910 (1961); Lasagna & von Felsinger, *The Volunteer Subject in Research*, 120 SCI. 359 (1954); Perlin, Pollin & Butler, *The Experimental Subject*, 80 ARCH. NEUROL. & PSYCH. 65 (1958).

[45] See generally *Ethics Governing the Service of Prisoners as Subjects in Medical Experiments*, 136 J.A.M.A. 447 (1948) (report of a Committee appointed by Governor Dwight H. Green of Illinois); Newman, *The Participation of Prisoners in Clinical Research*, in I. LADIMER & R. NEWMAN, supra note 1, at 467.

[46] See generally Remarks of T. Starzl, in ETHICS IN MEDICAL PROGRESS 75-77; Daube, *Transplantation: Acceptability of Procedures and the Required Legal Sanctions*, id. at 188, 197, 198. Daube makes his rule absolute, which in my estimation is too strong, since in ethics to say "never" is to remove oneself from historical possibility.

[47] See, e.g., Beecher, supra note 40.

doctor's goodness or helpfulness, and out of his own sense of need his power of discrimination is affected.

There are also factors of the same order to consider in those who are asked to consent for others. The attitudes of parents of mentally ill or retarded children are known, in some instances, to be quite ambivalent, a mixture of love, pity, and anger. Such feelings might present themselves in a response to a request for experimentation involving the child. Thus, the psychological situation of the patient's representative may be an effective restriction on "freely given" consent, even though the legalities are observed as carefully as possible with an explanation and signed consent forms.[48]

Related to the patient's education and his sophistication in science is the ability of the investigator to communicate, in lay language, technical aspects of the study to the patient or volunteer. Although reduction to simple terms may suffice to communicate to the patient *what* is going to happen to him, it is not so simple always to communicate *why* it is happening. Understanding the purpose of the experiment does assist the patient, in most cases, to give a more informed consent, as Alexander notes.[49] In actual consent situations with volunteers in which requests were made for explanations of the "purpose" of the study, investigators were observed to experience some difficulty in explanation. Volunteers could be seen to lose their attention in the consent situation when the technical aspects of the study were explained in simple scientific terms. If legal significance is attached to the subject's understanding the technicalities of the experiment, many physicians will express concern.

For a significant number of investigators the Southam-Mandel case assumed large legal proportions. In eight of twenty interviews, the investigator brought up the legal significance of this case voluntarily. Investigators sense their legal insecurity, not only because of the risks inherent in their professional work but also because the laws which do affect the practice of medical research are born in malpractice cases. Medical research is perceived to be far out in front of legal and moral consensus as to what is permissible in human experimentation. New definitions and limitations have not been clearly perceived in medicine's new social situation. Part of the striving for new definitions of justifiable behavior and rules to govern new conditions can be interpreted as a desire to harmonize new and innovative acts with the communal conscience. When men take risks with the life and health of members of the community, even when these risks are scientifically sanctioned, and they sense that these risks are questionable in the communal conscience, they can take at least three attitudes: they can become defensive and defend their pursuit of science as a "right"; they can become secretive; or they can share their dilemmas in a dialogue with the public conscience in the attempt to work out

---

[48] Silverman, *Informed Consent*, 38 PEDIATRICS 373 (1966).
[49] Alexander, *supra* note 2, at 63.

the actual practice of experimentation in relation to values and commitments held within our pluralist culture.

B. Constituted Rules for Consent: Heteronomy and Autonomy

The search for legal rules and guidelines for the experimental medical situation, as well as for clarification of moral issues in all aspects of human experimentation, provides a most interesting piece of social history of a segment of modern professional society. It has also become clear to the observer of social ethics that, as in the case of all instances of the protection of the individual against accumulations of power, the issues are never decided once and for all but find continuous outlet in the push and shove of social existence. In the highly organized and specialized climate of science, however, there have been renewed appeals for rules and revisions of rules to provide guidance for new contingencies.[50] The debate about rules can be seen as swinging between two extremes, between threats of heteronomy (external controls on experimentation) on the one hand and claims of the scientist for autonomy in the research situation on the other.

1. *Rules Governing Use of Minors and Mental Incompetents*

The Nuremberg rules, if interpreted as the only ones applicable to the consent situation, would prohibit research of a general nature in any group of persons who did not possess legal capacity to give consent. Thus, all research done within the mentally ill or with children which is of a nonbeneficial nature and conducted for general information, would be barred. Also prohibited would be research with unconscious or comatose persons, or anyone whose personal environment was so restricted as to fail to meet the demand of capacity. Alexander proposed, in 1947, six points as a basis for permissible experiments on human beings in a memorandum to the United States Chief of Council for War Crimes and the Court. Alexander noted later that, although all of his points were incorporated and expanded into the final ten criteria, his provisions for obtaining legal and morally valid consent from mentally ill subjects by consultation with the next of kin or from the patient where possible were omitted from Article 1. He ventured the opinion that the exceptions were excluded from the final version of the first rule "probably because they did not apply in the specific cases under trial."[51]

Would it be justifiable to enforce the Nuremberg rule to the letter? Perhaps the most intensely felt objection to a strict or legalistic interpretation of the consent rule originates from highly motivated researchers who feel a moral imperative to pursue general studies of a nonbeneficial nature in those areas which would be proscribed by the letter of the rule. They consider it morally irresponsible to neglect research in diseases of children or in mental illness. Thus strict application of the Nuremberg

---

[50] *See* Robin, *Rapid Scientific Advances Bring New Ethical Questions*, 189 J.A.M.A. 624 (1964).
[51] Alexander, *supra* note 2, at 62.

rule would approach the extreme of heteronomy, for while the rule has great and deserved standing it does not take account of exceptions which can be controlled and makes no allowance whatsoever for the exercise of professional judgment and the investigator's ethical discrimination. The price to be paid would be exacted from gains in knowledge of the sensitive areas mentioned, thus cutting across the general social principle of least suffering.

Following the promulgation of the Nuremberg Code, as we have noted, other statements and regulations incorporated the exception for the representative of the subject, when he is incapacitated or a minor, to substitute in consent giving. An additional example of an institutional formulation assuring protection to incapacitated individuals while making provision for including them in investigative research is the policy of the M. D. Anderson Hospital and Tumor Institute, University of Texas. Following a verbatim statement of the first article of the Nuremberg Code, this qualification appears:

> If the subject is not competent, the person responsible shall be the legally appointed guardian or next of kin. If the subject is a minor under 21 years of age, the person responsible shall be the mother or father or legally appointed guardian.[52]

Similar provisions appear in most other codes and guidelines published in recent years. Some of these, however, have included additional safeguards that appear useful and not obstructive of legitimate scientific inquiry. Thus, (1) the AMA permits a minor or mentally incompetent person to be used only if the research could not be conducted with adults or mentally competent individuals as subjects—a principle that should probably always be considered implicit in provisions permitting use of such subjects; (2) the Public Health Service requires obtaining the minor's consent, as well as his parent's or guardian's, if he is mature enough to have some understanding of the procedure and the risks; and (3) several formulations distinguish between therapeutic and nonbeneficial procedures, varying the need for consent accordingly.[53] These refinements appear to strike an appropriate balance between heteronomy and autonomy, especially as one recognizes the scientist's obligation to apply the formulated standards as meaningfully as possible in particular circumstances.

2. *Resistance to Excessive Scientific Autonomy*

Questions now need to be raised about the second type of exception noted earlier, namely the professional right of the investigator, if he deems it in the subject's interest, to withhold information or to suspend any interaction with the subject in consent giving. Just as there is a danger for the public interest in the rigid insistence on literal obedience to rules requiring informed consent, there is an equal

---

[52] M.D. Anderson Hospital and Tumor Institute, University of Texas Medical Center, *Research Investigation Involving Human Beings: Code and Methods of Procedure* (1963).
[53] *See, e.g.,* Medical Research Council, *supra* note 4.

danger in allowing the physician autonomy to determine what the subject shall know. The danger is that physicians will choose—on the basis of their own inhibitions against disclosing a research procedure—to withhold facts which seriously affect the subject's power of discrimination.

Certainly this is the lesson of the Southam-Mandel incident, quite apart from any reflection on the moral quality of these doctors' actions. The researchers withheld a description which, in their estimation, would have caused the patients unnecessary alarm, since in their judgment there was no reason to believe injection of these cells threatened harm. It was the withholding of that information, however, that provoked the Regents' sharpest criticism and occasioned their most specific statement about what constitutes satisfactory consent:

> No consent is valid unless it is made by a person with legal and mental capacity to make it, and is based on a disclosure of all material facts. Any fact which might influence the giving or withholding of consent is material.[54]

Thus, the Regents clearly concluded that the wrongdoing in this instance lay in omission of a material fact which could be instrumental in the patient's decision. In other words, it is up to the patient or his representative to decide whether the words "cancer cells" frighten him or not, and not up to the doctors to prejudge the validity of the patient's reaction. There can be little doubt that the reason this central fact about the experiment was suppressed was the investigators' expectation that patients would not volunteer if fully informed.

There were further warnings in the Regents' decision about autonomous decisions by physicians:

> There is evidenced in the record in this proceeding an attitude on the part of some physicians that they can go ahead and do anything which they conclude is good for the patient, or which is of benefit experimentally or educationally and is not harmful to the patient, and that the patient's consent is an empty formality. With this we cannot agree.[55]

In other words, there is not adequate public protection in the guiding assumption that the investigator possesses an unqualified power to decide what constitutes adequate and sufficient consent; even though the physician has confidence in the design of his study, abuses of the consent procedure can still occur. On the other side of this observation lies the necessity for the free exercise of the physician's professional judgment and perception as to the subject's personal receptivity to any information that would damage him psychologically or in any other way. Some "mediate" rule would seem to be required, perhaps the sharing of the decision to withhold certain information with a responsible relative, representative, or physician-friend of the subject.

---

[54] Board of Regents of the State of New York, reprinted in Langer, *supra* note 13, at 664.
[55] *Id.*

The newly developed Food and Drug Administration regulation requiring written consent in the use of new investigational drugs appears to incorporate such a "mediate" rule, falling between rigid external control and total dependence on the autonomy of the investigator.[56] The regulation presupposes that consent will be obtained in every case, and the only possible exception is based on the patient's own well-being, after the physician has concluded, on the basis of professional judgment, that the exception is relevant. No argument precluding consent which is based on the convenience of the physician is acceptable.

The FDA regulation recognizes many of the limitations to freely given consent which have been discussed. For example, there may be occasions when it is not feasible to receive consent; for example, where it is impossible to communicate with the patient or his representative, such as when the patient is in a coma and the drug must be quickly administered. In requiring written consent at that stage of drug experiments when it is initiated in treatment, the regulation makes an additional exception to the basic written consent requirement that is based solely on the health and welfare of the patient, but it still requires oral consent and a statement of the fact of consent in medical records. This regulation appears to be an attempt to resolve the possible conflict of interest in the case of experimental drugs by coming out fundamentally on the side of the patient's interests.

3. *Experimental Necessity as a Basis for Dispensing With Consent*

A particularly troublesome objection to the consent requirement in experimental situations is the attitude that, if full disclosure of the experimental design and variables which are operative is made to the subject, the observed results will be less reliable because of the psychological variables induced. The use of placebos is intended to determine to what extent the subject's psychological state is responsible for the observed change. The principle behind the placebo may be extended to keeping the investigator or physician who is in contact with the subject from knowledge of the identity of the variable in question.

Not all experienced investigators agree that disclosure of the use of a placebo will actually inhibit valuable results. Alexander, writing specifically out of consent situations with psychiatric patients, gives evidence that disclosure of use of a placebo can be made to patients without interference with the unbiased attitude necessary for establishing the results of the test.[57] The findings of Park and Covi correlate with Alexander's experience. In a study before which patients were told frankly that a placebo was to be used and the word defined for them, they later

---

[56] See note 10 *supra*. In interviews with officials of the Food and Drug Administration, the author asked how the new regulation was working out in the field. In general the response was that it was too early to tell. The "mediate" approach which is noted in the paper is corroborated by the fact that the FDA does not require evidence as to written consent, but the sponsor of the experiment must certify that the expectation is being met.

[57] Alexander, *supra* note 2, at 63.

reported that the patients accepted treatment and responded with a wealth of fascinating subjective material.[58] These remarks would indicate that preconceived opinions about disclosure need to be more widely tested. Park and his associates comment on some of the underlying causes of overly scrupulous secrecy in research:

> [T]he importance of being honest and straightforward with patients should be considered in setting up research procedures. We tend to become inappropriately secretive because of our own apprehensions that the patient might discern the experimental nature of procedures and/or might be able to infer that our primary purpose may be research findings rather than immediate alleviation of distress.[59]

The conflict with a legal or moral consent requirement is most marked when the fact of experimentation itself is withheld from the subject on the ground of experimental necessity. It may be the sincere judgment of the investigator that the subject's psychological response to the fact of experimentation may invalidate the obtained result, even when the subject has consented to participate. On the other hand, knowledge of the experiment may itself be the variable being manipulated. In either case, if participation involves any risk, the legal and moral problems are immense.

The conflict between the consent requirement and experimental necessity cannot, of course, be resolved here. Research is needed on the validity of research conducted under conditions of full disclosure and on other means of eliminating, detecting, and accounting for, or otherwise minimizing psychological factors in experimental situations. There is a strong and understandable tendency on the part of investigators to wish all psychological factors out of any experimental situations in order that results might be more reliably quantified. Unfortunately, the desire to eliminate such variables may reflect, in some cases and in some immeasurable part, an exaggerated mistrust by the physician of the validity of patients' judgment and understanding, a mistrust that may also cause the physician to undervalue the importance of the patient's informed consent. Because of this possibility, that conviction about the experimental necessity of dispensing with consent may accompany an undervaluation of consent's ethical importance, special care is called for.

Perhaps nowhere are the ethical issues apt to be drawn so clearly as where experimental necessity is advanced to warrant a dispensation from the consent requirement. Certainly approval of an interdisciplinary peer-group should be a prerequisite to the granting of exceptions in this area, and the burden on the investigator should be a heavy one. Moreover, scientific ingenuity should be insisted upon to avoid easy escape from disclosure requirements; for example, increased use of psychological tests might be recommended, or emphasis might be placed on two-stage experimental designs which first use informed subjects and only later use blind

---

[58] Park & Covi, *Non-blind Placebo Trial*, 12 ARCH. GEN. PSYCH. 336, 344 (1965).
[59] *Id.*

or double-blind techniques to verify the initial results when the risk factor has been shown to be minimal. The burden on the medical profession is to reconcile the scientific mission with the rights of its experimental subjects. Some autonomy must be accorded here, but the community conscience must likewise be accorded a role in decision making.

4. *Conclusions on the Roles of Rules and Professional Responsibility*

Who will set and enforce the rules as to the adequacy of consent? Posing the question in this fashion constellates the tension between heteronomy and autonomy, and every move is interpreted as constraint. Neither type of rule will serve medical research at this juncture. Constituted rules born out of constitutive principles of cooperation between skilled investigators and informed subjects have more promise. The polarity between those who feel that there should be no interference at all in research procedure and the possibility revealed in the Regents' decision for external regulation of consent practices can be broken down by more cooperative approaches to consent problems.

There is a genuine public interest to be protected in the practice of human experimentation; namely, candidates for experiments do not, with few exceptions, come to the experimental situation seeking employment. They are brought there by virtue of their being ill or in a specific situation which presents a researcher with a problem to study. Physical, social, and psychological conditions, each a part of personal and social existence, present themselves to the research group through the subject. Usually the investigator himself is the party who seeks out the candidate. Insofar as he has no *a priori* right—after the fashion of the government to draft men for military service—to recruit candidates for research, the public interest is protected when assurance is given that the methods for the conduct of the research accord with the voluntary nature of its recruitment and that what transpires in the consent situation provides the subject with adequate information and sufficient freedom, in that particular situation, to have a meaningful choice.

The fact that some subjects in research are remunerated for participation in a study should in no way relieve the investigator of responsibility to obtain informed consent just as he would in the event of nonpaid participation. If some volunteers for experiments are motivated primarily by financial considerations, then special care must be exercised by the investigator to distinguish between the role of money in the research contract and the role of informed consent. Money compensates the subject for the use of his time and the cost of his cooperation, and it in no way replaces informed consent as the main facet of the research contract. It is possible that the subject's expectation of financial gain could even be a restriction on his judgment and choice, and thus the economic status of research subjects becomes a relevant factor in the dynamics of the consent situation. As Lord Henley noted in 1762, "Necessitous men are not, truly speaking, free men, but, to answer a present exigency, will submit to any terms that the crafty may impose upon them."[60]

On the other hand, the clinical investigator has good reason to resist rigid codes which attempt to give specific, coded instructions on how to meet the requirements of the consent situation. The consent situation is an interpersonal encounter involving many variables. No set of rules can cover all the possibilities. One of the differences between traditional and open societies is that, in the former, groups of people are governed by specific sets of regulations which are highly ordered, rigid, and numerous, while in the latter, characterized by high mobility and social movement, moral rules are considerably less clear, though more flexible and considerably variable in number.[61] Physicians tend toward a more "situational" moral approach (as do many other professionals), which allows specific data in each new situation to be weighed in a decision, and they generally insist on being free from any one intrinsically defined principle of right or wrong action.[62]

It is far easier simply to act on the basis of an abstract principle than it is to make a fitting response to new situations on the basis of concrete and immediate responsibility. But the former course does not lead to the quality of responsibility which is necessary in today's medical setting. The individual uniqueness of each patient is not served by the kind of codification which would require stereotyped actions in each situation. The existing ethical codes of medical research are sufficient to inform the public of the medical profession's recognition of the principles which underlie informed consent; what remains to be accomplished, in the author's opinion, is an adequate demonstration to the public that the problems of consent giving and its dilemmas are being explored in as attentive a fashion as other obligations of the social responsibility of science. Significantly new methods of cooperation between experimental science and the public must be attained in order for science to keep the confidence of the public, which bears the major costs for medical research. Along these lines, cooperative methods of communication need to be developed to keep the public informed and assured that subjects in research (or their representatives), especially those in whom nonbeneficial procedures are carried out, (a) know that they are in an experimental procedure; (b) have been informed as to all essential aspects; (c) have assistance in making a decision to perceive the factors relevant to consent giving; and (d) are free to withdraw from the experiment at any time. The wide public discussion of consent is one indication that these popular expectations are being heeded. Much more careful study of actual consent situations in research is necessary, however, to ascertain responsibly how effectively those broad expecta-

---

[60] Vernon v. Bethell, 28 Eng. Rep. 838, 839 (Ch. 1762).

[61] H.D. AIKEN, *supra* note 38, at 72.

[62] *See* Beecher, *Some Guiding Principles for Clinical Investigation*, 195 J.A.M.A. 1135 (1966); Merrill, *Clinical Experience is Tempered by Genuine Human Concern*, 189 J.A.M.A. 626, 627 (1964); JOSEPH FLETCHER, *supra* note 38, at 26.

tions are being met. Some concrete proposals for research will be made at the end of the article.

C. Ethical Principles

Adequate ethical reflection is rooted in the real, arises out of situations of actual conflict, and involves itself with the justifications which persons in society make of their specific decisions. The level of principles is reached on this level of moral language when the parties to a dispute or a decision reflect on the question: am I *really* justified in acting according to the mandate, imperative, or rule which I perceive as governing my decision?[63] Thus, the level of principle is reached in a deeper and more reflective moment in decision making than is ordinarily realized in the press and heat of a conflict. Ordinarily, what can be observed as a moral conflict involves justifications of actions taken or anticipated which the actors in the situation perceive as necessary.

"Principles" can be functionally interpreted as socio-psychic categories found at a deeper level of justification, upon which we fall back to uphold our ways of handling situations in which values and norms are perceived to be in conflict. Principles clearly have theological possibilities because they will ever involve, at their deepest symbolic level, some image of the way the actor interprets himself and his world. For example, in the report of a case of heterotransplantation of the heart, the authors justify the substituted transplantation of a primate heart into a man when the human donor planned to be used had not expired, on the grounds that "although survival was not achieved, the situation was one in which the patient had no chance, except for the slim possibility that the transplant could be made to support the circulatory requirements and rejection could be prevented."[64] If the authors had gone on to spell out what the implications to them of what "having no chance" meant, how the principle of life or vitality lent deeper sense or meaning to the action which is being justified, they would have been involved in justification at the level of principle.

Other authors from the religious, philosophical, and legal communities have attempted to identify principles at this level which would finally justify both the practice of medical experimentation and the legal safeguarding of those who surrender some of their autonomy and freedom to facilitate a socially desirable enterprise.[65] While remaining aware of the temptations of self-deception, on the theological level, in seeking any ultimate justification by principles, we must nevertheless employ them to bring some proximate order into the press and conflict of decision making in society. The author's basic orientation is to Christian com-

---

[63] H.D. AIKEN, *supra* note 38, at 75.
[64] Hardy et al., *Heart Transplantation in Man*, 188 J.A.M.A. 1132, 1139 (1964).
[65] *See generally* Leake, *Technical Triumph and Moral Muddle*, in T. STARZL, EXPERIENCE IN RENAL TRANSPLANTATION 363 (1964); Stumpf, *supra* note 2; Freund, *supra* note 2; Giuseppe, *Human Experimentation—A World Problem from the Standpoint of Spiritual Leaders*, 7 WORLD MED. J. 80 (1960); Pius XII, *The Moral Limits of Medical Research and Treatment*, 44 ACTA APOSTOLICAE SEDIS 779 (1952).

munities as agencies of the growth and renewal of communities of persons in modern culture. He has learned much from colleagues who, though not sharing an explicitly theological perspective, show deep reverence for the mystery of human existence and an active concern for those who are imperiled by catastrophic social changes. There is much to be said, in this day of gigantic organizations, for laboring for social arrangements which will enhance the autonomy of the person and his need to control his own physical and social environment. Concern for civil rights in the spheres of public action is compatible with concern for the maximum conscious participation of those involved in experiments, within the limits of the situation. Defining a principle helps to locate the argument in a social and historical sense and to identify oneself and provides an operational norm for judgment which must always be subject to change. Thus the author seeks to argue that the principle of *mutuality between persons,* or "perceived effective decision making" is the relevant ethical principle for the consent situation. This principle is seen as especially relevant to requests for participation in nonbeneficial studies.

To illustrate: Two group consent situations were observed by the author. Each included a meeting between a senior investigator, his associates, and a small group of normal volunteers. Each meeting was similar in its structure: (*a*) a careful and technically documented explanation of the study, its purpose, duration, risks, and discomforts; (*b*) a period for questions; and (*c*) the giving of instructions as to decision making and the signing of consent forms. The meetings varied in content only in the third point. The first senior investigator, after stressing that none of the group had to furnish a reason for deciding against participation, asked the members to go to their rooms if they cared to, study the consent form, which contained the appropriate information, and turn them in signed or unsigned when a decision had been reached. At the similar point in the other meeting, the senior investigator passed out consent forms, asked the members to read them there, sign them there, and after reminding them of their freedom to withdraw, suggested that if any member planned not to enter the study, he wanted them to "back out now instead of later," after the study had begun.

This observer concluded that there was more latitude, if a group member required it, for the exercise of personal choice in the way the first situation was handled than in the second. Time was afforded each individual to absorb the technicalities, study the form, and make a decision apart from the group. There was careful definition of the meaning of withdrawal insofar as the necessity for furnishing reasons was involved. In the second situation there was more opportunity for group pressure to work, no time was allowed for "second thoughts," and the request for withdrawal was made so that response was suggested immediately. If a member had entertained thoughts of withdrawal, it could possibly have been more difficult to have brought them out in the group than later. In both cases the majority of the members belonged to a religious service organization in which individual differences between members tended to be submerged in a common "service" aim. Perception that it would be more difficult, in this particular group, for individuals to express doubts or questions in front of fellow members would call for preference of the first means of instructing. How the consent-seeker perceives the opportunities for volunteers or patients to exercise what control they do possess over decision making and how he helps to open these opportunities can enhance the degree of self-possession and hence the degree of mutual cooperation.

In attaching significance to the principle of personal autonomy the author is cognizant of the degree to which the power of decision of the very ill person in an experimental setting is greatly diminished. An investigator cannot create a strong ego for a patient or subject, but there are leads he can follow to stimulate what he does find in the person. A sensitive investigator can enhance the consent situation for the normal subject or patient by assisting him to perceive what it is that he does have control over; that is, his consent. Some physicians when interviewed revealed confusion about the content of patients' consent. Some indicated that they thought informed consent meant that the patient is expected to agree intelligently to the design of the experiment or to the details of a new therapy, and thus they could easily despair of ever attaining consent or were wary of seeming to relinquish professional medical judgment. The expectation of informed consent was never that the patient be a judge of the medical procedure in the consent situation. What is hoped for is the most self-possessed decision to give consent, to say "yes" or "no" to participation. The roots of the word *consent* (*con-sentio*) point not only to mutual understanding between the parties but to an answer which proceeds from within the person, involving feeling and perception. The most serious moral question which can be addressed to those who participate in the consent situation is this: How can the subject be helped to employ what power of decision he does possess? Can the interaction be turned to the mutuality of the persons involved so that fears of manipulation and deception can be transmuted into meaningful cooperation between equals in the research procedure? Such questions are derived from the principle of persons-in-mutuality, so integrally related in its development to the personalizing meaning of *agape*, the central focus of Christian ethics.

The two values which could come into conflict in the consent situation, the general welfare and the welfare of the individual, must be balanced and harmonized in the consent situation itself. It is not accidental that nonscientists have become concerned and involved in the debate about consent. Some have taken care to develop the category of "private personality" in the research sphere.[66] The author's own convictions find accord here. One could also generalize from Bettelheim's studies of the loss of autonomy in modern man, as well as from his revealing work on the development of autism in children, to the lack of subject participation in the consent

---

[66] Ruebhausen & Brim, *supra* note 2, at 423.

situation.[67] Do patients and subjects in the research situation perceive that their decisions to consent actually "make a difference" or affect the environment in any real way? Is this situation similar to so many others in society in which the less the individual is able to solve the strains between what his environment demands and what he himself wants, the more he relies on those who appear in the environment to furnish the cues for his behavior? There has been much written on the "responsible investigator" in medical research as the most effective protection and safeguard to the patient.[68] This is not in dispute, but could not some potential be found in the concept of the "responsible subject"? Moves which have been made to study the subjective attitudes of research subjects are most welcome. What needs to follow is a responsible investigation of the consent situation in its many settings and forms. The first form for study should probably be the one to which investigators assign the most difficulty, consent for nonbeneficial procedures in ill persons.

IV
Hypotheses for Research

Means to deepen the legal, scientific, and personal effectiveness of the interactions of consent in medical research should be of interest to all who take responsibility for the conduct of investigative procedures in man. There has been extensive writing in the field of human experimentation in the realm of principles and constraints, namely, in the realm of "what ought to be." There have been no investigations, to the author's knowledge, of the dynamics and interactions of the consent situation in experimental research. Since consent situations occur as a requirement of engaging each new participant in nontherapeutic general studies, and since the consent situation is the subject of many opinions in the fields of ethics, law, and science, it would seem reasonable to investigate the consent situation more thoroughly and deliberately.

Suggestions have arisen in several quarters that two physicians in the consent situation would improve the quality of consent obtained.[69] One of them would be the principal investigator, of whom the rule requires that he be the seeker of consent and the judge of its quality; he may not delegate this responsibility to another. Also in the situation would be another physician, either the patient's attending physician or one known to the patient. In the case of the volunteer, he could be an informed physician who had no vested interest in the experiment. The hypothesis for study would be this: there are fewer second thoughts and fears about participating in an experiment of the nonbeneficial type when the attending physician, or some other informed person known to the patient, is present in the consent situation when the principal investigator is obtaining consent.

---

[67] B. Bettelheim, The Informed Heart 72 (1960); B. Bettelheim, The Empty Fortress 45 (1967).
[68] Beecher, *supra* note 62.
[69] Guttentag, *supra* note 36; Beecher, *supra* note 62.

A second area of study would center on the restrictions of choice which operate on patients and volunteers in research situations. These forces and inhibitions need to be specified so that, by generalizing from findings, the sensitive investigator can respond more fittingly. Since we know that patients will generally accede to any reasonable request in a medical setting and that some physicians have noted that consent giving has an "automatic" quality about it, another hypothesis for research is this: patients whose consent is requested for nonbeneficial procedures perceive that their decision is more "under their control" and "makes a difference" when there are two visits for consent, one in which the investigator makes an explanation of the purpose, duration, and risks of the study and another when he returns to receive the patient's decision. Implementing these and similar studies would not resolve the basic moral dilemmas, but much could be learned about the decisions which men are asked to make and about the impediments which keep them from making a fitting personal choice. By looking more deeply within its own situation, medical research can perhaps be an agent of more human management of a problem area which has become a source of major public and legal concern.

REGULATION OF PRESCRIPTION DRUG ADVERTISING: MEDICAL PROGRESS AND PRIVATE ENTERPRISE

RICHARD B. RUGE*

Communication of new developments in medicine to practicing physicians is an essential step in implementing scientific progress. Each year the pharmaceutical industry spends an estimated $750 million in promoting drug products.[1] As a result of this barrage of advertising, amounting to $3000 for every doctor in the United States, a new drug may be widely prescribed within weeks after it has been placed on the market. Recently, the Food and Drug Administration (FDA) has increasingly questioned whether the advertising techniques of drug firms contribute to sound medical progress by helping doctors make informed choices among competing products or instead succeed in selling drugs by misleading claims, omission of crucial data, and inappropriate emotional appeals.

This article examines recent conflicts between the FDA and the drug industry over the purpose of prescription drug "advertising," as that term is peculiarly defined under the Food and Drug Act.[2] To the FDA, advertisements in medical journals should constitute "post-graduate education" through which doctors learn both the advantages and drawbacks of new drugs.[3] To industry, advertisements function only to provoke doctors into investigating new drugs through detailed information available in other manufacturer-supplied literature ("labeling") or from independent sources.[4] The FDA has warned industry to comply with its regulations or find itself altered "significantly, . . . beyond your present fears, and . . . beyond recall."[5] Replying that the FDA exploits the consumer "as a device, or a pretext, for adding further to government power at the expense of the strength and independence of private enterprise,"[6] the pharmaceutical industry in 1963 brought the first law suit challenging FDA rules since passage of the basic act in 1938.[7]

---

* A.B. 1963, LL.B. 1966, Harvard University. Associate, Hogan & Hartson, Attorneys, Washington, D.C. Member of the District of Columbia bar.

[1] May, *Selling Drugs by "Educating" Physicians*, 36 J. MEDICAL ED. 1, 5, 7 (1961). See generally S. REP. No. 448, 87th Cong., 1st Sess. 156-64 (1961) [hereinafter cited as S. REP. No. 448].

[2] Federal Food, Drug, and Cosmetic Act, 52 Stat. 1040 (1938), *as amended*, 21 U.S.C. §§ 301-392 (1964, Supp. II, 1965-66).

[3] Address by FDA Commissioner James L. Goddard, Advertising and Government Relations Conference, Washington, D.C., Feb. 8, 1967, in F.D. COSM. L. REP., para. 80,161 (1967).

[4] Jurow, *Safe and Effective Prescription-Drug Advertising*, 22 FOOD DRUG COSM. L.J. 57, 63 (1967).

[5] Address by FDA Commissioner Goddard, meeting of the Pharmaceutical Manufacturers Association, Boca Raton, Fla., April 6, 1966, *reported in* N.Y. Times, April 7, 1966, at 24, col. 4.

[6] Address by PMA President C. Joseph Stetler, N.Y.C. Pharmaceutical Advertising Club, Inc., Seminar, Oct. 20, 1966, *reported in* 28 F.D.C. REPORTS No. 43, at S-5, S-6 (Oct. 24, 1966).

[7] Abbott Laboratories v. Celebrezze, 228 F. Supp. 855 (D. Del. 1964), *rev'd*, 352 F.2d 286 (3d Cir. 1965), *rev'd and remanded*, 387 U.S. 136 (1967). This case is discussed in the text accompanying notes 38-47 *infra*.

I

BACKGROUND OF THE KEFAUVER AMENDMENTS

Prior to the enactment in 1962 of the so-called Kefauver amendments[8] to the 1938 act, the jurisdiction of the Food and Drug Administration reached prescription drug "labeling" but not its "advertising." The statute both before and after the amendments defined *labeling* to include all "labels," plus other written material on a drug's immediate container or "accompanying such article."[9] Before 1962, the FDA gave *labeling* a broad construction (by expanding the term *accompanying*) to bring much of the informational type of drug promotion under its control. Thus the agency regulated direct mail advertising to doctors as well as material left in the office by detail men, drug industry salesmen. At the same time, the definition of *advertising* contracted to cover only newspaper and journal advertisements. This segment of drug promotion fell under the jurisdiction of the Federal Trade Commission (FTC).[10]

However narrow its definition, advertising was extensive in quantity and played an important role in selling drugs. In 1958, for example, the drug industry paid for 3,790,908,000 pages of advertising in medical journals. The American Medical Association (AMA), the largest publisher of prescription drug ads in the world, grossed $10.1 million in 1963 from ads in its twelve scientific journals and its laymen's monthly. This large volume of material plus the insistent intrusion of detail men have prompted doctors' complaints about the burden imposed on their time.[11]

Despite these facts, the FTC prior to 1962 possessed little power over drug ads. Advertisements directed solely at physicians—so long as they listed quantitative ingredient information and contained no false representation of a material fact—were specifically excluded from FTC control, on the theory that doctors have an expertise enabling them to evaluate drug claims. This rationale probably made sense prior to the prescription drug "revolution" which occurred at the end of the Second World War. Until then the number of drugs available had been relatively limited, and a doctor could fend for himself in selecting medicines; he needed little protection from the law or from regulatory agencies.

But today some eighty new drugs are cleared each year by the FDA;[12] and ninety per cent of all prescriptions call for drugs manufactured within the past fifteen years.[13] One economist attributes this extensive introduction of new drugs—or at

---

[8] Pub. L. No. 87-781, 76 Stat. 780 (1962).
[9] 21 U.S.C. § 321(m), (k) (1964).
[10] Federal Trade Commission Act, 15 U.S.C. §§ 52-57 (1964).
[11] *See* N.Y. Times, June 13, 1966, at 26, col. 1.
[12] *Hearings on Competitive Problems in the Drug Industry Before the Monopoly Subcomm. of the Senate Select Comm. on Small Business*, 90th Cong., 1st Sess. 4 (1967) (statement by James L. Goddard, Commissioner of Food and Drugs).
[13] *Hearings on Drug Safety Before the Subcomm. on Intergovernmental Relations of the House Comm. on Governmental Operations*, 88th Cong., 2d Sess. 14 (1964) (statement by George P. Larrick, Commissioner of Food and Drugs).

least of new combinations and dosage forms of old drugs—to industry's efforts to replace price competition among relatively standardized drugs with product differentiation or competition "in innovation."[14] As a part of these efforts, companies make heavy advertising outlays to maintain their existing market share through constant introduction of "new" drugs. A new product will reach its peak in the second year following its introduction, then decline "rapidly in relative importance."[15]

More important, today advertising not only sells new drugs but also tells the physician about their existence and their claimed effectiveness for the first time. An AMA study,[16] for example, disclosed that medical journal ads constitute one of the largest sources of information to practitioners about newly discovered drugs. Forced to "contend with subtle overpowering promotion and the complexities of modern medicine," today's doctor cannot effectively fend for himself, "especially if he is to be 'educated' by the very purveyors of products which require his prescriptions."[17]

Prior to 1962 responsible doctors began to question the propriety of educating physicians through unpoliced ads. Pointing out that many doctors assume that at least some reputable firms consistently disseminate reliable information, Dr. Charles D. May wrote:[18]

> The traditional independence of physicians and the welfare of the public are being threatened by the new vogue among drug manufacturers to promote their products by assuming an aggressive role in the "education" of doctors. . . . Is the public likely to benefit if practicing physicians and medical educators must perform their duties amidst the clamor and striving of merchants seeking to increase the sales of drugs by conscripting "education" in the service of promotion? Is it prudent for physicians to become greatly dependent upon pharmaceutical manufacturers for support of scientific journals and medical societies, for entertainment, and now also for a large part of their education?

Another distinguished doctor has more recently charged that "persuasive propaganda of advertising literature and of visiting detail men" causes physicians to shift "repeatedly and needlessly from one drug to another."[19]

> [Doctors] are being systematically brainwashed by expensive advertising in the pages of medical journals, by the daily influx of mountains of advertising mail, by free throw-away "educational" pamphlets published by commercial agencies for the promotion of drug sales, and by visiting detail men, who go from door to

---

[14] Comanor, *Research and Competitive Product Differentiation in the Pharmaceutical Industry in the United States*, 31 ECONOMICA 372-73, 375 (1964). *See* Steele, *Monopoly and Competition in the Ethical Drugs Market*, 5 J. LAW & ECON. 131, 141 (1962). *See generally* J. BACKMAN, ADVERTISING AND COMPETITION (1967).

[15] Comanor, *supra* note 14, at 376.

[16] Attitudes of U.S. Physicians Toward the American Pharmaceutical Industry, Study conducted by Ben Gaffin and Associates, Inc., Chicago, Ill., in 1959 for the AMA, cited in S. REP. NO. 448, at 190. *See also* Demeritt, *Effectiveness of Pharmaceutical Promotion to Hospital Pharmacists*, 23 AM. J. HOSP. PHARMACY 13, 16-17 (1966).

[17] May, *supra* note 1, at 8-9.

[18] *Id.* at 1.

[19] Baehr, *Drug Costs and the Consumer*, in DRUGS IN OUR SOCIETY 179, 182 (P. Talalay ed. 1964).

door of physicians' offices leaving elaborate samples of new drugs and valueless combinations of old drugs, together with reams of impressive but biased literature. It is utterly impossible for most busy physicians to separate the wheat from the chaff in this enormous volume of information and misinformation.[20]

Hearings held by Senator Estes Kefauver before the Senate Subcommittee on Antitrust and Monopoly in 1961 and 1962 focused attention on such abuses. Out of these hearings, with the help of public concern aroused by the thalidomide tragedy, there developed the Drug Amendments of 1962.

The amended law placed on the pharmaceutical industry a greater responsibility to present factual and undistorted information to doctors than did the 1938 act, and gave jurisdiction to regulate prescription drug advertising to the Food and Drug Administration,[21] leaving control over nonprescription drug advertising to the FTC. Although FDA regulations issued under the 1962 amendments have imposed similar requirements for both advertising and labeling, the distinction between the two kinds of printed literature remains important—for example, side effects must be fully stated in labeling but may be summarized in advertising.[22]

The amended statute does not specifically give the FDA authority over oral promotional statements made by detail men. These salesmen are also an important source of information about new drugs, making an estimated 18 to 20 million calls a year on doctors and druggists.[23] The original version of the 1962 amendments included oral claims as advertising; this provision,[24] not enacted, would have required detailers to supply the generic name and warnings for drugs. Absent such a rule, promotional statements by detailers cannot be easily categorized as either labeling or advertising. The FDA does, however, have jurisdiction over literature left by detailers with doctors. The judiciary may fill this legislative gap. A recent case held a manufacturer liable where the company had warned doctors of a newly discovered side effect by product cards and letters but its detailers had remained silent.[25]

President Johnson has proposed legislation to control the unsolicited distribution of samples,[26] another major form of drug promotion costing $100 million per year.[27] The proposed Drug Safety Act of 1967 would not restrict person-to-person distribution from detailer to physician but would forbid drug companies to send samples through the mails except to a doctor requesting samples of a particular drug in writing.

Regulations covering prescription drug advertising can be divided into three

---

[20] *Id.* at 181-82.
[21] 21 U.S.C. § 352(n) (1964).
[22] *Compare* 21 C.F.R. §§ 1.106(b)(3)(i), (4)(i) (1967) *with* 21 C.F.R. § 1.105(e) (1967).
[23] R. HARRIS, THE REAL VOICE 89 (1964).
[24] S. 1552, 87th Cong., 1st Sess. § 4(A)(7) (1961).
[25] Yarrow v. Sterling Drug, Inc., 263 F. Supp. 159 (D. S.D. 1967).
[26] H.R. 3913, 90th Cong., 1st Sess. (1967).
[27] Medical Tribune, April 4, 1966, at 1, col. 2.

general areas. First, the FDA has issued controversial rules controlling drug names; related to these requirements are FDA rules compelling disclosure of certain essential ingredient information. Second, additional information needed before prescribing a drug—its side effects and contraindications—must also be listed. Finally, the FDA has recently moved to regulate the content of drug advertisements to ensure that the limits of the drug's effectiveness are accurately portrayed. These subjects are taken up below.

II

REGULATION OF DRUG NAMES

A discrete drug substance may be known by three types of names. Its chemical name simply lists every part of a drug's molecular structure. Its generic name abbreviates the components but still informs a doctor of the drug's chemical composition, from which he can determine its general effect on the body. Ordinarily a drug will have only one generic or nonproprietary name. Finally, a drug is sold under a trade or brand name which identifies the drug with a particular manufacturer but conveys little information about its nature or composition. Several manufacturers often market the same chemical substance under different trade names.

Senator Kefauver felt that the purpose of the vast sums spent by the drug industry on promotion was to persuade doctors to prescribe by trade name rather than by generic name.[28] Since the same product sold by trade name may cost several times as much as when sold by generic name,[29] advertising which planted the brand name firmly in the prescribing doctor's mind left the ultimate consumers "captives of the drug industry."[30] This promotional effort largely succeeded; 91.9 per cent of 1964 prescriptions called for trade name drugs.[31]

Although Congress rejected Senator Kefauver's chief proposal for encouraging prescription by generic name (government licensing of drug manufacturers),[32] the 1962 amendments require that a drug's "established name" must appear on each piece of promotional material in "direct" conjunction with its trade name.[33] To alert doctors to the exact relationship between the two designations, the established name must be surrounded by brackets or preceded by a phrase such as "brand of." The established name must be "printed prominently and in type at least half as large as

---

[28] S. REP. NO. 448, at 105, 231-44; 107 CONG. REC. 5638 (1961) (remarks of Senator Kefauver).

[29] S. REP. NO. 448, at 105, 231-44. *See generally* R. BURACK, THE HANDBOOK OF PRESCRIPTION DRUGS (1967). However, a survey conducted for the AMA of 100 Chicago drug retailers concluded that generic name prescribing did not necessarily cut drug costs. N.Y. Times, June 9, 1967, at 26, col. 3.

[30] 107 CONG. REC. 5638 (1961) (remarks of Senator Kefauver).

[31] N.Y. Times, June 13, 1966, at 27, col. 1. Additional factors may explain this fact. The generic name is often omitted in drug advertising and labeling; the trade name may be easier to pronounce, spell, and therefore remember; and it has been suggested by industry detail men that drugs produced and sold by smaller companies are of substandard quality. S. REP. No. 448, at 231-34.

[32] S. 1552, 87th Cong., 1st Sess. §§ 4(A)(7), (13) (1961).

[33] 21 U.S.C. §§ 352(e), (n) (1964).

that used for any trade or brand name."[34] In addition, the amendments seek to assure doctors of drug quality by certain safeguards over manufacturing, including registration and inspection.[35]

Early in 1963 the Food and Drug Administration issued regulations requiring that the established name of a prescription medicine accompany every appearance of the drug's trade name on all labels, labeling, and advertising, no matter how many times the brand name may be repeated on any single page.[36] The FDA contended that the "every-time" regulations were crucial to the 1962 amendment in light of the "evident intent" of Congress to popularize established names.[37] Arguing that the statute dictates only the manner in which the generic name must appear, and not its frequency, the Pharmaceutical Manufacturers Asssociation and thirty-seven of its members sought a declaratory judgment in the U.S. District Court for Delaware, invalidating the regulations as exceeding the FDA's statutory authority.[38]

This suit in 1963[39] was the first legal challenge to FDA regulations since passage of the basic act in 1938. The drug industry's concern extended beyond the estimated million-dollar cost of reprinting its existing labels to comply with the every-time requirement.[40] The regulations struck at the purpose of drug promotion, the implantation of trade names in the doctor's mind; they sought to lower drug prices by educating physicians to prescribe by generic names. But increased familiarity with nonproprietary names, the industry feared, would endanger its investment in brand names and in research for new and better products, little of which is undertaken by smaller, generic-name producers.

It was claimed that conspicuous disclosure of the generic name, to which the industry did not object, would notify the physician of the drug's active ingredients. He could then choose among the various sources producing the same or comparable chemical substances at different prices. Constant repetition of the established name, on the other hand, might make advertising and labeling less readable. (In fact, compliance with the every-time rule does not substantially affect over-all appearance.[41]) Finally, the industry complained that the regulations would induce doctors to believe that drugs "with the same established name are always and in all respects

---

[34] 21 C.F.R. §§ 1.104(g), 1.105(b) (1967). The regulations prescribe that "[T]he established name shall have a prominence commensurate with the prominence with which such proprietary name or designation appears, taking into account all pertinent factors, including typography, layout, contrast, and other printing features." 21 C.F.R. § 1.105(b)(2) (1967).

[35] 21 U.S.C. §§ 331(p), 351(a), 352(o), 374 (1964); § 360 (1964, Supp. II, 1965-66).

[36] 21 C.F.R. §§ 1.104(g)(1), 1.105(b)(1) (1967).

[37] F.D. Cosm. L. Rep., para. 40,060 (1963).

[38] Complaint, Abbott Laboratories v. Celebrezze, Civil No. 2737 (D. Del. 1963), *reported in* F.D. Cosm. L. Rep., para. 40,060 (1963).

[39] Abbott Laboratories v. Celebrezze, 228 F. Supp. 855 (D. Del. 1964), *rev'd*, 352 F.2d 286 (3d Cir. 1965), *rev'd and remanded sub nom.*, Abbott Laboratories v. Gardner, 387 U.S. 136 (1967).

[40] N.Y. Times, Sept. 6, 1963, at 1, col. 5.

[41] *See, e.g.*, Advertisement for Polycillin (ampicillin trihydrate), J.A.M.A. July 31, 1967, at 1-3.

identical," when in fact drugs with the same generic name but different proprietary names "can and do differ in their therapeutic effect."[42]

The district court invalidated the regulations as contrary to the intent of the 1962 amendments.[43] The Third Circuit reversed on procedural grounds, holding that there was no actual case or controversy as required for justiciability under the Declaratory Judgment Act[44] because no real threat of immediate prosecution had been presented.[45] On May 22, 1967, the Supreme Court reversed this decision, finding that "the impact of the regulations . . . is sufficiently direct and immediate so as to render the issue appropriate for judicial review at this stage,"[46] and remanded the case to the court of appeals for decision on the substantive issues.

On October 20, 1967, the day set for further argument in the Third Circuit, the FDA and PMA announced settlement of the litigation.[47] The FDA will replace the contested every-time rules with new regulations. On any page of advertising or labeling which "features" a drug's trade name, the generic name must appear "in direct conjunction with" and in type one-half as large as the brand name each time the latter is featured, but need not appear again in promotional copy on the same page. If a trade name is used but not "featured," the generic name must appear at least once with the most prominent display of the trade name. In addition, each column of text providing detailed information on effectiveness or side effects must include the generic name at least once "in association with" the trade name, if used, in the same size type as that used for the text. If the trade name appears in type size larger than that used for the column text, the generic name must again be half as large as the trade name.

In light of publicity recently given to generic-name prescribing in recent congressional hearings,[48] however, the FDA need not insist vigorously on "educating" doctors to use generic name drugs, so long as the generic name is "prominently" disclosed in drug advertising. A survey of ads in recent journals shows that, contrary to FDA regulations, the generic name type face does not always appear half as bold or wide as that used for the trade name; in many cases, the generic name is not preceded by a phrase such as "brand of" nor surrounded by brackets or parentheses.

---

[42] For the industry's position, see the complaint and plaintiff's briefs filed in 228 F. Supp. 855. Recently, the FDA ordered generic manufacturers to stop marketing their versions of the antibiotic chloramphenicol, sold as Chloromycetin by Parke, Davis, & Co. Parke-Davis had submitted test data to the FDA indicating that its version entered the blood stream quicker than the others. Some medical experts attribute this advantage to the different shapes of chloramphenicol crystals used in the trade-name drug. Wall Street Journal, Jan. 22, 1968, at 6, col. 2; id., Dec. 26, 1967, at 4, col. 3. The FDA has not, however, announced any rule requiring generic manufacturers to show that their products work as effectively in patients as the chemically equivalent brand-name products.
[43] 228 F. Supp. at 864.
[44] 28 U.S.C. § 2201 (1964).
[45] 352 F.2d at 291.
[46] 387 U.S. at 152.
[47] See Food and Drug Reg., 21 C.F.R. § 1.105, 33 Fed. Reg. 3217-18 (Feb. 21, 1968).
[48] Hearings on Competitive Problems in the Drug Industry Before the Monopoly Subcomm. of the Senate Select Comm. on Small Business, 90th Cong., 1st Sess. (1967).

The new rules, of course, may lead to new controversies over their exact interpretation, but they appear to be a reasonable compromise. Commentators have split on the question whether the now-withdrawn every-time regulations were consonant with congressional purpose.[49] Ambiguity in the statutory provision on generic names and in its legislative history probably indicate that Congress had no "intent" on the question of frequency. The AMA, which generally supports the industry against the FDA, urges doctors to prescribe by trade name.[50]

III

DISCLOSURE OF SIDE EFFECTS

More than one million adverse reactions to drugs occur annually in the United States. These unwanted effects often occur even when a drug is administered according to the manufacturer's directions. Information on a drug's recurrent side effects, or rarer but serious adverse reactions, is obviously important to a doctor weighing alternative medications, especially since many side effects are not allergic or unusual genetic reactions peculiar to the patient but pharmacological effects of the drugs.[51] Similarly, the doctor must know what pathological conditions contraindicate use of the drug. The Kefauver hearings found, however, that drug manufacturers sometimes failed to disclose to doctors or to the FDA reports in their possession of serious and even fatal side effects.[52]

In particular, the hearing revealed that prescription drug advertisements failed to list or discuss possible adverse reactions. A survey of promotion in six leading medical journals,[53] covering thirty-four important trade name drugs advertised in a total of 2033 pages during a nine-month period ending in March 1959, found that in eighty-nine per cent of the ads there was "no reference to side effects at all or only a short dismissal phrase which was typically less a warning than a reason for prescribing." Among the advertisements surveyed were several for Diabinese (chlorpropamide), an oral antidiabetic introduced in 1958 by Chas. Pfizer & Co., Inc. Although its promotion claimed an "almost complete absence of unfavorable side effects," a report prepared for Pfizer showed twenty-seven per cent incidence of side effects, including jaundice.[54] Doctors polled by an AMA study on misleading advertising termed such failure to cite side effects "the most heinous crime a pharmaceutical company can commit."[55]

---

[49] *Compare* Note, *Drug Amendments of 1962—Generic Name Prescribing: Drug Price Panacea?*, 16 STAN. L. REV. 649 (1964) *with* Note, *The Drug Amendments of 1962: How Much Regulation?*, 18 RUTGERS L. REV. 101, 127-30 (1963) *and* Sweeney, *The "Generic Every Time" Case: Prescription Drug Industry in Extremis*, 21 FOOD DRUG COSM. L.J. 226 (1966).

[50] Editorial, *Drug Names*, 190 J.A.M.A. 542 (1964).

[51] N.Y. Times, May 5, 1965, at 63, col. 1 (study at Johns Hopkins University).

[52] M. MINTZ, THE THERAPEUTIC NIGHTMARE 13-32 (1965).

[53] S. REP. No. 448, at 199. The journals surveyed included *JAMA*, the *New England Journal of Medicine*, and *Medical Economics*.

[54] *Id.* at 211, 218.

[55] *See* 108 CONG. REC. 21,086 (1962) (remarks of Representative Dingell).

Drug industry spokesmen counter that physicians can obtain full side-effect information elsewhere, particularly on the package insert which must accompany each prescription drug and sample and on all promotional labeling.[56] They contend that advertisements, aimed solely at doctors, serve only as "product reminders" and thus should not be treated as labeling. However, this argument begs the question of the importance of journal advertising in presenting drug news and overstates the adequacy of alternative sources of information on side effects. First, doctors often ignore the vast quantities of promotional labeling sent to their offices; they are most apt to study ads appearing next to scientific articles in prestigious medical publications such as the *Journal of the American Medical Association* (*JAMA*) and the *New England Journal of Medicine*.[57] Second, the package insert goes not to the doctor who needs the "full disclosure" labeling but to pharmacists.

The better journals do carry reports critical of new drugs. In early 1960, for example, *JAMA* noted thirty-five cases of baby girls with male characteristics born to women who had been given Norlutin (norethindrone), a hormone used in gynecologic disorders, during pregnancy.[58] But ads for Norlutin in *JAMA* during the following three months did not cite this side effect. Despite the fact that warnings given only in journal articles (which generally would appear but once) may be ineffective to deter improper use of a drug, *JAMA* did not request the advertiser to add a warning.[59]

Moreover, the responsible medical publications may not review all the new drug products unleashed yearly. Another potential source of information, *Physicians' Desk Reference,* a commercially produced manual of therapeutic agents distributed free to doctors, carries warnings supplied by manufacturers. The FDA has filed criminal informations against two drug compaines for allegedly failing to make full side-effect disclosures in *PDR*, which the agency considers labeling; Pfizer Laboratories recently notified doctors that the FDA considered its 1967 *PDR* entries for two drugs inadequate.[60] The sharpest critic of new drugs is the *Medical Letter*, which carries no advertising. Its effectiveness is limited, however, because fewer than 35,000 doctors subscribe.

To meet this need for disclosure, the 1962 amendments require any prescription drug advertisement listing indications or dosage recommendations—that is, any ad except a strictly reminder piece—to contain "a true statement of . . . information in brief summary relating to side effects, contraindications, and effectiveness" as called for by regulations.[61] In what detail must relevant side effects and contraindications

---

[56] N.Y. Times, July 20, 1963, at 19, col. 1 (criticism of FDA by PMA).
[57] S. REP. No. 448, at 160-64.
[58] Wilkins, *Masculinization of Female Fetus Due to Use of Orally Given Progestins*, 172 J.A.M.A. 1028 (1960).
[59] M. MINTZ, *supra* note 52, at 84.
[60] Washington Post, May 24, 1967, at 2, col. 1.
[61] 21 U.S.C. § 352(n) (1964); 21 C.F.R. § 1.105(e) (1967).

be presented? The answer depends on the size of the advertisement and the quantity of side effects. An ad of three pages or less, condensing information on effectiveness, may "concisely" present each side effect found in the drug's full-disclosure labeling; in an ad of more than three pages presenting extensive claims of effectiveness, the side effect information should similarly expand into a "discussion" of precautions.[62] But there is not precise matching requirement for stating the two types of information in an equal number of words, an equal amount of space, or in the same type size. Thus, if headlines, advertising leads, and photographs are used to convey information on effectiveness, similar techniques need not be used to communicate side effect information.

While the FDA may consider the size of the ad and the conditions for which the drug is offered in determining whether there has been adequate disclosure, the statute only requires a "brief summary," which Senator Kefauver described as a "fair condensation of the full disclosure information already required in labeling. . . ."[63] To comply with the advertising regulations, the manufacturer ordinarily summarizes the precaution and side-effect section of the package insert. For example, compare the 1966 package insert warning as to renal impairment and the corresponding advertising side-effect information for Declomycin (demethylchlortetracycline HCl):

Labeling[64]	*Advertising*[65]
If renal impairment exists, even usual oral or parenteral doses may lead to excessive systemic accumulation of the drug and possible liver toxicity. Under such conditions, lower than usual doses are indicated and if therapy is prolonged, . . . serum level determinations may be advisable.	Reduce dosage in impaired renal function.

To test compliance with its disclosure regulations, the FDA must gather and evaluate reports on adverse reactions, especially those occurring after a new drug is first sold. Until recently, there were no reliable systems for retrieving such information; for example, most hospitals did not encourage members to record recognized drug reactions. Today, side-effect data from numerous sources feeds into the FDA's Information Center on Adverse Reactions and Hazards, where it is studied and catalogued. Some 6600 hospitals supply the FDA with drug information. The agency also collaborates with the AMA central registry of adverse reactions, which receives drug news from hospitals not reporting to the FDA and from doctors in private practice. All federal medical services and agencies send side-effect

---

[62] Food and Drug Reg. § 1.105(e)(5)(xxix), 32 Fed. Reg. 7535 (May 23, 1967). *See* letters from George P. Larrick, former FDA Commissioner, to Gerhard A. Gesell, Oct. 1, 1963, Oct. 9, 1963, *reported in* F.D. Cosm. L. Rep., para. 40,063 (1963).

[63] 108 Cong. Rec. 22,039-40 (remarks of Senator Kefauver).

[64] Labeling for Declomycin (demethylchlortetracycline), dated February 1965.

[65] Advertisement for Declomycin (demethylchlortetracycline), J.A.M.A., Feb. 7, 1966, at 48.

reports to the FDA, and eight countries will exchange information through an international center created by the World Health Organization to provide a worldwide early warning system for drug news.[66]

Under the 1962 amendments the FDA requires manufacturers to record side effects and other clinical data as received and to report information relating to the drug's safety and effectiveness.[67] The reporting regulations are important because the manufacturer has more knowledge about the marketing experience of his drug than any other source, since he picks up information from doctors and his detail men.[68] The regulations have already brought to the FDA reports of adverse reactions which would not have been previously available. These are screened by the Information Center on Adverse Reactions and Hazards, which receives 150,000 reports annually and may get significant information on reactions to a new drug within three months after it is first sold. The Center may then recommend precautionary labeling, changes in existing labeling, issuance of a warning letter, or withdrawal of the drug from use.

In turn, the FDA publishes monthly reports on adverse reactions and a weekly journal of literature abstracts, which are sent to cooperating hospitals and other groups. FDA Commissioner James L. Goddard has proposed that a compendium of drug information approved by the FDA be distributed free to doctors; if this were done, the agency would drop its requirements that full-disclosure package inserts accompany the marketed or dispensing package of all prescription drugs.[69]

In December 1965, the Food and Drug Administration initiated its first prosecution under the advertising provisions of the 1962 amendments.[70] The FDA charged that ads for Pree MT, marketed by Wallace Laboratories, a division of Carter-Wallace, Inc. (formerly Carter Products), omitted essential side effect and contraindication information. The United States District Court for New Jersey imposed the maximum $2,000 fine after the defendant pleaded no contest.

Pree MT combines meprobamate, a tranquilizer sold separately as Equanil or Miltown, with hydrochlorothiazide, which removes excess fluids from body tissues. An ad appearing in four June 1964 issues of *JAMA* claimed, "Contraindications: None known," and urged doctors to prescribe the drug for premenstrual tension. The FDA insisted that the ad's brief summary omitted warnings that hydrochlorothiazide is contraindicated in patients who have had suppressed urine flow and that patients given it should be watched for signs of serious and sometimes fatal blood diseases; that Pree MT can precipitate gout, and that its use should be halted in patients with severe kidney disease or liver disease; and that meprobamate may cause skin rash, bronchial spasm, skin hemorrhages, and blood-vessel disturbances.

---

[66] 52 Dep't State Bull. 814 (1965).
[67] See 21 U.S.C. §§ 355(i), (j) (1964).
[68] Pisani, *Drug Safety and the FDA*, 21 Food Drug Cosm. L.J. 68, 74 (1966).
[69] Washington Evening Star, Aug. 11, 1967, at C-6, col. 5.
[70] Washington Post, Dec. 7, 1965, at 12, col. 1; *id.*, Jan. 18, 1966, at 4, col. 1.

The FDA has also charged that Ciba Pharmaceutical Co. "kept secret" reports showing that Elipten (amino-glutethimide), prescribed for control of epilepsy, caused sexual precocity, masculinization of young females, and other "untoward effects";[71] that Wyeth Laboratories and Merck & Co. delayed in reporting adverse effects on the eyes of dogs caused by the controversial experimental drug DMSO (dimethyl sulfoxide);[72] and that Merck, Sharp, & Dohme failed to report immediately (as required) "alarming" findings of breast cancer in four of six dogs given an experimental birth control pill, MK-665, combining mestranol and ethynerone.[73]

IV

REGULATION OF ADVERTISING CONTENT

The drug industry contends that once the FDA assures adequate disclosure of effectiveness, side-effect, and contraindication information within the "brief summary" portion of an advertisement, the agency has no further jurisdiction to regulate the content of the ad or the promotional techniques used.[74] The FDA asserts that Congress intended the 1962 amendments to grant power "to deal completely, and not partially, with the problems of false and misleading advertising which had been called to its attention" during the Kefauver hearings.[75] Thus, it is argued that Congress introduced the phrase "brief summary" only to authorize "a stripped-down statement of the drug's effectiveness, side effects, and contraindications when the sponsor wished to limit the size of his ad"; and so the agency retains jurisdiction over the entire advertisement. Exercising this power, the FDA has issued regulations which utilize the "brief summary" provision as a counterbalance to overpromotion.

Hearings conducted by Senator Kefauver repeatedly aired criticism by physicians of the promotional tactics used in drug advertising.[76] The problem of selling doctors on new drug products each year, of which as few as thirteen may be new single chemical entities,[77] has led to "clamorous competitive claims" presented in a style designed "to achieve uncritical acceptance of a preconceived message—to captivate the mind."[78] For example, Dr. Charles D. May of Columbia University has charged that from 1958 to 1961 drug firms launched an "exuberant" and "hectic" campaign to increase sales of antibiotics; the "confused and misleading barrage of promotion" presented "inadequate and irrelevant data" in a "triumphant tone." "The 'educational' effect on doctors was to confuse them and lead them to believe wonderful

---

[71] Washington Post, Feb. 16, 1966, at 8, col. 3.
[72] Washington Post, March 10, 1966, at 1, col. 5.
[73] Washington Post, March 11, 1966, at 1, col. 3.
[74] *See* Pharmaceutical Manufacturers Association, Comments on Proposed Prescription Drug Advertising Regulations, 32 Fed. Reg. 7533-37 (May 23, 1967), filed with the FDA on August 29, 1967.
[75] Letter of Oct. 1, 1963, *supra* note 62.
[76] S. REP. No. 448, at 164-90.
[77] N.Y. Times, June 4, 1967, § 3, at 1, col. 2.
[78] May, *supra* note 1, at 10.

new drugs were available" when in fact what development there had been was altogether minor.[79]

Need for government regulation in this area exists partly because leading medical publications have not strictly supervised the drug advertising which they publish. From 1953 through 1960 the AMA, which reaches over 200,000 subscribers through *JAMA*, gradually relinquished its earlier policing powers over advertisements.[80] Although the AMA today asserts that ads in *JAMA* "have been reviewed to comply with the principles governing scientific advertising in AMA scientific publications," it responded to the Pree MT prosecution by stating that censorship of advertisements is "fundamentally a matter for manufacturers."[81]

A drug advertising writer, in turn, places responsibility for misleading overpromotion on the doctor. Pointing out that few physicians subscribe to the *Medical Letter*, an independent newsletter attacked by industry "for presuming to pass on advertising claims, the validity of supporting evidence, and the inherent merit of drugs," the late Pierre R. Garai asked:[82] "In light of this kind of response, is it any wonder that drug advertisers should be unimpressed by the professional maturity of the bulk of their audience or that campaigns for ethical drugs should sometimes seek to manipulate physicians rather than communicate with them?" To avoid becoming "a sitting duck for color spreads," the doctor should develop a healthy skepticism concerning ads: "He must cultivate a flair for spotting the logical loophole, the invalid clinical trial, the unreliable or meaningless testimonial, the unneeded improvement and the unlikely claim. Above all, he must develop greater resistance to the lure of the fashionable and the new."[83] The industry would presumably react to critical appraisal of its ads by supplying more reliable information.

Aside from the dubiousness of his proposition that responsibility for providing accurate advertising lies with the reader, Garai's argument can be criticized on two grounds. Doctors do not have time to check claims by ferreting out more authentic analyses elsewhere. And the evidence cited in the ads themselves as backing up claims made may consist of unpublished data ("personal communications"), case reports in the company's files, exhibits at meetings, testimonials from anonymous sources, and citations from inaccessible or inferior journals.[84]

To fill this gap in control over drug ad content, the FDA issued in 1963 two important regulations. The first required a "fair balance . . . in presenting the information on effectiveness and that on side effects and contraindications."[85] The second, which the FDA considered part of the "fair balance" requirement, stated

---

[79] *Id.* at 3.
[80] R. HARRIS, THE REAL VOICE 126 (1964).
[81] Washington Post, Dec. 7, 1965, at 12, col. 1.
[82] Garai, *Advertising and Promotion of Drugs*, in DRUGS IN OUR SOCIETY 189, 196 (P. Talalay ed. 1964).
[83] *Id.* at 199.
[84] May, *supra* note 1, at 11.
[85] 21 C.F.R. § 1.105(e) (1967).

that information concerning side effects and contraindications "shall appear in reasonably close association with the information concerning effectiveness and shall have the same relative degree of prominence as the information concerning effectiveness, taking into account all pertinent factors, including typography, layout, contrast, and other printing features."[86]

The FDA interpreted these regulations to require at least that information on side effects given as part of the brief summary be readable, that is, that disclosure of precautions must be effective as well as adequate. Thus the type size used should compare reasonably with that describing the drug's benefits and in no case be unduly compressed.[87] Headings such as "Side Effects," "Contraindications," and "Precautions"—and not meaningless terms such as "In Summary" or "Special Considerations"—must introduce and plainly identify the warning data.

In addition to ensuring the readability of the cautionary portion of advertisements, the FDA required that ads be arranged so that "this important information *will* be read." Photographs, headlines, and type size must not overwhelm "essential side effect and contraindication information . . . [or] minimize its disclosure as part of the total message the advertisement conveys." For example, although the fair balance regulation does not require an ad containing a picture relating to a drug's effectiveness also to contain a picture relating to side effects, the former should not overplay the effectiveness, nor suggest use of a drug when contraindicated, nor create an impression that minimizes pertinent side effects. Similarly, information on indications already presented by graphic means, headlines, or discussion in the body of the ad should not be unnecessarily repeated in the brief summary portion so as to divert doctors from reading the side-effect information. Visual appeal of the summary report, as compared with the information on effectiveness, must be sufficient to make it a "conspicuous and easily perceived part of the total advertisement."

The FDA rules rest on the concept that precautionary information about drugs "should be presented as a part of the central message of the advertisement" to give a fair and balanced picture of the "good and the bad" of the drug.[88] The brief summary thus plays a more important role than that of merely supplying a list of warnings for the conscientious doctor to read. Even if the side-effect information may be obtained elsewhere, and even if the doctor does not scrutinize the summary, its prominence reminds him that there are limits to the drug's effectiveness. And it provides a measuring rod against which the more extravagant claims in the ad may be tested.

---

[86] 21 C.F.R. § 1.105(i) (1967). These regulations have been carried forward, in modified language, in the new FDA advertising rules.
[87] Statements in this and following paragraphs based on Letters, *supra* note 62.
[88] Letter of Oct. 9, 1963, *supra* note 62; Yakowitz, *Drug Labeling and Promotion* (Comments), 20 FOOD DRUG COSM. L.J. 97 (1965).

New regulations[89] issued by the FDA on May 17, 1967, to which industry has entered strong opposition, spell out that the FDA sees a third kind of fair balance required for prescription drug advertising beyond that (1) *within* the brief summary portion of the ad and (2) *between* the brief summary portion and the promotional copy—namely, (3) *within* the promotional copy itself. Thus the new regulations, as originally worded, order as follows:

> *Scope of information to be included in brief summary.* (i) The advertisement as a whole and each representation and suggestion in the advertisement shall be consistent with the requirement that it present a true statement of information in brief summary relating to side effects, contraindications, and effectiveness whether or not it relies on a distinct part of the advertisement to present information relating to side effects and contraindications.

This means that the ad must display the drug's limitations "in immediate conjunction with and as prominently as any claim for effectiveness," and that specific side effects must appear in "immediate conjunction with" each claim for safety *whether or not* such limitations and side effects are listed in a separate portion of the advertisement. For ads of over three pages, the side-effect information must appear as a "Brief Discussion Summary" which is "comparable in depth and detail" to that in full-disclosure labeling, even if effectiveness claims are summarized, in addition to appearing in the text next to any safety claims. In final form, the language of the regulations will be modified to assure the industry that each sentence of an ad need not present a complete report on the drug, although the ad as a whole must comply with the FDA's requirements.

Although the FDA has disclaimed any intention of regulating advertising techniques per se,[90] the new rules cover comparative claims, traditionally disregarded by the law as mere "puffing" which all but the most gullible consumers ignore. The rules forbid any claim or suggestion—either directly or through cited references—that a drug is better, safer, or more effective than its competitors, unless the claim has been approved by the FDA for labeling or has been demonstrated by "substantial evidence." Moreover, any assertion of superiority must be balanced by disclosure of those disadvantages shared with the "inferior" drugs plus those drawbacks unique to the "better" drug.

The agency's concern in this area may have stemmed from advertising for two oral contraceptives. The FDA charged[91] that Mead Johnson's description of Oracon (ethinyl estradiol, dimethisterone) as safer than and superior to other birth control pills was deceptive because there is no substantial evidence that one oral contraceptive

---

[89] The regulations referred to in this and succeeding paragraphs may be found at 32 Fed. Reg. 7533-37 (May 23, 1967).

[90] Goodrich, *Responsibilities and Problems of Government*, in Drugs in Our Society 141, 146 (P. Talalay ed. 1964).

[91] Address by FDA General Counsel William W. Goodrich, N.Y.C. Pharmaceutical Advertising Club Seminar, Oct. 20, 1966, *reported in* 28 F.D.C. Reports No. 43, at S-10, S-11 (Oct. 24, 1966).

outperforms the others, and that Eli Lilly wrongly claimed that women using its C-Quens (mestranol, chlormadione acetate) will gain less weight than those using nonsequential pills. The agency then required that labeling for all oral contraceptive brands display exactly the same prescribing warnings, thereby effecting some equalization of sales appeal.[92] Because six million American women are using these pills, and because their safety has not yet been conclusively shown, such stringent actions may be justified.

Exaggerated claims of superiority may achieve credibility when backed by an impressive-looking block of citations. Many of the thirty-four specific practices condemned in the new regulations pertain to the use of quotations and references in ads. A kind of "fair balance" is required here also; thus an ad is misleading if it

—ignores recent literature references for more favorable obsolete data;
—ignores published articles detailing side effects for literature reporting none;
—implies that a study reflects greater experience with the drug than it does in fact;
—fails to reveal that favorable studies conflict with other reliable studies; or
—improperly suggests that animal studies have clinical significance.

Even when accurately reported, studies cited in ads must have independent validity. Drug firms may not cite a study "that lacks significance because it was uncontrolled or for other reasons;" they must disclose the extent to which results claimed in studies "may be due to placebo effect or concomitant therapy."

An alleged violation of the 1963 fair-balance rules, involving some of the factors outlined above, led to the first seizure action under the advertising provisions of the 1962 amendments. On February 28, 1966, U.S. marshals seized sixty-eight bottles containing 100 capsules each of Peritrate SA (pentaerythritol tetranitrate), sold by the Warner-Chilcott Laboratories Division of the Warner-Lambert Pharmaceutical Co.,[93] which did not contest the action. Peritrate has been widely used since 1952 to relieve the vise-like chest pain of angina pectoris, a coronary artery disease. Taken by millions of patients, the drug enlarges blood vessels narrowed by fatty deposits building up on their walls. But five-page journal ads[94] suggested a new use for Peritrate—prolonging the life of heart patients by reducing the chance of subsequent attacks. Cited as support for this conclusion was one "long-range study of survival in 100 patients," in "well-matched treatment groups." Charts printed against a dramatic background of a sunset-lit ocean indicate that two years after myocardial infarction, 77.1 per cent of the patients on Peritrate were still alive, in comparison with 44.7 per cent of those given a placebo, demonstrating "a significant trend toward

---

[92] Washington Post, Nov. 14, 1966, at 3, col. 1.
[93] The discussion of Peritrate seizure is based on Wall Street Journal, March 1, 1966, at 1, col. 1; N.Y. Times, March 1, 1966, at 22, col. 1; MEDICAL LETTER, Jan. 28, 1966; Washington Post, March 4, 1966, at 3, col. 1.
[94] E.g., J.A.M.A., Dec. 6, 1965, at 75-79.

increased survival with Peritrate." On the last page of the ad a hand stretches toward the sun; superimposed on the full-color picture is the question: "Is Peritrate life-sustaining?"

The author of the cited study and the FDA answer that it is not. Dr. Alexander Oscharoff, chief of cardiology at Queens Hospital Center and Union Health Center in New York City, stated that he had never claimed "that Peritrate is the life-saving, dramatic drug that the advertising makes it." Dr. Oscharoff said that the ads were "distasteful," that he had "nothing to do" with them, and that after seeing them he had "objected" to the manufacturer. The FDA similarly charged that the Peritrate ads "falsely represented" Dr. Oscharoff's investigation. In addition, the *Medical Letter* has questioned the experiment itself, contesting the advertisement's claim that the two groups of patients were "well-matched."[95] In fact, patients in the placebo group were older and more severely ill from the start than those on Peritrate, and therefore had dimmer chances of survival. The *Letter* concluded that "it seems unlikely that the FDA would accept a single . . . study by a single investigator" as meaningful evidence for "one of the most intensive drug advertising campaigns of recent years . . . [which] promotes a drug as a lifesaving agent in a serious disease."

The advertisement contains three references in addition to Dr. Oscharoff's study, which was published in a medical journal. Two were from inaccessible sources—a paper presented by Dr. Oscharoff at the 1964 annual meeting in Detroit, Michigan, of the Michigan Academy of General Practice, and "data on file" in the medical department of the manufacturer. The other reference supposedly supports a claim that Peritrate "stimulates development of collateral circulation." As the FDA charged, the ad does not disclose that this study was made on piglets "in a manner which in no way approximates the human disease situation." A second study by Dr. Oscharoff was not cited; this revealed that the number of deaths among Peritrate patients in the post-attack period was exactly the same as that among patients given a placebo.[96] A spokesman for *JAMA*, however, said that the Peritrate ads "met our standards," which the *Journal*'s advertising evaluation director has described as limiting "claims for useful products to those which can be documented by scientific fact."

In contrast, a recent three-page ad[97] for Peritrate SA (billed as a "vignette of angina pectoris") claims merely that the drug has "been reported in clinical usage to reduce in number and severity the incidence of angina pectoris attacks," warning in the next paragraph of the promotional text that "the published literature contains both favorable and unfavorable clinical reports." The brief summary portion of the ad, which occupies two-thirds of a page, discusses the tests on pigs and adds that "these animal experiments cannot be translated to human behavior." However, the only

---

[95] MEDICAL LETTER, Jan. 28, 1966.
[96] Washington Post, March 4, 1966, at 3, col. 1.
[97] J.A.M.A., July 31, 1967, at 60-62.

reference to this and other warning information on the two pages containing the promotional copy (but largely consisting of irrelevancies) is the direction in small print at the bottom of the second page, "See next page for full prescribing information."

In a speech to the New York City Pharmaceutical Advertising Club on October 20, 1966,[98] FDA general counsel William W. Goodrich criticized advertising for the eight new drugs introduced in 1965 which within a year ranked among the 200 most frequently prescribed drugs. Among the advertisements termed false or deceptive were the following:

> Aventyl HCl (nortriptyline hydrochloride), Eli Lilly—Promotion uses "a new catch phrase to cover a host of 'target' symptoms, so that the drug is indicated and prescribed for the ordinary frustrations of daily living to reach a much larger patient population than the scientific data will support."
>
> Indocin (indomethacin), Merck, Sharp & Dohme—Ad claims greater long-term safety despite recent disclosure of new side effects; cites reference to support effectiveness claim without disclosing that the same study found "striking failures as well."
>
> Lincocin (lincomycin hydrochloride monohydrate), Upjohn—Ad for antibiotic "obscures the most important information that the MD needs in using this drug—that hematologic toxicity can occur, and that the frequency of severe diarrhea is a unique feature of Lincocin therapy."
>
> Tegopen (sodium cloxacillin monohydrate), Bristol—"The artwork, layout, and design of the ad" were meant "to impress the reader with the frequency with which Tegopen can be used, and not to carry the real message which the approval of the drug intended."

For the most part, the new regulations collect and codify advertising standards previously communicated to industry through letters, articles, and speeches by agency officials. By enumerating thirty or so specific practices as improper, the FDA hopes to overcome the genuine difficulties involved in translating the few words of the 1962 statute and the generalities of the 1963 regulations into decisions made on particular ads by the agency and by manufacturers (some of whom may not have adequate legal staffs). The industry withdrew its demands for a public hearing on the 1963 rules after then FDA Commissioner George P. Larrick sent two letters to industry counsel commenting on specific ads, although industry stated that it did not thereby concede that the FDA had broad regulatory powers over drug ad content.[99] Following Dr. Goddard's appointment, agency officials have given a series of some ten speeches to industry and its advertising agencies calling attention to

---

[98] Address by FDA General Counsel Goodrich, *supra* note 91, at S-10 to S-12.
[99] Record at 131, 135, 137, In the Matter of Drugs: Prescription Drug Advertisements (Docket No. FDC-D-78), Prehearing Conference (Sept. 26, 1963).

faults in drug ads and urging greater self-regulation. The new regulations should give more precise content to terms such as "fair balance."

Publicity attending the regulatory techniques used against defective ads has also disseminated the FDA's interpretation of the law. More recently, the agency has favored "dear doctor" letters from manufacturers to doctors to correct misleading ads. These warning letters fine the alleged offender the amount of their cost (about $40,000), force a confession from him, and communicate the confession directly to those persons whom the ad may have misled. Also, the advertiser has in effect agreed to change all future promotion to match the correction. In contrast, either an injunction against the ad or seizure of the drug would come too late. A seizure action is effective from the FDA's point of view only if widely publicized. But the industry complains that unfavorable publicity flowing from seizures may result in sharp drops in sales because some doctors do not distinguish between defects in advertising and total lack of efficacy and safety of the drug itself. Of course, some danger exists that through the threat of seizure, injunction, criminal prosecution, and consequent publicity, the FDA may be able to force its views on industry on points that are reasonably debatable.

While it is true that FDA enforcement of its rules plus voluntary compliance by industry have effected great changes in the format and content of drug ads, this writer's survey of ads in recent journal issues indicates a wide divergence in understanding of the thrust of FDA policy. The separate, brief-summary portions of prescription drug ads do not always conform to a standard of "readability." The type size may be very small;[100] headings such as "side effects" may not clearly stand out from the text;[101] all the information may be lumped into one paragraph and not separated by white space;[102] indications already presented in the ad body may be unnecessarily repeated; and warning data may be placed on the last page of a multi-page spread where it can be overlooked. At the same time, many ads, especially one and two-page spreads, present the summary of limitations in readable type close to promotional claims.[103] One ad varied this approach by stating in the promotional text, in the same type face and size: "Side effects, occurring in 9% of patients, seldom interfered with therapy. (For a description of side effects reported, see last page of this advertisement.)"[104] As the extreme case, an ad for Indocin (indomethacin) presented four X-ray pictures, one sentence on uses, and twenty-five sentences of warnings.[105]

In a number of journal ads, promotional claims in large type, colorful drawings

---

[100] E.g., Advertisement for Tepanil Ten-tab (diethylpropion hydrochloride), J.A.M.A., July 31, 1967, at 12.
[101] E.g., Advertisement for Dilantin (diphenylhydantoin), J.A.M.A., July 24, 1967, at 64-65.
[102] E.g., Advertisement for Miltrate (meprobamate, pentaerythritol tetranitrate), J.A.M.A., July 24, 1967, at 24-25.
[103] E.g., Advertisement for Kenalog (triamcinolone acetonide), J.A.M.A., Aug. 21, 1967, at 46-47.
[104] Advertisement for Vontrol (diphenidol), NEW ENG. J. MED., July 6, 1967, at viii-x.
[105] Advertisement for Indocin (indomethacin), J.A.M.A., July 31, 1967, at 7.

and cartoons, and dramatic scenes portraying patients may overwhelm the cautionary information. A two-page ad for Hygroton (chlorthalidone), an oral diuretic, was composed of three horizontal strips running across facing pages. At the top was the promotional text ("to get rid of the fussiness, get rid of the puffiness"); underneath, and dominating the ad, a six-and-one-half-inch high picture of a woman's piercing eyes and nose; under the picture, the small print of the warnings (one-half inch high) was barely noticeable.[106]

Although the FDA states that its regulations require an adequate explanation of the limits of effectiveness, considerably different treatment is given to information supporting effectiveness and information restricting a drug's usefulness—the former appears in large type in the body of the ad, often with a citation, while the latter is conveyed to the doctor through a summary statement without reference as a side effect or contraindication, sometimes in an obscure part of the ad. Perhaps after the issuance of the 1963 rules there arose some legitimate confusion over the requirement that warning information must become "part of the central message of the advertisement." In two recent ads, statements that under certain conditions the drug must be used only as adjunctive therapy appeared in the promotional text of one ad[107] but in the brief summary "indications" portion of the other.[108]

According to a study cited at the Kefauver hearings,[109] doctors want less exaggerated and more informative ads, aimed at a higher level, accompanied by complete, clear research statistics, without cartoons or sensationalism. Many drug companies seem to have a low regard for the intellect of the average doctor. Consider, for example, a twelve-page ad placed in *JAMA*[110] in December 1965 by Warner-Chilcott (which manufactures Peritrate SA) for Tedral and Brondecon. The ad begins: "Like the Riders of the Apocalypse, to whom power was given to kill, there are abroad in the land Four Horsemen of the Alveoli." The first three of the pathologic "Horsemen" are identified as asthma, chronic bronchitis, and emphysema; the fourth, "the pale rider of therapeutic despair and diagnostic discouragement," is portrayed in a one-page color drawing as a naked man slumped wearily on a horse amidst dark clouds. In large type, the ad asks "What can be done?" and ominously warns doctors of impending influenza epidemics and air pollution—"There is cause for alarm." "Much can be done," of course, by prescribing Tedral, "the air that comes in tablets."

Advertisements for tranquilizers and sedatives are particularly offensive, and have more than likely contributed to the "astonishing expansion" in the use of such drugs

---

[106] J.A.M.A., July 24, 1967, at 20-21.
[107] Advertisement for Depo-Medrol (methylprednisolone acetate), J.A.M.A., July 24, 1967, at 32-33. The ad text reads in part: "In such chronic diseases as arthritis, Medrol should be regarded as adjunctive therapy and not as replacement for standard measures."
[108] Advertisement for Miltown (meprobamate), J.A.M.A., Aug. 21, 1967, at 218-19. The ad's brief summary portion reads in part: "Indications: Effective in relief of anxiety and tension states; adjunctively when anxiety may be causative or disturbing factor."
[109] S. REP. No. 448, at 163-64.
[110] J.A.M.A., Dec. 6, 1965, at 11-22.

and their "phenomenal abuse" by doctors within the past several years.[111] Vividly illustrated, these ads suggest that tranquilizers supply the answer to almost all social problems—for the elderly woman "in senile agitation" clutching her dog, worried because her pension check is late; for the husband yelling at his wife over a bill; for the young woman crawling into bed with her teddy bear, nudged to sleep by a drug; for the man who has lost his wife, job, or self-esteem; and for the unhappy person experiencing "the fluctuating symptoms of Behavioral Drift." ("I keep pacing back and forth. I think I'm going to pieces.") An ad promotes Miltown (meprobamate) as helping to "control the underlying problem—anxiety— . . . when reassurance is not enough,"[112] an open-ended claim that sweeps broadly to catch a large proportion of today's urban population who need more than reassurance, although not necessarily Miltown. It is not surprising, therefore, that tranquilizers are being used less as a medication than as agents for producing sleep, a sense of happiness, and relaxation.[113] Although the FDA could not order that advertisements be more dignified, enforcement of the fair balance regulations plus general pressure toward scientific presentation of drug claims might incidentally result in ads aimed at a higher scientific level.

V

FUTURE DEVELOPMENTS

The Kefauver Drug Amendments of 1962, and regulations issued by the Food and Drug Administration to implement them, have produced significant and desirable changes in prescription drug promotion. At the minimum, drug maufacturers have complied with rules that are relatively unambiguous—that is, where noncompliance would be conspicuous. Thus drug ads today at least list the side effects associated with the promoted drug. And although it may be impossible to estimate to what extent lack of full disclosure or unsubstantiated claims made in pre-1962 drug literature caused misuse of drugs with consequent adverse effects, the new law provides some safeguards against such occurrences.[114]

Promotion for prescription drugs differs significantly from that for ordinary consumer goods. Ads for consumer goods may stimulate aggregate demand for an industry's product in addition to shifting demand among fungible brands of goods (such as perfumes) which are quasi-useful and which lack any real potential for good or harm. But no color photograph of a sunset[115] will ever create greater demand for medication to treat one class of diseases (such as epilepsy). In fact, it is the constant need for genuine medical progress, for the discovery and immediate use of drugs with proven greater effectiveness and safety, that justifies regulatory control.

---

[111] N.Y. Times, March 13, 1966, at 32, col. 3 (city ed.).
[112] J.A.M.A., Aug. 21, 1967, at 218-19.
[113] N.Y. Times, March 13, 1966, at 32, col. 3 (city ed.).
[114] Pisani, *supra* note 68, at 75.
[115] Advertisement for Dilantin, *supra* note 101.

When such drugs are marketed, the "art of persuasion" and exaggerated claims—or the failure to stress the unique limitation of a new drug among others used to treat the same illness—must not lull doctors looking to ads for information into easy acceptance either of inferior drugs or of equally effective drugs which may be inappropriate for a particular patient.

While physicians may be no more "immune to the contemporary scene" than other persons, it does not follow that one cannot, "in a world dominated by singing commercials and neon lights . . . expect to attract attention to *any* message if you clothe it in dull, eighteenth-century garb."[116] Doctors are not the ultimate consumers of drugs; they are agents entrusted to exercise dispassionate scientific judgment on scientific questions.[117] Communications phrased more like letters than billboards, with relevant illustrations, are just as likely to catch the attention of a doctor treating a patient for a painful, crippling disease as are more flamboyant, enthusiastic, and colorful reviews. And if it is true that misleading advertising destroys doctors' confidence in the pharmaceutical industry,[118] manufacturers should not hesitate to rely on facts to sell drugs, "facts presented in a professional way for professional men to read with care and respect."[119]

Dr. James L. Goddard, FDA Commissioner, has asked physicians to assist the agency to review drug effectiveness and eliminate abuses in clinical testing of new drugs. The medical profession could also take a more responsible stand in helping the FDA monitor drug advertising by reporting adverse reactions not adequately revealed in the brief summary; by expressing to detailers and manufacturers their distaste for overpromotion; and by using publications such as the *Medical Letter* to obtain more balanced pictures of drugs. Medical schools should take the initiative in teaching doctors how to evaluate promotional literature and how to supplement it with drug data from other sources.

Future relations between the FDA and industry will continue to include minor skirmishing, with industry contesting some FDA regulatory actions against drug promotion but acquiescing in others. The industry may contest the new advertising regulations in court, having forced the FDA to retreat on the every-time requirement. Recently drug companies have voluntarily submitted many ads for new drugs, which the FDA watches carefully, for advance clearance by the agency. (The statute bars the FDA from requiring advance approval except in "extraordinary circumstances."[120]) The industry has complained that the agency has been arbitrary in its choice of ads to criticize and its choice of regulatory techniques to employ in individual cases.

---

[116] Jurow, *supra* note 4, at 62, 63.
[117] The fact that doctors act as purchasing agents for their patients minimizes the influences of prices on the volume of prescription drug sales. Steele, *supra* note 14, at 132.
[118] S. REP. No. 448, at 155.
[119] Address by FDA Commissioner Goddard, *supra* note 5.
[120] 21 U.S.C. § 352(n) (1964).

Ironically, just as the conflict over drug advertising intensifies, the importance of medical journal advertising may be on the decline for a variety of reasons, which the following paragraphs suggest.

First, companies may direct their promotional efforts more at hospitals and government agencies and less at individual doctors reached through journals. Here the detailers, over whose oral statements the FDA exercises little control, may play a larger role. But large institutions cannot be misled or overawed as easily as can the single practitioner; in addition, hospitals have programs for monitoring drug reactions and effectiveness. In reviewing new drug labeling, the FDA has recently been carefully examining the material prepared for the detailer to leave with doctors during sales talks. And as more doctors become associated with hospitals or medical centers, more will learn of the effectiveness and limitations of new drugs through hospital and clinic committees.

Second, government agencies buying drugs under Medicare, Medicaid, and other programs may limit buying to little-advertised generic name drugs. The sheer volume of advertising for trade name drugs may obscure the existence of these generic drugs from the general practitioner.[121]

Third, each year the number of new drugs, the most heavily advertised, decreases. Thus, while forty-five new chemical entities were introduced in 1960, only thirteen were introduced in 1966. Reasons for this decline may include the FDA's tightening of rules on advertising content, which has diminished the manufacturers' ability to differentiate their trade-name products. But more stringent FDA policies with regard to testing and approving new drugs may have played a greater role in the reduction in the flow of new drug products.[122]

Fourth, techniques such as films and company-sponsored seminars may be stressed to a greater extent. Today detailers may show films on drug use at medical conventions and hospital meetings. Promotional films for one drug, or for a class of drugs one of which is marketed by a sponsoring company, when used in a promotional setting, are classified as labeling. In a concession to industry, the proposed regulations require only that such films spell out the drug's "major" side effects, provided they mention that full-disclosure information will be distributed to the audience.

Fifth, publication of a government-approved manual on drugs, reproducing full-disclosure labeling and updated with frequent supplements, may eventually replace advertisements as a major source of drug information for doctors. As yet, however, the industry has not agreed to subsidize such a publication, which would list drugs by generic name.

---

[121] Steele, *supra* note 14, at 147. According to William S. Comanor, assistant professor of economics at Harvard University, the volume of advertising for a particular drug may in some cases be more important than the ad content in inducing prescriptions from doctors who are uncertain about the relative merits of competing products. Washington Post, Jan. 26, 1968, at 6, col. 1 (capital ed.).

[122] N.Y. Times, June 4, 1967, § 3, at 1, col. 2.

During the next several years industry and government, either in a spirit of cooperation or in a mood of mutual and militant hostility, will determine the extent of legal control over the advertising of prescription drugs. The final result will be of great significance, for "except only those great decisions that lead to peace or war, it is difficult to think of any that affect so many lives for so long to come or affect them in such important ways."[123]

[123] Address by Alanson W. Willcox, General Counsel, Department of Health, Education, and Welfare, Charles Wesley Dunn Lecture at Harvard Law School, March 15, 1963.

LEGAL ASPECTS OF COMPUTER USE IN MEDICINE

Roy N. Freed*

Introduction

On July 5, 1967, a computer in Washington, D.C., analyzed electrocardiograms of patients in France and returned interpretations within thirty seconds.[1] That feat, which utilized a communications satellite, dramatized the intimate involvement of medicine with the current interrelated technological revolutions in electronic information processing and communications. Since the rendering of medical care largely is a series of information processing functions, increasingly those functions will be delegated to computers with varying degrees of responsibility.[2] Being alerted to that development, laymen and lawyers alike promptly become curious about the legal rights and liabilities of the various participants in the process of using computers in medicine. These participants include not only patients and doctors but also hospitals and other suppliers of specialized data processing services, manufacturers of computers and other equipment, system designers, and programmers.

Imaginative doctors and medical engineers foresee great benefits to patients from the use of the new technology. They are working actively to develop a wide variety of applications.[3] Equally imaginative plaintiffs' lawyers, on the other hand, undoubtedly will develop new applications of tort liability theory to secure damages for harm suffered by patients. Those lawyers might inquire, for example, along the following, very diverse lines: Can a doctor escape liability to a patient injured by his using a computer system to administer anesthesia? Is it legally safe for a doctor to fail to use a computer diagnosis system or simulation system for pretesting treatment? May the operator of a diagnosis system cater to laymen? Do hospital charity patients have a right of privacy that guarantees freedom from routine treatment by medical students when computer-operated teaching dummies are available? May a patient harmed by a flaw in a computerized intensive care monitor sue the system manufacturer on the basis of strict liability?

This article considers some representative legal considerations related to uses of

---

*B.S. 1937, LL.B. 1940, Yale University. Division Counsel, Computer Control Division, Honeywell Inc., Framingham, Mass. Member of the Massachusetts, Connecticut, and Pennsylvania bars. Contributor to legal and engineering periodicals.

The opinions expressed in this article are entirely those of the author and are not to be attributed to Honeywell Inc.

[1] N.Y. Times, July 6, 1967, at 37, col. 8.
[2] *See* Davis, *Computers in Medicine*, Int'l Sci. & Technology, Dec. 1966, at 40.
[3] *See generally id.*; Baruch & Barnett, *Joint Venture at Massachusetts General*, Datamation, Dec. 1965, at 29; Caceres, *Computer Analysis of Medical Signals, id.* at 34; Greanias, *The Computer in Medicine, id.* at 24; Kleinmuntz, *Clinical Information Processing, id.* at 40; Shaw, *Rx for Medical Instrumentation: Realism, Patience, Communication*, Electronics, July 10, 1967, at 96; Spinrad, *Automation in the Laboratory*, 158 Sci. 55 (1967).

computers in medicine that are reasonably to be anticipated. In developing the topic, attention is given first to the nature of the related computer and communications technologies as they are involved with medicine generally. Then, successively but with no indication of relative significance, some of the most likely computer uses in medicine are described in sufficient detail to provide factual background for legal review, and the legal impact of each use is explored to suggest how the various questions might be approached, if not resolved. Since the medical applications discussed are just being introduced or developed, no direct precedents are available.[4]

Fortunately, it is not necessary for this purpose to prove the technical feasibility of the various applications identified or to describe them accurately or in full detail. In view of the importance of computers to medicine and the momentum already developed for their use, it is reasonable to assume that the ingenuity of doctors and engineers will make the suggested applications practical in the not-too-distant future. Much, if not all, of their legal significance can be appreciated from the brief descriptions provided.

It is hoped that this study will dispel any unwarranted concerns over legal barriers to efficient use of computers in medicine that might inhibit the adoption of needed systems and will suggest how any genuine handicaps can be overcome. Its purpose also is to encourage regard for pertinent legal considerations in system planning and operation so that each computer use will have as sound a legal foundation as possible and affected legal rights will be respected.

This article will not cover the legal aspects of the use of computers in medicine peripherally to keep doctors' accounts, as research tools (rather than clinical devices) in medical laboratories, or to maintain central medical records for all persons.

I

COMPUTER TECHNOLOGY

It is essential to understand a number of general characteristics of computer technology in order to identify the legal aspects of its use in medicine and to suggest how they might be treated.[5] Those characteristics include not only how the devices work but also how their use is made available.

Essentially, computers are machines for processing information. They do so by performing mathematical operations and by making comparisons with predefined standards. In general, they can be set up to carry out any information processing operations that people know how to do and hence can describe in full detail. For this purpose, the operations must be reduced to their elementary logical steps. Most digital computers are general purpose machines, similar to typewriters, and can

---

[4] For a similarly anticipatory discussion, see Wasmuth, Homi & Hale, *Hyperbaric Medicine and Law*, 14 CLEV.-MAR. L. REV. 300 (1965).

[5] In view of the extremely dynamic nature of the technology, it should be recognized that the description provided, however general, well might be made inaccurate at any time by changes that occur continually.

use their abilities to carry out a wide variety of very different tasks, frequently doing so practically simultaneously.

Where feasible, computers generally are used as elements of larger systems rather than merely as advanced, independent calculating machines. In such systems the computer controls other equipment, processes and reports on information it receives, and assembles and analyzes large quantities of data. Computers can do these things because they are basically different from all other machines in that they work automatically in accordance with programs stored within themselves. The programs tell the computers how to cope with various circumstances that might be encountered during their operation. Only the instructions given will be performed. If an unanticipated situation occurs, at the present state of the art, the computer cannot cope with it without external assistance, but it can be instructed to call for such help. Computers also can be caused to adjust themselves, with considerable versatility, as the conditions they are working with change.

The programming is reflected in records often called "software documentation." That documentation normally will contain statements of the instructions and the circumstances under which they will be given, that can be understood, in large measure, by a nonspecialist. Since programs are changed frequently to accommodate new situations or newly acquired knowledge or to correct deficiencies, ideally documentation is kept up to date and logs of program usage are maintained. Hence, it generally is possible to find out much about what a particular computer could have done or probably actually did in the past.

Computers are analogous to human beings in that they can receive messages in various forms from the outside world, can store facts and instructions, can manipulate information to do arithmetic and to make comparisons, and can communicate to the outside world by many different media. They can handle input information on almost the entire range of physical phenomena, including color, temperature, pressure, viscosity, speed, weight, shape, and time, for example, as well as alphabetic, numeric, written, and audible material. With the ability to compare for magnitude and identity, they can make prearranged types of decisions or conclusions. They can manifest their decisions or conclusions by operating devices (such as valves, pumps, motors, and heaters), by activating alarms, and by printing words and numbers or displaying them on a cathode ray tube.

Computers function more rapidly and accurately than people. They operate at speeds measured in billionths or smaller fractions of a second. And they normally carry out their instructions reliably, without suffering from fatigue, distractibility, and other human frailties.

While computers can report their observations and conclusions more efficiently than people in terms of speed, accuracy of detail, and volume of material, they do not have the automatic memory of humans. They make no record of what they have observed or done unless directed to do so. When so instructed, however, they can record not only on magnetic tape and similar machine-readable media but also in such visual forms as written text, charts, and graphs.

Also, as distinguished from people, computer systems repeat exactly what they did before if they are rerun or otherwise encounter the identical situation. Similarly, a computer specialist generally can describe, with a substantial degree of certainty, what a computer system must or would have done, if he is told the elements of the system and the inputs at the time in question.

Where a computer is used as an element in a system rather than only as an advanced calculating machine, the entire system first is described or designed by a person knowledgeable primarily in the particular subject matter, who specifies the nature and extent of action to be taken and the circumstances in which it should occur. Then, the design is reduced to a program by a programmer, who normally is adept at some aspect of that general skill. The design might exist in the records in narrative form or as a flow diagram.

Error rates in computer system operations generally are substantially lower than in nonmechanized activities. Moreover, errors that do occur usually are caused by people, either when introducing information into the system or in designing or programming the system, rather than by the operation of the computer and related equipment. The risk at input is greatest when people communicate their observations of phenomena to computers and least when accurate sensing devices send such information directly to the machines. Considerable error prevention is achieved by the "debugging" of programs in advance and by including in programs and the machines themselves measures that will detect the possibility of error and lead to corrective action. Normally, so-called benchmarks are selected as the critical items to be tested to see if the system is working correctly. However, debugging many systems challenges the ingenuity of man and usually is not foolproof, because of the extreme difficulty of anticipating all possible situations that might confront the particular computer system as it operates.

Although complete failures are unavoidable in machine systems, techniques are available to minimize their effects through standby arrangements, manual backup measures, and fail-safe alarms. Furthermore, many computers have power interrupt features that automatically record the status of operations when electricity is lost.

As indicated, it is the distinct trend to use computers as integral elements in continually operating systems, rather than merely as processing machines run intermittently when batches of information are collected. In the newer approach, the computers are said to be *on line,* working in *real time.* There also is a tendency to set up *integrated systems,* in which as many related tasks and operations as possible are combined in a single system, to be carried out routinely and without interruption. With increasing frequency, *closed loop* systems are set up where appropriate to provide fully self-regulating control of processes, such as chemical production and petroleum refining. In such systems, messages from sensors trigger adjustments necessary to maintain proper operation. Furthermore, in on-line, real-time systems, provision usually is made to treat people, as well as the machines, as elements of the system so that they are in the information flow as sources and recipients and can interact regularly. Similarly, by utilizing on-line communication links, such as provided by public or private telephone service, computer systems achieve greater capabilities and can function over long distances, as evidenced by the international electrocardiogram analysis project described at the beginning of this article.

Examples of computer applications outside medicine indicate the direction of mechanization in that field. For example, in an on-line, real-time system, information is gathered on pertinent phenomena as it is available; this information is processed by the computer promptly upon receipt and in accordance with rules; and decisions are made by the computer and action is taken by other elements of the system at the direction of the computer. Computers are used in industry at various levels of responsibility. Some run single machines or entire factories automatically; others monitor processes and warn personnel when dangerous conditions exist; and still others merely record or log data as operations progress. The three functions can be combined. Also, computers are used to simulate various activities in order to perform tests or provide a learning experience without the the need either to create a prototype or to carry out the actual operation. Some simulators have a physical resemblance to the real thing. For example, an aircraft or spacecraft simulator for teaching purposes will have a cockpit and controls. Other simulations are performed solely with mathematical models manipulated entirely within the computer. Such simulations can be used to pretest physical phenomena, such as the strength of an aircraft component in use. Computers also are used to check out complicated devices, such as space rockets ready for flight, and present their reports in words and numbers on a cathode ray display. It should take little imagination to identify counterparts of these applications in medicine.

The opportunity to use computers is expanding rapidly as more machines become available, as specialized application programs are created, and as the cost of computing time decreases. Computer use costs less because the prices of computers are being reduced at the same time that their capacities and speeds increase. Use costs are lower, too, because it is possible, in so-called *time-sharing* systems, to buy only the amount of time needed, on demand. Also, charges for use frequently reflect economies achieved in operating, on a fee basis, specialized computer services using either a particular file of information or a group of programs, such as credit verification or the making of engineering calculations, that can serve many customers.

Since computer systems are assemblages of computer central processing units, peripheral equipment (input-output and memory devices), system designs, programs, and other items, they can be created by any entity prepared for the task. Such an entity could be, for example, not only a system manufacturer that buys computers outside or a computer manufacturer itself but also a system operator. System designing and programming might be done either by one of those entities or by an independent contractor specialist.

It is hoped that this brief review of computer technology will contribute to a better appreciation of the legal aspects of the specific uses of the devices in medicine that are discussed in the remainder of this article. Those uses include diagnosis assistance, direct participation in therapy, simulations for teaching and pretesting treatment, and hospital record-keeping with the capability of checking on the propriety of prescribed medications.

II

Diagnosis by Computer

A. Nature of Computer Diagnosis Systems

With their remarkable ability to compare extensive data with pre-established norms, computers will be utilized widely to assist doctors in making diagnoses. Two different types of diagnosis systems can be expected.

Systems will be set up, on an operating basis, first to interpret relatively limited physical data on particular body functions or conditions, such as electrocardiograms and samples of blood or other body fluids. In that area, the computer systems probably will be regarded primarily as clinical laboratory instruments. With their restricted scopes, those laboratory systems can provide fairly conclusive opinions on the specific matters for which they will be designed, much as a specialist would render, only considerably faster.

Later, systems undoubtedly will be offered to suggest possible diagnoses based on more extensive symptom data. The great complexities of the general diagnostic process undoubtedly will preclude directly usable machine opinions based on such data. Instead, the output, being highly probabilistic, will serve merely as memory reinforcers for doctors, by indicating possible causes and other symptoms to be looked for. Actual diagnoses in those cases still will be made by doctors who will use the output along with other data. Despite all their very real limitations, good general diagnostic systems nevertheless could have the substantial merit of at least alerting their users to unusual medical problems that doctors ordinarily would not think of. Being replicative, they could be interrogated at a later date to show what they would have responded if they had been given particular symptoms.

In both types of systems, persons highly skilled in the particular medical subject matter will specify precisely how the computers will carry out their logical operations and what information they will have in their memories. That activity constitutes the designing of the system. The machine systems will be no better, as regards the technical information they contain, than the persons contributing that information are proficient in their special fields, although they might be superior at least in part in the way they function because of their ability to assimilate more data at one time.

In order to minimize exposure to error through sample switching and similar misfortunes, efforts undoubtedly will be made wherever possible to provide input information directly from the patient to the diagnostic computer, such as can be done with electrocardiograms. Comparable protection can be achieved where the doctor submits symptoms on line to the computer.

At the present state of the art, particularly the cost of acquiring and operating computers, it is likely that business concerns, hospitals, or professional associations, rather than practicing doctors as such, will operate computers for diagnostic purposes.[6] The systems usually can be economical only if they serve many users. For many applications, users can be located at a substantial distance from the site of the computer. Many systems probably will be run under the direction of doctors.

Initiative to use computer diagnostic systems that are offered would have to come primarily from doctors, who probably will be the ostensible customers of the services in most cases. In view of the nature of medical practice, they have to be convinced that the assistance is technically sound and that using it would be consistent with their best interests and would not entail undue professional, legal, or economic risks. To a lesser extent, patients might influence their doctors to resort to such services in the same way they induce consultations with specialists.

It is reasonable to expect that the use of diagnostic systems will be provided on a fee basis, since each use is separate and is identifiable, at least by the doctor, with a particular patient. With the precedent of fee charges for clinical laboratory work, the costs for such computer analyses undoubtedly will be passed on to patients routinely, without any awkwardness. This will be facilitated by the fact that the availability of computer services will be recognized fairly readily as socially beneficial. For example, computers will make available the skills of specialists in areas where they are not located and could result in the rendering of medical services at lower costs. Where fees of the outside service are paid by the patient directly, the operator necessarily will receive the patient's name, a fact relevant to the patient's right of privacy.

The handling of the costs of more general diagnostic aids probably will be more involved. Passing on of charges to patients could introduce professional complications and have resulting legal ramifications affecting a doctor's duty to use such systems. Doctors very likely will be reluctant in most cases to admit, by incurring charges for patients or by seeking reimbursement from them, that they have used

---

[6] The selection of the entity that will own and operate computer systems of the types discussed in this article will be influenced by the tax laws. Hospitals enjoying tax exemptions would have an economic advantage in that respect over taxpaying entities. A bill has been introduced in Congress to give hospital exemptions to cooperative data processing organizations serving hospitals and composed of hospitals. S. 2315, 90th Cong., 1st Sess. (1967). Other factors also might be influential. An alleged attempt by organized pathologists to monopolize medical laboratories is cited in note 24 *infra*.

a general computer diagnosis system on their own initiative. They will believe that patients normally expect their doctors to be competent to make substantially all diagnoses without outside assistance.[7] On the other hand, doctors will not want to use such a service and absorb the charges as part of their overhead, even if they could be recouped through increased fees. If doctors do not attempt to have their patients pay the computer diagnosis fees directly, they probably will give the operators some code designations for the patients, rather than their names, to protect confidentiality.

Incidentally, it also is possible that computer systems that deliver recommended therapy routines and similar information to doctors will be operated. Where such systems have the same qualities as those suggesting general diagnoses, their legal aspects should be comparable. In some instances the closer analogy may be to patient simulation by computer, a subject discussed further on.[8]

B. The Doctor

1. *Malpractice Liability*

As both actual and potential users of available computer diagnosis systems, doctors are exposed to malpractice liability to their patients. The test of such liability is the failure to use the degree of care and professional skill normally exercised by doctors in the same field of medicine practicing in a similar locality.[9] However, it would not necessarily be improper to use a treatment technique acceptable to a respectable minority of the profession in the area;[10] indeed, doctors are legally obliged to keep reasonably abreast of medical progress.[11] On the other hand, a doctor must make a referral to another doctor properly qualified if the patient's condition requires care beyond his competence or for which he lacks necessary equipment.[12] Consideration now will be given to how these general rules might apply to both types of diagnosis systems.

During the time in which the output of a particular laboratory diagnosis system is accepted by the profession on a par with the opinions of medical specialists, it could be an exercise of due professional care for a doctor to rely upon an erroneous opinion produced by that system, if the error was not obvious to a person with the

---

[7] It is unlikely that the increasingly frequent press descriptions for laymen of medical computer systems will dispel this consideration. In such a description, the following observation was made: "No one suggests that a computer will replace the physician in diagnosing diseases, but it is quite clear that it will be a great aid to a doctor's memory." Boston (Mass.) Globe, Nov. 14, 1967, at 30, col. 1.

[8] See pp. 697-700 *infra*.

[9] *E.g.*, Worster v. Caylor, 231 Ind. 625, 110 N.E.2d 337 (1953); Zoterell v. Repp, 187 Mich. 319, 153 N.W. 692 (1915).

[10] Gielskie v. State, 10 App. Div. 2d 471, 200 N.Y.S.2d 691 (1960), *aff'd mem.*, 9 N.Y.S.2d 834, 175 N.E.2d 455 (1961).

[11] Reed v. Church, 175 Va. 284, 293, 8 S.E.2d 285, 288 (1940) (dictum).

[12] Tvedt v. Haugen, 70 N.D. 338, 294 N.W. 183 (1940); Annot., 132 A.L.R. 392 (1941). "A physician should seek consultation . . . in doubtful or difficult cases . . . ." AMA PRINCIPLES OF MEDICAL ETHICS § 8 (Rev. 1957) [hereinafter cited as AMA ETHICS], reprinted in D. LOUISELL & H. WILLIAMS, TRIAL OF MEDICAL MALPRACTICE CASES, para. 2.04, at 19 n.8 (1960).

proper degree of skill.[13] However, if flaws in such a system become known in the profession, reliance on its output while its reputation is in question could be the basis for a malpractice claim against the doctor using it. In view of a doctor's duty to make a referral or consultation to provide necessary professional skill,[14] there might be situations in which that duty would be satisfied by use of such a computer diagnosis system as an alternative to resort to a specialist. Furthermore, if no qualified specialist is reasonably available but a computer system is, conceivably even by telecommunications, then failure to use the service could constitute malpractice, assuming that such a failure was the proximate cause of the harm suffered. Of course, where the proper input data are missing, such a malpractice claim would be handicapped by the difficulty of proving what the service would have stated if used.

Since the output of more general computer diagnosis assistance systems will constitute merely suggestions intended to reinforce the memory of the doctor who actually will make the diagnosis, there probably can be no legal claim by a patient based on any reliance by his doctor on erroneous output. The diagnosis is made by the practicing doctor, not the computer system, and any malpractice stems from the doctor's own failure to meet the applicable test of competence. Were the doctor to rely wholly upon the computer diagnosis, he would be substituting it for his own judgment, an act of delegation he ordinarily could not properly make. On the other hand, if the system is acknowledged to reflect high professional quality, its output consistent with an erroneous diagnosis of a doctor using it might be persuasive evidence to support his defense that he used adequate professional skill.[15] It might be argued that such output, properly offered, is equivalent to the testimony of other doctors.[16] But, conversely, if a doctor makes an erroneous diagnosis despite his receipt of system output suggesting the actual problem, it is possible that such receipt would bolster a malpractice charge, thereby creating a legal situation worse for him than if he had not consulted the system.

If a doctor does not use a general diagnosis system and makes an erroneous diagnosis, the mere failure to seek machine aid probably would not constitute compensable malpractice unless the system is acknowledged by the profession to be useful, unless it is economical to use or the patient agrees to pay the cost, and unless the patient has a rare problem that would have been suggested in response

---

[13] *Cf.* Pilgrim v. Landham, 63 Ga. App. 451, 11 S.E.2d 420 (1940); *In re* Johnson's Estate, 145 Neb. 333, 16 N.W.2d 504 (1944).

[14] JOINT COMM'N ON ACCREDITATION OF HOSPITALS, STANDARDS FOR HOSPITAL ACCREDITATION 5 (Dec. 1965).

[15] *Cf.* Redwood v. Raskind, 49 Tenn. App. 69, 350 S.W.2d 414 (1961), *noted in* 25 GA. B.J. 103 (1962).

[16] In some states, published material written by recognized experts is admissible in malpractice actions as proof of facts or as opinions. *E.g.,* Stoudenmeier v. Williamson, 29 Ala. 558 (1857); MASS. ANN. LAWS ch. 233, § 79C (Supp. 1966); NEV. REV. STAT. § 51.040 (1957). Since they specifically cover published treatises, periodicals, books, and pamphlets, statutes providing for the admissibility of such evidence probably would not provide a basis for the admission of computer output.

to symptoms the doctor actually identified or a reasonably competent doctor would have observed. If a doctor misdiagnoses a common condition, any malpractice would be the result of his personal error rather than his failure to use a computer system. Again, the fact that the system output would have included the correct diagnosis could be evidence of lack of skill if the system enjoys general professional respect. As indicated, what the system would have told the doctor generally can be determined by giving it the symptoms, and making allowances for any system changes in the interim. In many cases, the doctor's records on the patient will disclose the symptoms he noted and relied upon.

Liability very likely would exist for avoidable harm if a physician failed to use an acceptable system requested by a patient who offered to pay its cost unless he expressly indicated that he would not do so.[17] If a doctor is so requested by a patient and indicates that he will use a computer system but then does not, he probably would be liable, although more likely for fraud rather than malpractice.[18] However, if he expressly refuses, he would not be liable unless it was professionally acceptable to use the service and the patient had no genuine opportunity to secure another doctor.[19] A patient who had such an opportunity to switch and failed to use it could be held to have consented to the doctor's course of action and to have assumed the risk of the doctor's not consulting the outside service.[20]

Since imposition of malpractice liability usually requires proof through the defendant's fellow professionals,[21] injured patients will have a strong incentive, where possible, to sue persons who might be liable on more easily proved grounds of negligence or strict liability. Those persons might include diagnosis system and component manufacturers and operators.

2. *Insurance*

Most of the legal exposure of doctors to their patients related to computer diagnosis systems appears to be covered by malpractice insurance, which generally encompasses all damage because of injury arising out of malpractice, error, or mistake in rendering or failing to render medical services.[22] However, some situations might be beyond the scope of that coverage. For example, an intentional failure to comply with a promise to a patient to consult a service might be characterized as

---

[17] Ethical principles require a doctor to seek consultation upon request of the patient. AMA ETHICS § 8.

[18] *See* Berkson v. Chandler, 5 Ill. App. 2d 583, 126 N.E.2d 389 (1955).

[19] Abandonment can constitute malpractice. Carroll v. Griffin, 96 Ga. App. 826, 101 S.E.2d 764 (1958); D. LOUISELL & H. WILLIAMS, TRIAL OF MEDICAL MALPRACTICE CASES, para. 8.08 (1960, Supp. 1966) [hereinafter cited as LOUISELL & WILLIAMS].

[20] *See* Champs v. Stone, 74 Ohio App. 344, 58 N.E.2d 803 (1944).

[21] This rule is subject to exception where res ipsa loquitur applies. *See generally* Comment, *Medical Malpractice—Expert Testimony*, 60 NW. U.L. REV. 834 (1966); Comment, *The Application of Res Ipsa Loquitur in Medical Malpractice Cases*, *id.* at 852.

[22] *See generally* LOUISELL & WILLIAMS, para. 20.03; Hirsh, *Insuring Against Medical Professional Liability*, 12 VAND. L. REV. 667 (1959).

fraud or some other type of actionable conduct, in which case the doctor would have to explore the availability of a different kind of insurance.[23]

3. *Antitrust*

Since some computer laboratory diagnosis systems will be performing functions that otherwise would have been performed by doctors, many doctors might resent the competition, especially at a lower price.[24] If doctors are stimulated by such an attitude to use joint action to affect the prices charged or to exclude the service entirely, they could violate the federal antitrust laws if their steps interfere with interstate commerce or commerce within the District of Columbia.[25] They could also violate comparable state antitrust laws.

Similarly, some doctors might want to discourage resort to general computer diagnostic assistance services lest their use become the custom in the area and hence a general professional responsibility, especially if the charges have to be absorbed by doctors. Again, concerted effort might constitute an antitrust breach.[26]

On the other hand, an attempt to capitalize economically on such a service by means of kickbacks or comparable techniques, such as was alleged to have been made by some opthalmologists with respect to dispensing opticians,[27] also could violate those laws. Of course, arrangements under which doctors contributing to the design of computer diagnosis systems would secure compensation for that work measured by system use normally would escape such a legal risk.

Just as medical associations are expected to maintain responsible oversight over the professional competence of practitioners in their localities,[28] so they very likely will take an interest in the operations of computer systems performing medical functions, particularly the laboratory-type systems which make diagnoses themselves.[29] Even if there are federal clearance requirements for such machine systems, that would not necessarily eliminate the proper continuing interest of medical associa-

---

[23] Nevertheless, a malpractice insurer probably would be well advised to assume the defense of a suit against the insured doctor for intentional harm, Gray v. Zurich Ins. Co., 65 Cal. 2d 263, 54 Cal. Rptr. 104, 419 P.2d 168 (1966); but the doctor would risk the strong incentive of the attorney so defending to resist any effort to amend the complaint to cover malpractice.

[24] In United States v. College of Am. Pathologists, Civil No. 66C1253 (N.D. Ill., filed July 7, 1966), an attempt by pathologist members of the defendant association to monopolize the commercial medical laboratory business in the United States is alleged.

[25] American Medical Ass'n v. United States, 317 U.S. 519 (1943).

[26] *See id.*

[27] United States v. White-Haines Optical Co., 1950-1951 Trade Cas., para. 62,882 (S.D. Ohio 1951) (consent decree). *See also Hearings on Physician Ownership in Pharmacies and Drug Companies Before the Subcomm. on Antitrust and Monopoly of the Senate Comm. on the Judiciary,* 88th Cong., 2d Sess. (1964), concerning the practices of doctors who prescribed drugs manufactured by firms in which they owned substantial interests.

[28] AMA ETHICS § 4; *see* Comment, *Medical Societies and Medical Service Plans—From the Law of Associations to the Law of Antitrust,* 22 U. CHI. L. REV. 694, 695 (1955).

[29] *See* FTC v. Raladam Co., 283 U.S. 643, 653 (1931). By way of comparison, the Amercian Bar Association, through its Special Committee on Electronic Data Retrieval, is considering measures to protect users of computerized systems for searching for legal literature, which probably will entail primarily disclosure of information on the details of each system.

tions. Manifestations of such interest, however, must fall within the scope of reasonable activities of a truly professional nature as distinguished from joint efforts primarily to protect the economic position of doctors.

C. The System Operator

The business entities operating computer diagnosis systems probably would be exposed to claims of patients or doctors only where clinical laboratory systems are involved. It seems unlikely that general systems will be offered, for some time to come, if ever, that do any more than jog the doctor's memory. In that respect, they will have much the same function as books. Hence, defects in those general systems would not be the proximate cause of injury to patients. The cause, instead, would be the doctor's lack of skill. The remaining discussion of operator liability relates only to clinical laboratory systems unless indicated otherwise.[30]

1. Negligence

Unless the system operator is an institution enjoying charitable or governmental immunity when performing the service,[31] it probably would be liable directly to a patient injured through its fault. Lack of privity through the ostensible interposition of the doctor should constitute no problem in view of the widespread elimination of that requirement. If required, privity probably would be found to exist where the patient is billed for the service, despite the fact that he personally neither ordered it from the operator nor received the output directly.

Patients might choose to sue system operators for negligence in a number of situations. For example, where it was reasonable for a doctor to rely upon an erroneous machine laboratory diagnosis, the operator, on the other hand, well might have been careless in running a system that would produce such a result, because it knew or should have known of deficiencies in information content or machine operation. However, as suggested under the next subheading, it might be proper to alter the test of negligence where harm is attributable to the medical information used in the system.

It is entirely possible that a hospital might be negligent for neither having a laboratory computer system nor using one available outside. That could be the case where such a system is significantly more rapid or accurate than the traditional analytical tools and is economical to acquire and its use would have avoided harm.

2. Strict Liability

Since system operators might be exposed to strict liability, patients injured by their output (generated on the basis of proper input) and not handicapped by the

---

[30] *See generally* Mills, *Malpractice and the Clinical Laboratory*, 144 Sci. 638 (1964), for a review of legal exposure of clinical laboratories.

[31] *See generally* LOUISELL & WILLIAMS, paras. 17.07-.57, for summaries of the condition of the immunity doctrine in the fifty states and the District of Columbia; Horty, *The Status of the Doctrine of Charitable Immunity in Hospital Cases*, 25 OHIO ST. L.J. 343 (1964).

disappearing requirement of privity or by charitable or governmental immunity certainly would prefer to sue them on that ground rather than their doctors, whose liability rests only on fault. Such a suit against the system operator might be based on the argument that the erroneous output that caused the harm is a defective product manufactured by the operator in accordance with methods it chose. The analogy might be drawn to a poorly designed or manufactured product that caused injury. Even though the computer output is only nominally physical and really is information, nevertheless it is delivered to be used and can cause as much harm in the hands of the doctor as a tangible instrument. The fact that the doctor using the system induces the output of a laboratory diagnosis system (by submitting the input in the form of a sample of body fluid or the like) and hence causes it to be made to order does not detract from the analogy.

Along these lines, if the output of the service were considered to be "goods" under the Uniform Commercial Code,[32] the operator could be liable for breach of warranty of merchantability.[33] Since the patient will pay for the laboratory work, he probably is the "buyer" entitled to the rights and remedies provided by the Code, and his doctor would be acting as his agent in dealing with the system operator.[34]

In defense, it might be contended that functioning of the laboratory diagnosis system is equivalent to the work of a doctor making the same type of diagnosis and hence should be subjected, with respect to the medical information stored within it, to a test of legal liability no more stringent than is that of the doctor or to at least the test of ordinary negligence. In practice, many system reports probably would be signed by a doctor. That argument probably would be stronger (very likely merely on an *ad hominem* basis) if made by a nonprofit organization rather than a commercial company. Similarly, it might be contended that the system output is analogous to the report of a noncomputerized medical laboratory that relies primarily on the conclusions of people.

3. *Operational Formalities*

The creation of laboratory reports by computer would not obviate formal require-

---

[32] UNIFORM COMMERCIAL CODE § 2-105. However, § 2-102 provides that "this Article applies to transactions in goods." Thus, the operator would argue that although his report fell within the definition of "goods," the transaction was essentially a contract for services and not, therefore, subject to the Code provisions.

[33] UNIFORM COMMERCIAL CODE § 2-314. It should be recognized that courts have been reluctant to imply warranties in connection with services of professionals and hospitals. Lovett v. Emory Univ. Inc., CCH PROD. LIAB. REP., para. 5836 (Ga. Ct. App. 1967) (supplying blood not a sale); Perlmutter v. Beth David Hosp., 308 N.Y. 100, 123 N.E.2d 792 (1954) (supplying blood not a sale); Dorfman v. Austenal Inc., 3 UCC REP. 856 (N.Y. Sup. Ct. 1966) (supplying surgical pin to patient not a sale); Texas State Optical, Inc. v. Barbee, CCH PROD. LIAB. REP., para. 5837 (Tex. Civ. App. 1967) (fitting of contact lenses by optometrist). However, it has been held more recently that hospitals are subject to strict liability, including such warranties. Jackson v. Muhlenberg Hosp., 96 N.J. Super. 314, 232 A.2d 879 (L. Div. 1967) (delivery of blood; no liability for hepatitis because of specific disclaimer and fact that blood was not unreasonably dangerous in view of risk of shock if it were not supplied).

[34] Jackson v. Muhlenberg Hosp., 96 N.J. Super. 314, 232 A.2d 879 (L. Div. 1967).

ments such as signatures,[35] and they should not be overlooked. Where reports are transmitted directly in machine language, it is impractical to use signatures. Even where they are sent as print-outs and hence can be signed, it is burdensome to have to preserve the signed reports since the working record will be in machine language. It can be anticipated that many such requirements will be changed to accommodate new types of systems.[36]

Substantially more extensive requirements might exist, such as licensing, demonstrations of proficiency, and maintenance of copies of reports for inspection.[37]

4. *Injury to Doctor's Reputation*

Although attention has been focused on compensation for harm to patients, doctors also might suffer injury from a defective computer system and seek damages from the system operator. If a doctor's professional reputation is tarnished by his proper reliance on the output of a laboratory diagnosis system that was operated carelessly, the operator could be required to reimburse him for the loss.[38] Since it would be unreasonable to rely on the suggestions of a general diagnosis system, no similar legal claim could be pressed against its operator.

5. *Unauthorized or Unethical Practice of Medicine*

So long as the computer diagnosis system operator restricts its clientele to doctors, it probably could withstand any charge of unauthorized or unethical practice of medicine. Normally, operators would prefer to limit their customers in that manner. Exposure to such a charge, however, is not entirely remote. Traditional medical laboratories, which analyze body fluids and give opinions that are comparable to the output of computer systems, have escaped such a challenge at least in part because they perform functions most doctors do not want to perform themselves. But some computer systems will do desirable work that has been done by doctors, such as interpreting electrocardiograms, thereby stimulating possible resentment on essentially economic grounds. If a system operator is a doctor licensed in the state in which he functions and not a corporation[39] and if he does not advertise,[40] he would probably be safe in even the most hostile environment.

---

[35] JOINT COMM'N ON ACCREDITATION OF HOSPITALS, *supra* note 14, at 4 (clinical pathology, X-ray, and tissue reports must be signed).

[36] For example, it is understood that the Department of Health of the City of New York is waiving the requirement that clinical laboratory test results be stated on the requisition form. This problem is further discussed at pp. 700-02 *infra*. Incidentally, it is possible for computer output to state the input that stimulated it as well as the results.

[37] *E.g.*, ILL. REV. STAT. ch. 111½, §§ 622-103, 623-101, 624-103, 627-106 (1965).

[38] Stott v. Johnston, 36 Cal. 2d 864, 229 P.2d 348 (1951) (damage to goodwill of painting contractor by inferior paint made by defendant was actionable).

[39] *See* People v. United Medical Serv., Inc., 362 Ill. 442, 200 N.E. 157 (1936); Annot., 103 A.L.R. 1240 (1936).

[40] N.Y. EDUC. LAW § 6514 (McKinney Supp. 1967) (advertising or soliciting grounds for revocation of license to practice medicine); ILL. REV. STAT. ch. 111½, § 629-101(c) (1965) (clinical laboratory may not advertise to the public).

However, an operator well might be tempted to try to serve the undoubtedly large market represented by laymen interested in their own medical problems. In doing so, it probably would encounter the suggested legal barriers to corporate practice of medicine and to the advertising of medical or clinical laboratory service; moreover, in some states, clinical laboratories may serve only physicians and other qualified persons.[41] But even if these handicaps do not exist, the venture might be attacked for fostering self-medication. In this respect, a violation of medical ethics might be found in the making of diagnoses for laymen without any intention of undertaking treatment. Normally, doctors who limit their practice to diagnosis are specialists serving only other doctors. Similarly, it might be against public policy as facilitating self-medication, by laymen, of nonminor illnesses. Self-treatment is not legally protected as is self-representation in court, witness the restriction on the dispensing of many medications without a doctor's prescription. It should be noted that medical laboratories generally do not serve laymen directly, although probably largely to avoid offending doctors, who are their major customers. However, some laboratories do cater to laymen in connection with tests for pregnancy, which is a unique medical condition. Where other medical tests are performed for laymen, such as chest X-rays, they usually are primarily screening procedures intended to detect persons with suspicious conditions who should see a doctor for proper diagnosis.[42]

6. *Defamation of Patient*

Computerized clinical laboratories probably are as vulnerable as their nonmechanized counterparts to defamation charges for reporting erroneously that patients have venereal and other "loathsome" diseases.[43] However, both are shielded by the same qualified privilege where publication is made to the types of persons who reasonably would be expected to receive the information, since those reports rarely, if ever, are made with actual malice.[44] Laboratories normally are not exposed to such charges as a practical matter because their reports go only to doctors, and patients are unaware of them unless the doctors make disclosure, thereby triggering legal action against themselves.[45] Although patients have been unsuccessful in contending that dictation of an erroneous laboratory report to a stenographer is unprivileged publication,[46] not even such disclosure occurs where a computer actually prints out the

---

[41] *E.g.*, ILL. REV. STAT. ch. 111½, § 627-101 (1965).
[42] Franklin, *Medical Mass Screening Programs: A Legal Appraisal*, 47 CORNELL L.Q. 205 (1962).
[43] Shoemaker v. Friedberg, 80 Cal. App. 2d 911, 183 P.2d 318 (1947). The reader may find humorous the appearance in this ultramodern context of the quaint old doctrine that to misrepresent another's health so flagrantly is libel per se.
[44] *Id.* *See also* Berry v. Moench, 8 Utah 2d 191, 331 P.2d 814 (1958); MASS. ANN. LAWS ch. 112, § 12 (1965) (in good faith, doctor may tell recipient of marriage promise that promisor has a venereal disease).
[45] These were the circumstances in Shoemaker v. Friedberg, 80 Cal. App. 2d 911, 183 P.2d 318 (1947).
[46] *Id.*

report or, as might be done in the future, sends it by telephone to be printed out in the doctor's office.

D. The System Manufacturer

1. *Negligence*

An injured patient might want to sue a diagnosis system manufacturer, even on the grounds of negligence, if the doctor was not negligent or if the system operator enjoys charitable or governmental immunity[47] or just because he feels that the manufacturer is the most vulnerable target on practical grounds. That manufacturer brings together and sells, or less frequently leases, the complete package consisting of the computer and other hardware, the system design, and the programs, and probably created one or more of those elements itself. It would be liable to the patient for fault, and, again, lack of privity should not be a handicap. If the offending element of the diagnosis system is something the manufacturer bought outside rather than made itself, there might be a question whether it was negligent in using that element.[48]

2. *Strict Liability*

As usual, it would be most advantageous to the injured patient to impose strict liability on the system manufacturer for harm from a defective system, where privity is not a factor.[49] That application of that theory probably is closer to the commonly accepted one than the similar approach[50] with respect to output of the system operator. Since the thing causing the harm includes a computer, which is a machine, the computer system more closely resembles the traditional manufactured product than does mere computer output. In fact, the cause of the erroneous output, insofar as the manufacturer is concerned, most likely would be the system design or the program, with the result that the computer system would suffer from defective design, a well recognized basis for strict liability.[51] Of course, under the normal rule, strict liability cannot be escaped even if due care was exercised in using a defective part acquired elsewhere.[52]

As suggested briefly in discussing the system operator's liability, diagnosis and other medical types of computer systems might be unique because of the special nature of the stored information with which they work, and consequently might

---

[47] *See* Sevits v. McKiernan-Terry Corp., 264 F. Supp. 810 (S.D.N.Y. 1966), which held that a member of the U.S. Navy could sue the manufacturer of a component of a vessel manufactured by the federal government.

[48] Pabon v. Hackensack Auto Sales, Inc., 63 N.J. Super. 476, 164 A.2d 773 (App. Div. 1960).

[49] Goldberg v. Kollsman Instrument Corp., 12 N.Y.2d 432, 240 N.Y.S.2d 592, 191 N.E.2d 81 (1963) (passenger may sue aircraft manufacturer for breach of implied warranty of fitness for contemplated use by virtue of faulty design or manufacture).

[50] Discussed at pp. 685-86 *supra*.

[51] Goldberg v. Kollsman Instrument Corp., 12 N.Y.2d 432, 240 N.Y.S.2d 592, 191 N.E.2d 81 (1963).

[52] Ford Motor Co. v. Mathis, 322 F.2d 267 (5th Cir. 1963); Vandermark v. Ford Motor Co., 61 Cal. 2d 256, 37 Cal. Rptr. 896, 391 P.2d 168 (1964).

deserve a special liability rule. Just as the malpractice standard of care is less stringent than ordinary negligence, presumably because of the difficulty of applying medical knowledge, so computer systems applying that same knowledge well might be spared the rigors of strict liability to that extent.[53] It would not seem reasonable that the substitution of machine systems for doctors in order to provide better or less expensive medical care ipso facto should enlarge patients' legal rights. A doctrinaire approach to strict liability in this area might inhibit the introduction of needed machine aids in medicine.

If strict liability is applicable, the fact that input is submitted by the doctor to the system for it to work on should not detract from any such liability. Each such submission represents use of the system for its intended purpose, much like driving an automobile or eating packaged food. If the system operator has bought a complete system, its role relative to a design defect is essentially nominal, similar to that of the retailer of packaged food. Its own responsibility would involve, in fact, its failure to have preventive maintenance done on the computer or to have corrections made for system design or programming errors uncovered.

E. The System Designer and the System Programmer

1. *Negligence*

If not protected by the privity requirement, the business entity that designed or programmed the system could be liable for negligence to a patient harmed by its error.[54]

2. *Strict Liability*

The designing or programming business entity might be exposed to strict tort liability to injured patients if its defective design or program caused the diagnosis system to inflict the harm.[55] Its work product could be considered to be the offending element in a defective machine sold or leased by the system manufacturer.

III

PERFORMANCE OF MEDICAL PROCEDURES BY COMPUTER

A. Nature of Computer Treatment Systems

Computers will play a direct, major role in the performance of many medical treatment procedures, as distinguished from the diagnostic uses discussed above. In therapy, a great advantage of computers is their ability to operate on-line, in real

---

[53] It is recognized, however, that lack of knowledge and hence inability to foresee harm usually is no defense to strict liability. Gottsdanker v. Cutter Laboratories, 182 Cal. App. 2d 602, 6 Cal. Rptr. 320 (1960); Green v. American Tobacco Co., 154 So. 2d 169 (Fla. 1963). *Contra,* Lartigue v. R.J. Reynolds Tobacco Co., 317 F.2d 19 (5th Cir. 1963).

[54] *See* Katz, *Negligence in Design: A Current Look,* 1965 INS. L.J. 5.

[55] It might be that the component manufacturer's implied warranty of fitness and merchantability applies only if the producer of the major item is immune to suit. *Cf.* Sevits v. McKiernan-Terry Corp., 264 F. Supp. 810 (S.D.N.Y. 1966).

time, and, whenever feasible, in a closed loop, to supplement unique human judgment with machine reliability, data processing capacity, persistence, and speed. Such medical applications are comparable to factory process control uses in industry, because the living human, for purposes of this discussion, is as much an operating system as is a chemical factory or a railroad. Of course, human functioning is much more complex than any nonanimal system and presents difficult problems of measurement and control, especially in closed loop applications. Computer systems will be used at various levels of responsibility. For example, such systems might be used to record details they observe on the conditions of patients (data logging); to monitor the functioning of patients whenever observation is required, especially during medical procedures (particularly operations) and in postoperative situations; and to carry out medical procedures, such as the administration of anesthesia or medications. Each higher order approach can, and probably will, include functions of the lower ones.

Substantially all computer treatment systems will involve considerable man-machine interaction. Each such element will perform the functions it can do best, and both will operate in close coordination. If the computer merely logs data, it probably will display the information for medical personnel. If the system does monitoring, it will call for professional help when the patient requires it. On the other hand, if the machine performs medical procedures, the doctor or nurse will be in close proximity to intervene as needed.

Incidentally, it is feasible to use data logging and monitoring systems on patients who are at a substantial distance from the computer itself. Patients at home or even performing their normal activities can be served by devices that pick up signals of body functions and transmit them by radio. They and their doctors could even be warned by the computer of impending danger. Although the distances that can be spanned are not as great as that in the international electrocardiogram project described earlier, the application of remote monitoring probably will be very useful.

Treatment systems will have a greater variety of hardware than most diagnosis systems. They will include many different sensors and transducers to pick up and convert input signals from different parts of the patient's body and output means to give audible and visual alarms and to report current conditions and trends. For the latter purpose, cathode ray tube displays that can project graphs as well as words and numbers will play a major role.

Treatment-type computer systems are attractive because they can perform many important functions better than people.[56] For example, they can check on many aspects of a patient's condition constantly and can compare their observations with pre-established norms. They also can record the data as well as announce it to

---

[56] Davis, *supra* note 2, at 45-46.

observers. Equally important, they can perform essential data reduction at the same time, analyzing the significance of concomitant trends of different aspects of body functions to determine whether they are compatible. On occasion, those functions might be within acceptable limits individually but might be moving in directions that spell trouble.

Many elements of computer treatment systems, if not the entire systems themselves, might require clearance by a federal agency prior to regular use, in much the same manner as the Food and Drug Administration clears drugs.[57]

At the present state of the art, computer treatment systems very likely will be provided under the auspices of hospitals. They resemble the services traditionally furnished by those institutions, and the information they will collect would be very useful to the hospital staff for research and medical audit purposes as well as to attending doctors. It seems improbable that the operation of those systems would be the type of activity an independent entity would undertake to offer to doctors. However, cooperatives of smaller hospitals or other organizations might actually run the systems. Under the circumstances, any charges for system use probably will be billed by the hospitals directly to the patients.

Since practicing doctors are responsible for the conduct of the activities in which treatment systems would be included, the major initiative for the use of such systems will come from them. While doctors still will have to be satisfied that the treatment systems are technically satisfactory, when using them they will not be confronted, as in the case of general diagnostic systems, with possible adverse reflections on their competence in the minds of their patients. On the contrary, such use probably will evoke favorable reactions because they appear to be modern medical tools. Patients, on the other hand, very likely will have little occasion to prod their doctors to use the new devices in the way they might induce resort to a consultant.

B. The Doctor's Malpractice Liability

The liability exposure of a doctor prescribing use of a computer system in therapy will vary widely, depending upon the type of application. With all types of systems,

---

[57] An administration bill to expand the Food, Drug, and Cosmetic Act to authorize the setting of standards for medical devices (other than those intended solely for diagnostic use) was introduced on June 8, 1967. H.R. 10726, 90th Cong., 1st Sess. (1967). This bill would extend the safety, reliability, and effectiveness provisions of the Federal Food, Drug, and Cosmetic Act, now applicable to drugs, to medical devices. Thus, the Food and Drug Administration would have the authority to require that medical devices be safe, reliable, and effective, both in their uses and in terms of the claims made for their use. Computers, their ancillaries, and their programs might well be considered "medical devices" when used in a medical or hospital application. The FDA has identified categories of devices it would be likely to regulate if H.R. 10726 is enacted. Electronic News, Oct. 23, 1967, at 34, cols. 1-2.

Previously, on February 27, 1967, a bill was introduced to establish an independent study commission to determine the need for and the extent of federal regulation of medical devices and equipment. H.R. 6165, 90th Cong., 1st Sess. (1967). Under this approach, direct government action would presumably be postponed until the commission recommended methods for determining minimum performance standards and feasible methods for federal regulation.

injury might be caused by the attachment of sensors and other equipment to the patient's body. Harm also might result from reliance on erroneous information collected by a data logging or monitoring system, from malfunctioning of a therapy system otherwise used in a proper situation, or from use of a therapy system where inappropriate.

In selecting and applying those devices, the doctor must use the regular degree of care expected of him in performing his work. He normally would not have to examine them for latent defects,[58] but should be on the alert for information on problems experienced with particular devices. If medical systems are cleared by a government body, such use authorization for a device that caused harm very likely would support a doctor's contention that he exercised due care in selecting it for a proper application, until he actually had or should have had knowledge that it was deficient.[59] Similarly, if such clearance is required, the regulatory body well might require statements by the manufacturers of situations in which use is contraindicated.[60] Failure to observe those limitations of which he should have been aware would expose a doctor to liability for resulting harm. Manufacturers undoubtedly would have to use methods for publicizing device limitations at least similar to those followed with respect to drugs, which largely involve distribution of literature through detail men and inclusion of notices with the products.[61]

Despite necessary recognition of possible adverse experiences, medical data logging and monitoring systems have so many potential advantages to patients that eventually they will be recognized items in the medical armamentarium. Then, use of such devices, when available in particular situations, very likely will constitute due care and a failure to take advantage of the proper one would be malpractice if harm resulted. Although closed loop therapy systems seem to be further in the future, they also might achieve the same status.

There is a real danger that doctors' concerns over malpractice suits might discourage them from pioneering in the use of closed loop computer therapy systems, thereby delaying the introduction of many devices that could be very beneficial in rendering medical care. The present standard of legal care supports such conservatism, relying as heavily as it does, in the case of new techniques, on the extent to which the particular approach is used by an appropriate segment of the profession. The importance of facilitating the adoption of computer devices that substantially advance medical practice requires close attention to the

---

[58] Hine v. Fox, 89 So. 2d 13 (Fla. 1956); cf. Smith v. American Cystoscope Makers, Inc., 44 Wash. 2d 202, 266 P.2d 792 (1954). Probably the more professional and ostensibly qualified is the organization operating the system, the less the doctor would be expected to investigate the details of its system design and programming.

[59] See Lewis v. Baker, 243 Ore. 317, 413 P.2d 400 (1966).

[60] See id.

[61] See generally Ruge, *Regulation of Prescription Drug Advertising: Medical Progress and Private Enterprise*, in this symposium, p. 650. As indicated in note 82 infra, manufacturers might use a constantly updated computer information system for the purpose of alerting doctors to device limitations.

elimination of any such inhibition. The situation is quite different from that with respect to other types of medical devices, which have been much simpler in operation and commensurately more limited in their impact on treatment. There are a number of possible solutions to the problem.

If doctors are willing to take the initiative, they might try to get consents from patients, at least until use of a device has become accepted medically.[62] The importance of promoting medical progress would seem to warrant serious consideration of such a step. Of course, it would be feasible only if the consent were carefully drawn to apply only to the particular measure and if there were adequate pretesting of the device.

An alternative approach might be for system manufacturers to undertake to indemnify doctors for any out-of-pocket loss from using devices as recommended, where such consents are not secured. This probably would be unacceptable to doctors because understandably they would prefer to avoid the risk of malpractice claims, with resultant damage to their reputations.

The most satisfactory solution would be to change the test of malpractice liability. Such a change probably could not be accomplished through the courts, as a practical matter, because of the hazard in exposure to litigation until a revised standard is adopted. However, it might be reasonable to try to secure state legislative relief for doctors with respect to devices that have been cleared by a federal agency. In effect, such a step would substitute federal clearance for wide professional use. That approach would not deprive patients of proper recovery in the event of harm since the doctor should remain liable for misuse of a cleared machine system and the manufacturer would be subject to suit if its product was defective in design or operation.[63]

Through actual operation rather than as a matter of law, the performance of machine data logging could affect the liability of doctors, both favorably and adversely, by making valuable evidence available in many malpractice situations not involving computer systems directly. It is reasonable to assume that logging results will be retained in patient records. They will be more extensive, and possibly even more objective, then records kept by many doctors personally. Computer system records also will provide essential information, with possibly similar results in many cases, to hospital medical audit units, such as tissue committees, that maintain oversight over the practices of staff doctors.[64]

---

[62] To be valid where the technique is new and hazardous, consent must be "informed." Natanson v. Kline, 186 Kan. 393, 350 P.2d 1093, *rehearing denied but opinion explained*, 187 Kan. 186, 354 P.2d 670 (1960). Such consent covers only the risks inherent in the treatment and not any negligence of the doctor in selecting or administering it.

[63] Such is the case with respect to cleared drugs. Lewis v. Baker, 243 Ore. 317, 413 P.2d 400 (1966).

[64] LOUISELL & WILLIAMS, para. 2.04, at 21; Appleman, *The Preparation of Medical Malpractice Cases*, in 12 TRIAL AND TORT TRENDS 452, 466 (M. Belli ed. 1962); Derrick & Wilber, *The Electronic Computer and Developing Concepts of Patient Monitoring*, INT'L ANESTHESIOLOGY CLINICS, May 1965, at 507.

C. The System Operator

1. *Negligence*

A patient could be interested in suing the business entity operating a treatment system for negligent harm caused by system malfunctioning, especially if his doctor was not negligent in using the system. The operator probably would be negligent if the negligence of any independent producer of any elements of the system, including the equipment manufacturers, the system designer, and the programmer, caused the harm. In view of his direct involvement with system use, particularly his payment for it, the patient should have no difficulty with the privity requirement, where it still exists. Occasionally, he might run up against the charitable or governmental immunity doctrine, however, since hospitals can be expected to be the operators.[65] Furthermore, the patient might have difficulty in proving negligence if harm results from the operation, in the recommended manner, of a system enjoying clearance by the cognizant federal agency, before the operator has had the opportunity to learn of weaknesses uncovered subsequently.[66]

On the other hand, a hospital that does not have a computer therapy system that would be appropriate for a particular problem has the legal duty to transfer the patient to one that does.[67] More realistically, hospitals worthy of the name must keep abreast of technological developments in medicine by making machine assistance available at their facilities when it is reasonable to do so.

2. *Strict Liability*

Where harm results from system use, patients would prefer to rely on the strict liability approach in suing the hospital to avoid the burdens of proving negligence, especially if there was compliance with official clearance requirements. By running an information processing machine that produces output information, the operator might be considered a manufacturer and hence responsible for harm resulting from the use of its products, regardless of fault. Although the delivery of information is less obvious in a closed loop therapy system, it does occur, if that factor is an essential ingredient for liability. Alternatively, the operator might be regarded as an element in the chain of distribution of the equipment, much as the lessor of an automobile,[68] and be liable on that basis. Although courts have been reluctant to impose strict liability on hospitals, the situation well might change.[69]

---

[65] An entity established by a group of hospitals cooperatively might not enjoy the immunity of its sponsors, just as it is considered not to enjoy their tax-exempt status without legislation. A bill now pending would confer such status. S. 2315, 90th Cong., 1st Sess. (1967).

[66] *See* Lewis v. Baker, 243 Ore. 317, 413 P.2d 400 (1966).

[67] *See* Carrasco v. Bankoff, 220 Cal. App. 2d 230, 33 Cal. Rptr. 673 (1963).

[68] *See* Cintrone v. Hertz Truck Leasing & Rental Serv., 45 N.J. 434, 212 A.2d 769 (1965) (lessor liable to helper of lessee's driver).

[69] *See* cases cited note 33 *supra.*

D. The System Manufacturer, Designer, and Programmer

1. *Negligence*

Where treatment systems are provided by hospitals, injured patients frequently might seek to sue the manufacturers rather than the hospitals, even if fault must be proved. The handicap of charitable or governmental immunity would be a reason for such a choice. In addition to the requirement of proper design and manufacture, the manufacturer's duty of due care would require it to notify operators and users of any propensities of its product to cause harm of which it knew or should have known.[70]

Independent designers and programmers of treatment systems would be subject to liability for negligence similar to that for faulty design and programming of diagnostic systems.

2. *Strict Liability*

Patients more likely would seek recovery from system manufacturers on the basis of strict liability. Since negligence is not relevant, clearance by a federal agency should not bar recovery if a defect existed nevertheless.[71] The considerations discussed in connection with such liability in the use of computer diagnosis systems would be pertinent to treatment systems. However, the propriety of tempering the strict liability rule with respect to the medical information stored in computer systems, as discussed with respect to the liabilities of operators and manufacturers of diagnosis systems, seems to be even more pertinent to therapy applications. In any event, strict liability applies even where products are not defective, if particular directions or warnings required for safe use are omitted.[72] Where strict liability is applicable, the system manufacturer is exposed to such liability notwithstanding the impossibility of anticipating the occurrence of harm, a particularly important consideration in view of the difficulties in designing computer systems.[73]

Independent designers and programmers may also be subject to strict liability, just as designers and programmers of diagnostic systems.

3. *Injury to Doctor's Reputation*

A doctor's professional reputation could be harmed by his use of a defective computer treatment system. Since he probably would be on the staff of the hospital

---

[70] Harmon v. Plapao Laboratories, 218 S.W. 701 (Mo. App. 1920); Cleary v. John M. Maris Co., 173 Misc. 954, 19 N.Y.S.2d 38 (Sup. Ct. 1940); Pariser v. Wappler Elec. Co., 145 Misc. 315, 260 N.Y.S. 35 (Sup. Ct. 1932); LaFrumento v. Kotex Co., 131 Misc. 314, 226 N.Y.S. 750 (New York City Ct. 1928). Food and Drug Administration regulations require warning labeling for medical devices that must be operated under a doctor's supervision because they have a "potentiality for harmful effect." 21 C.F.R. § 1.106(d) (1967).

[71] Lewis v. Baker, 243 Ore. 317, 413 P.2d 400 (1966).

[72] Crane v. Sears Roebuck & Co., 218 Cal. App.2d 855, 32 Cal. Rptr. 754 (1963); LaPlant v. E. I. duPont de Nemours & Co., 346 S.W.2d 231 (Mo. 1961).

[73] Gottsdanker v. Cutter Laboratories, 182 Cal. App. 2d 602, 6 Cal. Rptr. 320 (1960); Green v. American Tobacco Co., 154 So. 2d 169 (Fla. 1963).

making it available and might even have been involved in selecting the particular system, such a doctor more likely would sue the system manufacturer than the hospital. That type of claim has already been discussed in connection with diagnosis systems.[74]

4. *Misbranding*

Although equipment used in medicine is not subject to the clearance requirements of the present Food, Drug, and Cosmetic Act, the proscriptions against misbranding do apply to it.[75] That legal weapon might be used against manufacturers that do not provide adequate warnings of limitations in their therapy systems.[76]

IV

Patient Simulation by Computer

A. Nature of Patient Simulation Systems

As in the case of computer simulation applications elsewhere, simulation systems in medicine will exist in two different forms—physical models and mathematical models.

Physical models will consist of computer-linked mechanisms that respond to medical procedures in the same manner as the real human system. For example, already a dummy of a human being is being used for teaching purposes. Among other things, it reports, through its computer, when and in what respects injections have been given incorrectly. A similar device for training anesthesiologists has been constructed. It includes a manikin that manifests, in real time, lifelike reactions to medical procedures and a device that prints out reports.[77]

In the mathematical model approach, in contrast, the functioning of the genuine item is described by a series of mathematical formulae that can be manipulated by computer in terms of input data representing a particular situation. Such models probably will be available at least for a number of human organs. Using those models, adjusted (by the input data) to reflect the actual condition of the organ under consideration, a doctor should be able to pretest the results of various types of treatments and the effects of new drugs and to determine such information as the status of a disease in a person and the consequences of lack of treatment. Such a tool has utility in medical research, teaching, and especially treatment. This type of model system consists essentially of digital computers and mathematical models reduced to programs.

The physical simulators will be made available to students by medical schools. The mathematical model simulation systems very likely will be provided to

---

[74] See p. 687 *supra*.
[75] 21 U.S.C. §§ 321(g), (h), (n) (1964, Supp. II, 1965-66).
[76] 21 C.F.R. § 1.106(d) (1967).
[77] Loberman, *Computer Control of a Manikin for Anesthesiological Training*, in Council to Advance Programming, Proceedings Fall 1967 (Computer Control Division, Honeywell Inc., forthcoming).

students by their medical schools, to practicing doctors by their hospitals and possibly by other entities, and to research workers by their particular companies or other organizations. Patient charges would be involved only where model systems are used in treatment. They probably will be handled the same as for laboratory work.

As with treatment systems, the major initiative to use mathematical model systems in rendering medical care will come from practicing doctors. The assistance in pretesting contemplated treatment will be beneficial in performing normal medical work. Undoubtedly, patients will consider the tool to be an appropriate aid to doctors, and resort to it will not be construed as an admission of professional weakness, as distinguished from general diagnosis systems. Since charges for such service will be quite low and patients will pay them, doctors will have no economic objection to their use.

Where mathematical models are used with computers in connection with treatment, the results probably will appear on a computer printout along with the patient's name and file number, the input data reflecting the particular condition noted and submitted by the doctor, and identification of the program (and hence model) utilized. That tangible information properly would be included in the patient's record.

Although physical simulation machines will be located where they are used, the mathematical model devices will be able to be utilized from a substantial distance, by various economical telecommunications means.

Despite the fact that mathematical simulation systems will not be connected to patients' bodies, there is a good chance, since doctors will rely on them in therapy, that efforts will be made to subject them to advance clearance requirements. Against that step, it might be argued that such an approach carried to its logical conclusion would require similar clearance of medical treatises. On the other hand, it could be contended that books present relatively complete information for the using doctor to evaluate, whereas complex machine systems generally have to be utilized with considerable reliance on the representations of the manufacturers or operators.

The legal liabilities of operators, manufacturers, designers, and programmers of simulation systems are the same as in the case of computer treatment systems, which have already been discussed. Thus, the following treatment of simulation systems is limited to their significance for the physician and patient.

B. The Doctor

1. *Malpractice Liability*

Where a simulation system used in therapy produces incorrect information and a patient is harmed as a result, the doctor would be liable for malpractice if he relied on a technique not yet recognized by his colleagues or cleared by a cognizant government agency. Once either of those circumstances has occurred, the doctor probably would escape liability for resulting harm, unless he actually had or should have had reason to doubt either the value of the system for the particular purpose or the output received but used it nevertheless.

On the other hand, when a simulation technique is accepted by the profession, a failure to use it where it is available and where there is no economic barrier to its use probably would be actionable if harm to the patient could have been avoided in that manner. As indicated, telecommunications can make simulation service facilities located at a considerable distance available as a matter of fact. However, proof of liability could be difficult, unless the information about the patient that the doctor should have submitted for processing appears in the patient's record. If such information is known, what the computer system would have responded usually can be determined accurately.

2. *Access to Hospital Facilities*

Despite the unavoidable (to a lawyer) adversions to harmful involvement with computer medical systems, such systems promise great positive contributions. In fact, the doctor's duty of due care undoubtedly will require his increasing use of such systems. Since most types of systems very likely will be operated by hospitals (so-called private as well as admittedly public or, more properly, governmental), attention will tend to be drawn to the doctor's freedom of access to the new services. The initial reaction might be to consider that facet as a matter of the doctor's right of admission to hospital staffs or visiting privileges, which right appears to exist with respect to government hospitals but not private ones.[78] However, it actually might be entirely sufficient merely to make available to all doctors the services themselves that do not entail hospitalization of the patient. Such services would include both types of diagnosis, simulation in therapy, and recommended therapy routines, and might also include record-keeping for doctors' practice outside hospitals.

C. The Patient's Privacy

The availability of physical simulation models for teaching medical students eventually might provide the basis for the enlargement of the right of privacy of hospital patients to spare them from serving as subjects in routine teaching activities. With the broadening of the definition of that right generally, it reasonably could be contended that patients should not be subjected to observation and treatment by medical students any more than absolutely necessary for training purposes.[79] Certainly, the long accepted distinction that indigents should be available as teaching

---

[78] *See* Horty, *The Legal Right of Physicians to Hospital Privileges*, 44 CHI. B. RECORD 373 (1963).
[79] Prior to Medicare and similar programs, involvement as teaching subjects was a problem almost exclusively of the poor. *See generally* Handler & Rosenheim, *Privacy in Welfare: Public Assistance and Juvenile Justice*, 31 LAW & CONTEMP. PROB. 377 (1966), for a discussion of encroachments on the privacy of the poor.

subjects because they do not pay for medical care has even less validity when simulation devices can be used at reasonable cost.[80]

V

HOSPITAL COMPUTER RECORD SYSTEMS

A. Nature of Hospital Computer Records Systems

Hospitals are starting to adopt computers for a wide variety of uses, ranging from ordinary accounting to the maintenance of records on patients, operations performed, and other matters.[81] In the application involving patients' records, the usual information about each patient is kept in digital form so that it can be called out and supplemented by nurses and doctors at input-output terminals. Machine management of such information can remind nurses of medication schedules and check on their compliance and can screen doctors' orders and contemplated action against contraindicated medicines and procedures specified in the record. Similarly, it is possible to verify medication prescriptions against a general file of information, for proper spelling, dosage, and application.[82] Patient records kept in machine-readable form also can be examined easily for medical research purposes and to maintain oversight by hospital medical audit committees over treatment rendered by staff doctors. The other records could include not only logs of operations but also tissue committee reports.[83] In addition, they provide a source of evidence for litigation.[84]

The furnishing of hospital record systems will be the responsibility of the hospitals. Their cost will be defrayed through normal charges for hospital service rather than by specific fees. Their use will be routine once they are adopted and will not depend upon the discretion of doctors.

[80] Such situations could be considered to be improper intrusions, which Professor Bloustein believes to be illegal because they constitute "a blow to human dignity, an assault on human personality," and are "demeaning to individuality." Bloustein, *Privacy as an Aspect of Human Dignity: An Answer to Dean Prosser*, 39 N.Y.U.L. REV. 962, 974 (1964). *Cf.* Inderbitzen v. Lane Hosp., 124 Cal. App. 462, 12 P.2d 744 (1932); DeMay v. Roberts, 46 Mich. 160, 9 N.W. 146 (1881) (improper intrusion during childbirth).

[81] Eventually, when remote access is routine, hospitals might offer to keep the regular patient records of doctors not involving hospital treatment. In using such services, doctors should satisfy themselves that unauthorized access to those records is prevented in order to avoid legal exposure. *See* Note, *Action for Breach of Medical Secrecy Outside the Courtroom*, 36 U. CIN. L. REV. 103 (1967); Note, *Medical Practice and the Right to Privacy*, 43 MINN. L. REV. 943 (1959); *cf.* Boyd v. Wynn, 286 Ky. 173, 150 S.W.2d 648 (1941).

[82] It is possible that a service might be offered, either as a commercial venture or as a public service of pharmaceutical manufacturers or others, for clearing specified medicines, in light of current information, for use with indicated symptoms or diagnosed conditions. The output could include warnings of limitations of uses, such as are included in packages of medicines.

[83] Appleman, *supra* note 64, at 466.

[84] Morris, *Hospital Computer in Court*, M.U.L.L., June 1963, at 61; letters from Gerard Salton and R. Crawford Morris, M.U.L.L., March 1964, at 34 (hospital computer system searched 6.25 million patients' charts in 25 minutes and located chart that disclosed that plaintiff's expert witness previously made same erroneous diagnosis as did defendant). Tissue committee reports might not be admissible in evidence, Judd v. Park Avenue Hosp., 37 Misc. 2d 614, 235 N.Y.S.2d 843 (Sup. Ct. 1962), *aff'd*, 235 N.Y.S.2d 1023 (App. Div. 1962), and CALIF. EVID. CODE § 1156 (West 1966), but are subject to discovery in California. *Id. See The Tissue Committee*, 160 J.A.M.A. 1238 (1956).

When patient records can be handled in machine-readable form, reasons of economy suggest the elimination of most traditional paper records, many of which contain authorizing and validating signatures. Substitute means for signifying authorizations and validations by doctors in ways compatible with digital systems undoubtedly will be devised, since it is unlikely that either their elimination or the expense of continuing to use customary records for that limited purpose can be accepted. Paper consent, personal property acknowledgment, and similar forms signed by patients undoubtedly will continue for some time.

Use of records accessible remotely entirely by machine introduces a threat to the privacy of patient information. In traditional systems, the identity of each person requesting file data is known and his authority to receive the particular material can be verified. Efforts are being made to devise foolproof recognition techniques for use with machine inquiry terminals in all types of systems.[85] Hence, the preservation of privacy of medical information is a problem present in many types of computer systems that are shared by many persons. Solution of the general problem certainly will fill the need in the hospital area. However, since breach of a hospital system offers less valuable returns than check or credit forgery, less rigorous identification means probably will be acceptable.

On the other hand, maintenance of patient records by computer facilitates the distribution of information already required by or useful to a wide variety of outside agencies, such as vital statistics bureaus (births and deaths), police departments (gun wounds and other foul play[86]), local, state, and national public health units (crippled children,[87] communicable diseases,[88] and drug addiction), Social Security Board (births and deaths), and the Internal Revenue Service and other tax authorities (deaths).[89] That information can be disseminated automatically in either digital or printed form. Wherever appropriate, the patient or his representative should be informed of the making of such reports. Such notification can be given easily by having a computer print up the letters.

The efficiencies and other advantages achieved by computerization of hospital records should be available for equally important patient records kept by doctors in their own files. To achieve such advantages, hospitals might offer to keep those files for a fee, when telecommunications means with remote terminals are available economically for doctors' offices. Under such an arrangement, consideration should

---

[85] Ware, *Security and Privacy In Computer Use*, in AM. FEDERATION OF INFORMATION PROCESSING SOCIETIES, 1967 SPRING JOINT COMPUTER CONFERENCE PROCEEDINGS 279; Petersen & Turn, *System Implications of Information Privacy*, id. at 291.

[86] *E.g.*, MASS. ANN. LAWS ch. 112, § 12A (1965).

[87] *E.g.*, CONN. GEN. STATS. ANN. § 19-21 (1960); MASS. ANN. LAWS c. 111, § 67E (Supp. 1966) (state-furnished form required).

[88] *E.g.*, CONN. GEN. STATS. ANN. § 19-89 (1960); Shoemaker v. Friedberg, 80 Cal. App. 2d 911, 183 P.2d 318 (1947).

[89] The last two are suggested as possible information items that soon will be deemed to be useful, respectively, to trigger the issuance of Social Security numbers and to record the deaths of persons from whom income tax returns are expected because their names appear on the Service's master list.

be given to the extent to which the doctor's records should be processed similarly to the hospital's, such as for the automatic reporting of particular events to government agencies.

B. The Hospital

1. *Negligence*

If a hospital adopts a computer record-keeping system that permits harmful errors to be made in the patients' files, it probably would be liable for negligence, unless shielded by charitable or governmental immunity. At the present state of the computer art, it is unlikely that it would be reasonable to choose a system that is error-prone. Proof that a system is so vulnerable would be much easier if it is computerized than if it is operated solely by people, because of the availability of more complete documentation for machine systems. In fact, the requirements of due care, if not professional responsibility, probably would make it advisable to include in such a system the technique for monitoring the administration of medications since such a measure is feasible and its cost would be relatively low.

As was observed in other connections, computer use for recordkeeping could minimize the occurrence of negligent acts, thereby reducing legal liability in practice by preventing harm. For example, machine verification of patient identity, a routine but highly reliable operation, would avoid the insertion of data, such as clinical laboratory reports, in the wrong records.[90]

2. *Recordkeeping Requirements*

The hospital using a computer for record maintenance must comply with any legal and other requirements on documentation of treatment authorizations, laboratory reports, and other events, if it seeks to abandon traditional paperwork. Such requirements might be found in statutes, in rules adopted by professional bodies,[91] or merely in practical legal precautions.

Particularly troublesome is the general requirement that hospital medical records[92] and orders[93] be signed by the physician. Designers of hospital systems are planning to have special code identifications for doctors used at input terminals, to be entered either through a keyboard or by an embossed wafer, like a credit card, in lieu of signatures, with the reasonable expectation that the requirement will be changed. In some cases, the acceptable physical forms of the records are prescribed

---

[90] This problem is discussed in Mills, *supra* note 30, at 641. A recent study disclosed that almost fifteen per cent of the medications administered in a particular hospital were incorrect. Barker, Kimbrough & Hiller, *The Medication Error Problem in Hospitals*, 1 HOSP. FORMULARY MANAGEMENT 29 (1966).

[91] JOINT COMM'N ON ACCREDITATION OF HOSPITALS, *supra* note 14, at 3-4.

[92] *Id.* at 3; DEP'T OF PUBLIC HEALTH, COMMONWEALTH OF MASSACHUSETTS, LICENSURE RULES AND REGULATIONS FOR HOSPITALS AND SANATORIA 4 (1950).

[93] JOINT COMM'N ON ACCREDITATION OF HOSPITALS, MODEL MEDICAL STAFF RULES AND REGULATIONS 14 (1964).

by statutes,[94] which also will have to be altered. Fortunately, government and other authorities appear to be receptive to reasonable changes required for computer systems.[95]

The right of patients and others to inspect and secure copies of hospital records[96] should not inhibit the adoption of computer record-keeping systems. Printing and cathode ray tube display techniques usually provided so that hospital personnel can read those records that are not legible visually probably will be entirely adequate for outsiders as well. In lieu of actual copies of the records, it usually should be acceptable to furnish visually legible conversions in the form of either printouts or copies of the displays.[97]

As a matter of mechanics, hospitals might have to explore the use of new numbering systems to identify patients in their records in order to minimize identification errors (and resulting liability) and to facilitate integrated use of recorded information. Computers can verify numbers much more efficiently than can people. For example, they can utilize self-checking digits to uncover transpositions and similar errors. If a universal numbering system is considered desirable for integration with other files, such as those of other hospitals, doctors, laboratories, or vital statistics bureaus, consideration might be given to the approach of the Internal Revenue Service, in which the Social Security number is used with the first four letters of the person's name.

3. Evidence

The maintenance of hospital records in forms unique to digital computer systems and unreadable by sight does not diminish their admissibility as evidence in litigation. If they otherwise meet the standards of business records, such records will be accepted by courts to the extent that their visually legible counterparts will be received, even if made expressly for the litigation.[98] Of course, entry in a computer system will not improve the low evidentiary quality of recorded self-serving statements of the patient or his family on what occurred outside the hospital.[99] However, much evidence generated in the hospital of the type that is of probative value will

---

[94] *E.g.*, MASS. ANN. LAWS c. 111, § 70 (Supp. 1966) (handwriting, print, typewriting, photographs, or microphotographs).

[95] For example, the Joint Commission on Accreditation of Hospitals has so indicated but insists that responsible persons be identified clearly. Letter from J. D. Porterfield, M.D., 1 HEALTH SERVICES RESEARCH 119 (1966). Oral communications of the writer with some state authorities are consistent.

[96] CONN. GEN. STATS. ANN. §§ 4-104, -105 (1960); MASS. ANN. LAWS c. 111, § 70 (Supp. 1966); WIS. STAT. § 269.57 (1965).

[97] *See* Freed, *Providing by Statute for Inspection of Corporate Computer and Other Records Not Legible Visually—A Case Study on Legislating for Computer Technology*, 23 BUS. LAW. 457 (1968). Persons inspecting hospital medical records occasionally might want machine language copies for processing by computer on their own behalf.

[98] Transport Indem. Co. v. Seib, 178 Nev. 253, 132 N.W.2d 871 (1965). *See* Freed, *Computer Print-outs as Evidence*, in 16 AM. JUR. PROOF OF FACTS 273, 316 (1965); Freed, *supra* note 97.

[99] *See* Sheary v. Hallock's of Middletown, Inc., 149 Conn. 188, 177 A.2d 680 (1962) (to be admissible, entry must be based on entrant's own knowledge or that of a person who has a business duty to transmit the information).

be more accurate when it is collected and recorded either by machine or by people for a machine system.

C. The Patient's Privacy

Patients are entitled to protection from breaches of their privacy in the use of hospital record systems accessible widely. Hospitals must take reasonable measures to protect that privacy.[100]

D. The Doctor's Malpractice Liability

Computerization of patient records kept in hospitals and private practice should help doctors satisfy their duties to read prior records that are readily available and to warn patients of previous treatment that has been discovered to be harmful.[101] Fulfillment of those duties can be onerous with respect to traditional paper records because of the mechanical difficulties of securing an earlier record from another repository and of searching through voluminous records. By making both measures relatively easy to perform, computer systems will reduce human barriers and the disposition to gamble.

The exposure of doctors to malpractice liability also will be reduced substantially by the operation of hospital record systems that monitor the administration of medication and other treatment measures against patient records and general standards. Although patient records in the traditional form frequently specify contraindicated treatments, their administration often occurs nevertheless, with adverse results, because of the normal difficulty people have in using those records. Rigorous machine review, such as against both the particular patient's history and the standard cautions of drug identity, dosage, and propriety for the illness, will uncover the errors before they can cause harm. On the other hand, the inclusion in patient records, as already indicated, of greater quantities of detailed medical information increases the likelihood that doctors guilty of malpractice will be held liable because more evidence will be available.

SUMMARY AND CONCLUSION

The nature of medical practice can be expected to change substantially with the eventual widespread use of computer systems to aid in diagnosis, treatment, and administrative activities. The remarkably versatile machines will be used not only to help professionals perform their usual functions better but also to carry out procedures beyond the capabilities of people. In the adoption of the new tech-

---

[100] *Cf.* Tournier v. National Provincial & Union Bank of England, [1924] 1 K.B. 461 (under common law, bank is liable for damages to customer from nonprivileged disclosure of information).

[101] Schwartz v. United States, 230 F. Supp. 536, 540 (E.D. Pa. 1964):

"The negligence here is not in [the medication's] installation, but rather in not having affirmatively sought out those who had been endangered after there was knowledge of the danger in order to warn them that in the supposedly innocent treatment there had now been found to lurk the risk of devastating injury."

nology, there is substantial promise of improved medical care, of increased productivity of professionals, and even of lower costs in limited areas.

As in all phenomena of this nature, legal involvement is unavoidable. Hopefully, it will not represent a negative factor in the development and use of the technology. Fortunately, the requirements of sound business administration and responsible professionalism usually will influence the taking of appropriate steps in the design, construction, and use of computer systems in medicine to prevent harm. With the example of the manufacture and administration of drugs, however, there is no assurance of complete success, and lawsuits will be brought. The outcomes of such suits and their impact not only on the particular area but also on society generally will depend upon both the legal rules considered to be pertinent and how effectively they are applied.

Despite the considerable novelty of introducing engineering extensively into medicine, the possible legal transgressions are sufficiently similar in nature to legal involvement in other areas of society for existing, fairly general rules of law to be usable in substantially all situations. Those rules are essentially means for distributing the impacts of losses caused by mishaps. Their sound application to computer medical devices will depend upon how well lawyers and judges comprehend the very novel and highly complex technology involved. As frequently is true, factual aspects are of major importance in influencing the outcome of litigation through the selection of legal theories and the marshalling and evaluation of proof. Judges and lawyers must achieve a fairly deep understanding of the new technology because of its novelty and complexity. In defining legal duties respecting use of the machines, they must be able to attribute the appropriate strengths to them as well as to recognize their real weaknesses. Doctors as well as computer specialists have a major role in interpreting the technology for this purpose.

The introduction of computers into medicine probably will cause a shift among the entities currently exposed to legal claims. For example, as harm can be attributed to machines, patients will prefer manufacturer's strict liability to medical malpractice actions. Although doctors still will be subject to legal exposure, they have every reason, since computer systems promise substantial benefits in medicine, to undertake to use those devices that are carefully designed and operated. In most situations, applicable legal rules do not expose them to unreasonable legal risks in doing so and in many cases probably will favor such use eventually by making it an exercise of due care. As a practical matter, furthermore, use of computer systems should reduce the risk of malpractice claims by preventing the occurrence of harm. However, it must be recognized that, by collecting medical information more effectively, such systems can make it easier to spot and prove some types of malpractice that do occur.

Some few changes in legal rules may be advisable. For example, with respect to therapy systems, where the test of malpractice might cause doctors to be unduly conservative in adopting valuable machine help despite the fact that it has met federal standards, a conscious effort should be made, probably through state legislation, to create a more favorable legal climate without sacrificing patients' rights. While protecting the interests of patients, which are primary, such a step would remove a possible marketing handicap for manufactures whose products pass evaluations of objective official experts.

It is hoped that this discussion of some legal aspects of computer use in medicine identified at this relatively early stage will dispel unwarranted concerns over the impact of the law on the promising mechanization in that area and will contribute to the sound resolution of legal questions when they arise.

THE CHANGING STRUCTURE OF MEDICAL PRACTICE

David Mechanic*

Although medical practice has been continuously adapting to social and technological changes, American medicine will be confronted in the coming years with social, economic, and ideological challenges of a magnitude it has never before experienced. In almost every area of medical activity—in the distribution of services, allocation of costs, assessments of quality, recruitment into medical work, organization of care, ethics of practice—the traditional medical view that these matters are to be decided solely by doctors will be under scrutiny and re-evaluation. For it is increasingly recognized among public officials and the educated public—if not among doctors themselves—that medicine is most basically a social enterprise, and although doctors have the technical competence for treating the sick, they have no monopoly on wisdom in matters concerning the organization, distribution, and economics of medical care. Already the rumblings from such conflicts are evident, and in the coming years the various interested parties will require great patience and understanding if acrimony is to be minimized. Given the expected clashes between ideologies and perspectives in the medical field, it is important that we attempt to isolate those issues which are most basic to the organization of medical practice so that our attention is not diverted in the rhetoric of controversy.

I

Varying Perspectives Relevant to the Organization of Care

Medical practice in the United States is one of the last bulwarks of an individualized, entrepreneurial tradition. In comparison with the other professions and occupations, the ability of medicine to resist group organization to the extent that it has, despite the enormous complexity of medical technology, is in itself an extraordinary phenomenon. Despite the tremendous influences encouraging group organization, the persistence of the solo practitioner or partnership as modal forms of practice attests to the strength of the entrepreneurial ideology and its importance in molding the doctor's view of medical care. This ideology makes it all the more difficult to attract doctors to new organizational forms for meeting changing social conditions and developing technological and economic demands on medicine.

The pattern of medicine that continues to persist in the United States has a

---

* B.A. 1956, City College of New York; M.A. 1957, Ph.D. 1959, Stanford University. Professor of Sociology and Director of Graduate Training in Medical Sociology, University of Wisconsin. Author, Medical Sociology (1968), Students Under Stress (1962); co-author [with Henry Latané, George Strother, and George Strauss], Social Science of Organizations (1963). Consultant, Social and Rehabilitation Service, U.S. Department of Health, Education, and Welfare.

distinctive character. Although early American developments in medicine, as well as the development of the hospital, followed European patterns, they took on some unique features.[1] By the nineteenth century the European countries with the greatest influence on the colonies were already highly urbanized, and medical education and practice had taken on a specialized character with a growing separation of general practitioners from hospital doctors and clear distinctions between physicians, surgeons, and apothecaries.[2] But America was frontier country and largely rural, and such distinctions were inappropriate for a population scattered over a vast land area with a low population density.[3] Doctors functioned for the most part as generalists, doing whatever they thought was necessary to meet their responsibilities, and the jealousies and distinctions so important in European medicine did not take root. When the idea of the general voluntary hospital, borrowed from Great Britain, was implemented first in Philadelphia and later in other cities,[4] the doctors who offered their services free to the indigent obtained the privilege of using the hospital to treat their own private patients as well. This pattern, first established under conditions very different from those that now exist, has persisted as the dominant one to this very day and carries along with it certain merits, but also some important disadvantages. For example, despite the far-reaching trend toward specialized medical functions, access to the hospital and complexity of work undertaken by the individual doctor have only a very limited relationship to the length of his training and competence. Even today a vast bulk of the total surgical work in the United States is undertaken by doctors regarded as "nonqualified surgeons" by the American College of Surgeons.[5] In short, even in this most basic area—the specification of qualifications to undertake work graded in its complexity and difficulty—doctors who have met minimal qualifications for licensure are left for the most part to make their own individual decisions as to their competence and capacity to function in various medical spheres.

Understanding doctors' views of medical care requires awareness of the perspectives from which they perceive the medical scene—orientations which conceptualize the problems of medical practice from a personal rather than an organizational perspective. Unlike the organizational theorist, the doctor asks how medicine should be organized so that he can provide his patients with a high standard of care and also maximize his personal and professional satisfactions. The solutions thus obtained might look very different from those posed by medical care experts, who phrase the question in terms of how medical practice might be most effectively and efficiently organized so as to provide a high level of care through maximal use of

---

[1] *See* R. SHRYOCK, MEDICINE AND SOCIETY IN AMERICA: 1660-1860 (1960).
[2] *See* B. ABEL-SMITH, THE HOSPITALS, 1800-1948 (1964).
[3] *See* B. STERN, AMERICAN MEDICAL PRACTICE (1945).
[4] *See* R. SHRYOCK, MEDICINE IN AMERICA: HISTORICAL ESSAYS (1966).
[5] Roemer, *On Paying the Doctor and the Implications of Different Methods*, 3 J. HEALTH & HUMAN BEHAVIOR 4, 7 (1962).

health resources and personnel. Indeed, the optimal organization of medical resources may require a degree of control and surveillance over the doctor's work which is threatening and unattractive to him. One needs no theory of professional conspiracy to explain conflicts between the health professions and other groups; conflict is a natural product of the different perspectives from which they view the medical context.

II

The Elements of Medical Care

The concept of medical care applies not only to the care received by individual patients but also to the manner in which medical resources are provided and distributed to the population at large. Even if every patient treated received optimal patient care, the medical care system itself would be inadequate if a close congruency did not exist between need and the distribution of services. Thus, systems of medical care must be measured not only in terms of individual care but also in terms of the adequacy of personnel and facilities and the distribution of services among various economic strata and geographic areas. Persons of sufficient ability and motivation must be recruited into the health professions and trained, and the conditions for continuing innovation and adaptation to change must be maintained.

Given the growing demand for medical services[6]—inflated by an increasing rate of utilization for the average person, a growing population, a larger number of persons in age groups that require more concentrated medical attention, and greater health coverage stimulated by new government programs—the number of physicians available to the population in coming years will be inadequate.[7] At the end of 1964 there were 297,200 physicians and osteopaths (active and inactive) who were listed as part of the American health manpower pool. Although the number of doctors relative to the population has been maintained, a much larger part of the total medical work force is involved in nonclinical activities, such as medical research and administration, leaving relatively fewer doctors to meet the growing demands for medical services.[8] In comparing 1950 and 1964, there were more general practitioners in the early period than general practitioners, internists, and pediatricians combined in 1964.[9] There are basically two ways to respond to the situation: we can continue to stimulate the development and growth of medical schools to a much greater extent than has yet been attempted; or the resources available can be concentrated into programs and forms of organization designed to increase the doctor's

---

[6] See H. Somers & A. Somers, Doctors, Patients, and Health Insurance (1962).
[7] See U.S. Surgeon General's Consultant Group on Medical Education, Physicians for a Growing America (Public Health Service Pub. No. 709, 1959); R. Fein, The Doctor Shortage: An Economic Diagnosis (1967).
[8] N.Y. Times, Sept. 28, 1967, at 53, col. 2.
[9] Nat'l Comm'n on Community Health Services, Report of the Task Force on Health Manpower 40 (1967).

productivity.[10] Although it is necessary to take steps in both directions, it is not clear that these remedies will have much impact on the vast maldistribution of medical manpower and facilities throughout the United States.[11] Thus far, we have not been extremely bold in considering the development of incentives and subsidies that might stimulate a more adequate distribution of medical manpower.

There are few areas in medical care that can compete successfully with the manpower problem in evoking platitudinous comment. The manner in which we attempt to meet medical demands and the types of responses we evoke in meeting manpower problems will have a vast influence not only on the amount of medical care available but also in its patterning and structure. If we, indeed, decide that major emphasis should be given to increasing the doctor's productivity, then we must be cognizant of the fact that this is likely to change the nature of the physician's role itself with possible dangers of destroying the sustenance aspect of medical practice. The failure to tangle with the real analytical issues in the structuring of medical care is exemplified by the report to the President from the National Commission on Community Health Services.[12] Compare, for example, the two following notions suggested by the Commission:

> It is critically important to make full use of available medical manpower. The physician is neither nurse, social worker, nor physical therapist. He is a physician. His training and talents as a physician must not be dissipated by employing them—except in crisis situations—in any tangential, nonmedical discipline. There are not enough of him in the United States today to warrant wasting a minute of his education and experience on jobs others can do as well. Because it is necessary to face up to this fact squarely, and make the most efficient use of limited physician manpower, health care functions not requiring medical training should be delegated by the physician to other members of the health care team to the maximum extent practical.[13]

> The physician should be aware of the many and varied social, emotional, and environmental factors that influence the health of his patient and his patient's family. He will either render, or direct the patient to, whatever services best suit his needs. His concern will be for the patient as a whole and his relationship with the patient must be a continuing one. In order to carry out his coordinating role, it is essential that all pertinent health information be channeled through him regardless of what institution, agency, or individual renders the service. He will have knowledge of the access to all health resources of the community—social, preventive, diagnostic, therapeutic, and rehabilitative—and will mobilize them for the patient.[14]

---

[10] In defense of the latter argument, see Ginzberg, *Physician Shortage Reconsidered*, 275 NEW ENG. J. MED. 85 (1966).

[11] *See* NAT'L COMM'N ON COMMUNITY HEALTH SERVICES, *supra* note 9; Darley & Somers, *Medicine, Money and Manpower—The Challenge to Professional Education*, 276 NEW ENG. J. MED. 1414 (1967); N.Y. Times, Sept. 28, 1967, at 53, col. 2.

[12] NAT'L COMM'N ON COMMUNITY HEALTH SERVICES, HEALTH IS A COMMUNITY AFFAIR (1966).

[13] *Id.* at 22.

[14] *Id.* at 21. (Original in italics.)

To all but the most rampant optimists the goals defined in the two statements above will appear inconsistent. Continuing relationships with patients and concern for the patient as a whole by necessity require doctors to engage in tangential, nonmedical functions that do not require his technical medical education. Indeed, the kind of medical stance that maximizes technical forms of productivity is incompatible with the definition of the doctor's role as a coordinator of services and an attendant to the social and emotional welfare of patients. Since this issue is central to future decisions concerning the organization of medical practice, I turn now to a more complete discussion of the consequences of varying forms of practice organization.

III
MEDICAL PRACTICE AND BUREAUCRACY

As the needs for greater efficiency and productivity in the provision of medical care grow, and as increasing developments in medical technology demand greater organization and coordination, the arguments toward the bureaucratization of medicine are compelling. Many technical-scientific aspects of medicine can be efficiently organized within bureaucratic forms, thus making it possible to reach more people and to facilitate a more adequate pattern of distribution of medical services. Moreover, bureaucratic contexts facilitate the imposition of quality controls (for example, routine auditing of medical care) and enhance the possibilities for continuing education in a situation of rapid social and technological change. The trend toward greater bureaucratization of medical practice is not only a certainty because of the forces within medical practice, but it is also being encouraged through the growing involvement in medical affairs of other organizational forces; government agencies, labor unions, and other major purchasers of medical care are increasingly conscious of the value received for their investments and are concerned that their constituencies enjoy a standard of medical care at least equal to that of the individual consumer who purchases his own services.[15]

The solutions to some problems usually create others, and it is of the greatest importance that thought and energy be devoted to considering bureaucratic mechanisms and alternatives that counteract some of the more noxious side effects of the growing bureaucratization of medical practice. The great variety of life problems brought to doctors indicates that from the patient's perspective the nontechnical aspects of the doctor's role are important. Indeed, it seems apparent that the physician has to a great extent occupied a sustaining role in Western society, handling a wide range of problems outside the sphere of his technical-scientific expertise. The continuing importance of the social aspects of medical practice is attested to by the increase of utilization of medical resources despite the fact that the level of the population's health is probably higher than ever before. Certainly, the growing

---

[15] See R. MUNTS, BARGAINING FOR HEALTH (1967).

demand for medical services is in part a product of general affluence, increased consumer spending power, and the expanding provision of medical resources resulting from new medical and government developments. But the nature of medical demand and the wide-reaching character of problems brought to the physician suggest that increased utilization may also be a product partially of the changing organization of social life itself.[16]

As opportunities for intimate personal contacts diminish and as the American population becomes increasingly mobile, problems that have been previously handled in familial, social, and religious contexts may be transferred to formal sustaining professionals (doctors, lawyers, social workers, and the like). Although a wide variety of professionals deal with problems which in previous decades were handled by informal sources of help, it is generally believed that physicians appear to have experienced the most substantial part of this additional consumer demand. Because the formal structure and definition of the doctor-patient relationship provide a legitimate way for expressing intimacy and requesting help, it is only natural that various psychosocial problems and other problems in living should be brought to the physician.

There is little reason to believe that doctors presently deal adequately with the sustaining aspects of their role. But the continuing bureaucratization of medicine threatens even further danger in this sphere, as evidenced by the growing clamor over the contraction of general practice despite the fact that the average consumer of medical care receives better technical services than ever before. One possible source of such dissatisfaction is the commonly held feeling that it is necessary to have someone to rely on during times of trouble. And it is expected that such a relationship would allow an opportunity for expressing deeply felt attitudes, doubts, and uncertainties. Thus, if the sustaining professions are to be effective in responding to many patients' needs and expectations, these professions must be organized to insure some opportunity for the expression of intimacy and for the provision of close personal supports. It is essential that the patient feel that the person to whom he allows access to the private regions of his "self" be truly interested in him and his welfare, and not regard him as one more item on an assembly line.[17] Yet at the same time that societies and their various institutions become more bureaucratized, making the sustaining professions more important than ever before, these professions themselves are becoming more formalized. As already noted, there are many excellent reasons for formalizing medical care, but it is not clear to what extent such relationships can be bureaucratized without seriously damaging the potential emotional sustenance functions of the helping professions.

When we think of bureaucratizing medical practice, we usually conceive of medicine in its more narrow perspective—that is, as an applied science rather than as a

---

[16] *See* M. BALINT, THE DOCTOR, HIS PATIENT, AND THE ILLNESS (1957).
[17] *See* D. MECHANIC, MEDICAL SOCIOLOGY (1968).

sustaining profession. As doctors become more capable technically, they tend to think of medicine in its more restricted medical aspects. And increasingly doctors trained in modern, hospital-based, scientifically oriented medical schools, operating with heavy patient loads and faced with severe time pressures, resist rendering some of the services the "old family practitioner" saw as an integral part of his role. Moreover, in organizing the technical-scientific components of the doctor's role so that the same facilities reach more people, opportunities for the emotional aspects of medical practice diminish. As Freidson[18] has illustrated, bureaucratic roles facilitate high quality care in a technical-scientific sense, but a certain degree of inflexibility in dealing with patient definitions, expectations, and desires also results from such organizational forms.

Just as it is unnecessary that medical care be organized to fit every personal wish of the physician, so is it equally unnecessary to respond to every whim of the patient. Since medical resources are substantially limited, it is likely that the optimal pattern of medical care from a national perspective will require some compromises on all fronts. There is little point in encouraging a continued pattern of solo, entrepreneurial practice, as it will increasingly become as inappropriate to the dimensions of medical demand and technology as the individual tutor is to modern education and scientific development. However, the character of the particular bureaucratic forms we develop deserves very serious study since the future offers abundant opportunity for the exercise of administrative stupidity.

On a simple logical basis it would appear reasonable to attempt to separate the technical-scientific aspects of medical practice from the more amorphous sustaining function. Presumably large group clinics could provide separate professionals to deal with the needs of different kinds of patients, and some experiments along these lines have been attempted. For example, within the Health Insurance Plan of New York a demonstration program was attempted in which families were assigned to health teams including nurses and social workers as well as medical men.[19] Although many more such experiments need to be attempted, it appears that many patients are reluctant to deal with emotional problems outside the medical context, and they are clearly partial to the physician.[20] Thus, regardless of whether physicians agree to allocate certain problems of patients to other professionals, it is not unlikely that patients will continue to bring emotional problems to physicians despite the availability of other channels of help. Given such a tendency, it appears expedient to develop other social services around general medical services.[21]

The coordination of the doctor's work in conjunction with the work of other

---

[18] Freidson, *Medical Care and the Public: Case Study of a Medical Group*, 346 ANNALS 57 (1963).
[19] *See generally* G. SILVER, FAMILY MEDICAL CARE (1963).
[20] *See* Freidson, *Specialties Without Roots: The Utilization of New Services*, 18 HUMAN ORGANIZATION 112 (1959).
[21] *See* M. JEFFERYS, AN ANATOMY OF SOCIAL WELFARE SERVICES (1965).

professionals and related health workers raises certain difficulties. For example, if we are to take seriously the notion that work that does not require a medical education be delegated to other practitioners, then the reinstitution of midwifery appears reasonable. Experience in other developed countries suggests that well-trained midwives can provide a level of obstetrical care comparable to the care provided by physicians. But since medical care is largely private, patients may very well choose to receive such care from physicians; and individual doctors, making their own choices, would be agreeable to providing this service. There is danger, however, that even a more highly stratified medical care system than presently exists may develop where those with means buy the services they wish, while those who are less well-off receive what is socially defined as inferior care. Indeed, the social definition of midwifery under such circumstances may discourage the recruitment of competent personnel to this work, resulting, in fact, in inferior care. Midwifery is only offered as an example; it is the general issue to which I wish to draw attention. In a medical market which is largely private, persons with adequate income will be able to buy services from the practitioners of their choice, thus leaving the new physician-substitutes to provide similar services to those with lesser purchasing power. Given this threat of a highly stratified medical care system, as well as the unwillingness of the physician to share control over his work with "lesser specialties," it seems more appropriate to think in terms of new supporting specialties that facilitate the doctor's performance and efficiency but which do not operate in competition with him. In areas where there are, in fact, competing specialties (that is, professionals having a clearly defined sphere of activity), we should encourage independent practice which offers the consumer an alternative to the doctor. But even in such areas as social work, psychological counseling, and the like, there are compelling reasons for providing opportunities for help at the settings where the client is most likely to appear.

The future of medicine is faced with a dilemma common in organization life. Bureaucracy allows a more efficient and effective standard of medical practice and facilitates the use of available resources so that more people benefit. But bureaucracies also develop certain rigidities and inflexibilities in dealing with specific unique problems in that there is a tendency toward standardization of modes of professional practice. The dilemma we face is that the bureaucratic form most appropriate for the efficient organization of scientific medical work is not the best form to deal with the emotional sustenance aspects of medicine, nor does it encourage the flexibility and variation which are so useful in dealing with social and emotional problems.

There is a vast range of possible bureaucratic forms, and it is a serious error to assume that the most typical bureaucratic forms characteristic of government agencies are those best suited to medical practice.[22] Nor is it necessarily correct to assume that

---

[22] *See* Goss, *Patterns of Bureaucracy Among Hospital Staff Physicians*, in THE HOSPITAL IN MODERN SOCIETY 170 (E. Freidson ed. 1963).

bureaucracies need give priority to quantity over quality or to technical aspects of medicine over emotional and social sustenance. It is not difficult, for example, to conceive of a medical bureaucracy that defines its main goals in terms of the social and emotional needs of patients and gears its activities and procedures toward this end. The difficulty in modern medicine, however, is that although medical bureaucracies often give lip service to the social and emotional needs of patients, the bureaucratic organization of medicine continues to reflect the priority—and it may be a correct one—attached to the technical-scientific aspects of the medical role. Although medical bureaucracies can be organized so that they give emphasis to the patient's education, his social and emotional needs, and comprehensive care, few medical bureaucracies are truly committed to these ideas and willing to assume the necessary economic costs.

While bureaucratic forms may vary, thus fulfilling needs differently, bureaucratic organization regardless of its type poses certain problems from a social viewpoint. Bureaucracy encourages specialized activity, routinized procedures and modes of operation, formalized methods of requisition, and standardized modes of training and evaluating personnel, and there is a strong tendency for bureaucracies to limit client control.[23] On the assumption that professionals know best what is good for the client, patients are usually given little power or formal channels through which to express their dissatisfaction or influence the type of care they receive. Unless known channels for patient influence are available and used, doctor-patient relationships can take on a stereotyped form resulting in the medical staff's giving highest priority to organizational needs and values rather than to those of patients. As clinical settings become larger and more impersonal, the patient finds it difficult to contact his doctor without first dealing with a variety of intermediaries who may try to deflect the patient's request. Since the organization is unlikely to make the patient aware of its staff rotation policies, it is not unusual that he does not see the doctor he expected or wanted to see, and, indeed, the patient may have difficulty finding someone who assumes major responsibility for his care. Moreover, as medical bureaucracies not only develop in size but spread out in space, it is not uncommon for the patient to be sent on a wild-goose chase in attempting to complete some facet of his care. All of these problems, of course, are not unique to bureaucracy, but there is a strong tendency for them to be exacerbated in such organizational contexts.

Assuming that bureaucratic organization is essential in medicine—and I for one would take this position—there continue to be alternative choices open to us. Bureaucracies can be structured so that they offer flexibility and choice to patients with different needs and inclinations.[24] They can also be structured so that they

---

[23] *See* E. FREIDSON, PATIENTS' VIEWS OF MEDICAL PRACTICE (1961).
[24] For a provocative discussion of the issue of choice within welfare bureaucracies, see B. ABEL-SMITH, FREEDOM IN THE WELFARE STATE (Fabian Tract 353, 1964).

provide patients with power in those areas where critical patient scrutiny and evaluation are likely to improve the quality of services while, at the same time, protecting doctors from frivolous and trivial demands that detract from the over-all quality of medical care. It is not too farfetched to suggest that just as students are demanding some role in decisions at universities that concern their welfare, patients, too, ought to demand some voice in the structure, organization, and provision of services which they pay for directly and indirectly. Although such demands can be excessive, medical care—like education—has not been as responsive as it should be to the many legitimate criticisms of its clients.

In organizing new forms of medical practice, caution is required so that as we eliminate economic barriers to medical care, we do not substitute in their place a variety of other social barriers.[25] The success of new forms of organization in medical care will depend in large part on the flexibility, alternatives, and control mechanisms that are devised to mold bureaucratic processes in a direction which enhances choice and meets needs conducive to the health and welfare of patients as individuals.

IV

THE PRINCIPLE OF COUNTERVAILING FORCES IN MEDICINE

One of the most important social changes in medical care in recent decades has been the development of collective power among consumers of medical care. As labor unions moved into the medical care field, patients' interests were consolidated into powerful bargaining forces for the kinds of medical programs deemed desirable. These new attempts on the part of the consumer to structure care alternatives were frequently resisted, of course, but, having banded together, patients' interests were now consolidated into an effective bargaining framework. If the medical profession was not prepared to bargain in a reasonable fashion, the unions were in a position to build and develop their own facilities and disregard local practitioners; when these practitioners placed obstacles in the path of such developments, the vast legal resources available to major labor unions allowed them to carry the battle to the courts.[26] It was clear that public policy concerning health care would never again be the unique province of the medical profession.

The substantial and continually growing involvements of the federal and state governments as purchasers of medical care provide very powerful countervailing forces in the medical care field, and new programs such as Medicare, Medicaid, and the medical programs of the Office of Economic Opportunity afford tremendous

---

[25] *See* Rosenstock, *Health Behavior*, in THE POVERTY-ILLNESS COMPLEX: A SOCIOLOGICAL ANALYSIS (A. Antonovsky *et al.* eds. 1968) (forthcoming); Mechanic, *Response Factors in Illness*, 1 SOCIAL PSYCHIATRY 11 (1966).

[26] *E.g.*, Group Health Cooperative v. King County Medical Soc'y, 39 Wash. 2d 586, 237 P.2d 737 (1951). *See also* American Medical Ass'n v. United States, 317 U.S. 519 (1943). *See generally* R. MUNTS, *supra* note 15.

opportunities to affect organization of medical care, controls over standards of medical practice, and the qualifications of providers of medical services. For example, in its first year of operation it is estimated that the Medicare program covered five million hospital admissions at a cost of almost two and one-half billion dollars.[27] Under the voluntary part of the Medicare program, it is estimated that payments were made for twenty-five million bills covering physician and other services, at a cost of approximately seven hundred million dollars. Between 1966 and 1967, the proportion of personal health care expenditures involving public funds increased by ten percentage points—from twenty-two to thirty-two per cent—largely due to Medicare. In short, the magnitude and scope of such a program cannot help but have a deep impact on medical care, especially if government administrators have some clear notion as to the directions in which medical care should be moving.

In contrast, the community of physicians is very powerful not only by virtue of its tight and effective organization[28] and unity of sentiments but also because of the nature of the medical care market. Since there is a scarcity of physicians relative to medical demand and a growing scope of utilization stimulated by general affluence, doctors are in a position to boycott effectively new programs without excessive economic hardship, and thus they are in a position to bargain for conditions of service which are favorable in terms of their perspective. The federal government, appreciating the power of the medical community and the state of the medical market, has moved carefully and conservatively in attempting to protect the success of its new programs. In its Medicare program, for example, an exceedingly cautious position has been taken on such central concerns to the medical profession as fees. The willingness of the government to accept direct billing to the patient under the Medicare program and its agreement to accept the doctor's "customary charge" without insuring the concept of a "customary service" (which can be defined as the provision of a service comparable to that provided to fee-for-service patients in the same locality) reflect the caution with which the federal government has approached the sensitive area of bargaining with the medical profession. And there is little question but that the Medicare program has added some increment to the average doctor's income.[29] A panel study of a sample of physicians in New York State[30] found that

---

[27] U.S. Social Security Administration, Dep't of Health, Education, and Welfare, Health Insurance Statistics, Nov. 20, 1967.

[28] *See* Comment, *The American Medical Association: Power, Purpose, and Politics in Organized Medicine*, 63 YALE L.J. 937 (1954).

[29] There has been a continuing debate as to whether the 7.8% increase in physicians' fees in 1966—the largest annual increase since 1927—was in part a response to the acceptance of the "customary fee" criterion within the Medicare program. For a conservative review of the question, see U.S. DEP'T OF HEALTH, EDUCATION, AND WELFARE, A REPORT TO THE PRESIDENT ON MEDICAL CARE PRICES (1967); for a less conservative view, see Smedley, *Medicare*, THE AM. FEDERATIONIST (AFL-CIO), Sept. 1967, at 9, 14-15.

[30] J. Colombotos, Physicians and Medicare: A Before-After Study of the Effects of Legislation on Attitudes (unpublished paper presented at the annual meeting of the American Sociological Association, San Francisco, Cal., Aug. 31, 1967).

prior to Medicare only thirty-eight per cent of doctors favored the bill. Following the enactment of Medicare seventy per cent reported approval, and six months later the endorsement rate went up to eighty-one per cent. After the passage of the bill and also six months later, ninety-three per cent of the doctors interviewed indicated that they had planned or were planning to treat Medicare patients.

In contrast, the Medicaid program in New York State has had a much more stormy entrance. Six months following its enactment only forty-two per cent of a sample of New York State physicians favored the program, and a substantial number of doctors are alleged to be boycotting the program. Compared to Medicare, title 19 appears to be less popular among doctors, and although there are many explanations for their reactions, it is very likely that an important element involves a dispute over controls. Unlike Medicare, New York State's title 19 program has attempted to impose regulations dealing with the quality and costs of medical care by specifying criteria concerning who can render specialist care and by attempting to provide a fixed fee schedule rather than using the "customary fee" criterion. In this dispute one can see the clash of powerful countervailing forces, and one begins to get some view of what medical care politics will look like in the future.

As government programs in the medical care field expand in their coverage and as inclusion rules become more liberal over time, concern with costs and quality becomes inevitable. Such new programs provide the government with considerable opportunity to upgrade medical education and levels of medical skill at the same time that they encourage efficient practices. Such pressures obviously frighten professionals who are accustomed to unquestioned independence, and they disenfranchise others with lesser qualifications. If, for example, the government requires that providers of particular services be board-eligible or board-certified in the relevant specialties, such requirements arouse the opposition of many doctors who do not meet these qualifications but ordinarily undertake similar work. In the long run specification of such criteria will upgrade medical practice, but in the short range confrontations are inevitable.

One of the major problems in such confrontations is that the rhetoric of dispute is rarely in terms of the issues at hand. Doctors who are fearful of government regulations concerning the quality auditing of medical care find it more expedient to attack the government's alleged intrusion in the doctor-patient relationship rather than to bargain for a fair and reasonable auditing system that protects both sides from abuse. And the false rhetoric does little to refine and resolve such pertinent issues as what constitutes a fair auditing system, how penalties and authority will be administered, how reviews will be undertaken, how auditors will be selected, and the role doctors will have in their selection. Despite the pervasive paranoia among the medical profession concerning government, there are realistic problems resulting from growing government involvement in medicine, and negotiated safeguards for both doctor and patient are required. The obnoxious attachment of a loyalty provision to the original enactment of title 18 is symptomatic of possible dangers to the patient's privacy[31] and to the worthy ethics of the Hippocratic oath. Although such problems can be exaggerated, it remains important to insure that government's role in medicine is structured so as to protect the integrity of patients and those aspects of independence which are necessary among professionals. Despite one's attitudes toward the degree of benevolence exercised by the medical profession, it is too much to expect doctors to passively await developments while the structure of their work situation is so radically changing. We can, however, attempt to channel the discourse into more pertinent and constructive areas of discussion.

Just as the medical profession chooses its own rhetoric, so do government officials. Although they may promise "equal access to quality care" to all persons covered by their programs, the powers of implementation are frequently insufficient to induce the appropriate organizational changes. Making medical care a right rather than a dole does not necessarily change the organization of clinics and how they operate, the attitudes of physicians toward their clients, and the liberties medical organizations take with patients of differing social status. Indeed, the increased provision of medical services to underprivileged groups faces problems in many respects identical to those involved in welfare administration generally.[32] If the government pays medical bills directly, they have better opportunity to control the quality and costs of care and to influence the structure of medical practice. In contrast, if the patient pays his own fees, he has greater opportunity to escape the stigma of receiving a welfare service and whatever consequences flow from such a definition. But in the latter circumstance the government has no way of using its influence to insure that the patient receives a good value for his money. Moreover, under the direct billing scheme recommended by the American Medical Association, there is no protection to the Medicare patient that the doctor will not charge an exorbitant fee in excess of the reimbursement possible under the government program. Furthermore, requirements to pay bills before reimbursement can produce difficulties for elderly patients on limited incomes.

In my opinion direct billing would be desirable and conducive to good quality care only if local medical societies would protect the patient against exorbitant fees by accepting a standardized fee schedule within the limits of government reimbursement. Under such conditions patients would have greater freedom in seeking sources of medical care without being labeled as welfare recipients and would, at the same time, have assurance that they would not be held for expenditures beyond those allowable by the government. From the government's standpoint, if there

---

[31] The Justice Department has conceded in response to ACLU's objections that the Medicare loyalty oath is unconstitutional. 46 ACLU ANN. REP. 31-32 (1967).
[32] *See generally* Handler & Rosenheim, *Privacy in Welfare: Public Assistance and Juvenile Justice*, 31 LAW & CONTEMP. PROB. 377 (1966).

is a predetermined agreement on medical fees reimbursement could be expedited, thus protecting the patient from incurring unnecessary loans to pay medical expenses and negating the need for such obnoxious mechanisms as promissory notes used by some physicians. Here, it appears, is an opportunity to substantially improve the patient's position in the medical care structure, if only the medical societies were willing to undertake action consonant with their verbalized philosophy concerning the freedom of patient choice of doctor and if the federal bureaucracy was able to overcome the inefficiencies of its reimbursement mechanisms.

The field of medical care administration in the United States is complicated by the fact that doctors function in a "seller's market." Unlike England and Wales, where government medicine is used by the mass of the population[33] and where nearly all doctors must depend on the Health Service for their livelihood, doctors in the United States, as noted earlier, are sufficiently busy so that if necessary they can work outside of government schemes. This allows the medical profession a powerful bargaining position, one which permits it to resist to a considerable extent government pressures for change. But there is also evidence that the power of the medical profession is becoming more fragmented as the changing technology and structure of medical practice produce within the health professions new pressure groups who come into conflict with the policies of the American Medical Association. Doctors can no longer work effectively without the availability of the hospital, but hospitals are faced with their own problems and increasingly are looking toward the government for financial support and are showing a willingness to accommodate to administrative pressures from the government. Similarly, medical educational institutions and particular medical specialties are to a greater extent identifying with their own particular problems and spheres of concern, and when their interests are at stake they are willing to form coalitions with the government against the American Medical Association. In the past few years we have had the opportunity to see several such instances: the American Hospital Association supporting the government on Medicare; the medical schools supporting regional government-supported clinics for chronic disease; and the American Psychiatric Association supporting government investments in staffing community mental health centers. The changing political and social climate in the country at large and the growing ferment among the young also have not failed to penetrate the medical schools, where there is a growing consciousness of the social responsibilities of the medical profession.

V

THE CHANGING CONTEXTS OF MEDICAL PRACTICE

The greatest problem in health care evident in the United States involves the lack of congruency between the need for medical care and its distribution. Those groups in the United States with the most abundant health problems and need for

---

[33] *See* A. CARTWRIGHT, PATIENTS AND THEIR DOCTORS: A STUDY OF GENERAL PRACTICE (1967).

adequate medical attention use proportionately the smallest share of health services.[34] Whatever the defects of nationalized systems of care—and there are many—they have made impressive progress in closing the gap between the need for services and their availability.[35] In comparison to the United States there are few developed countries in the Western world that have such great discrepancies in access to care and health status between the rich and the poor.[36] Much of the problem in the United States stems from large pockets of "impoverished health" in underprivileged areas which have not been reached effectively by medical programs already available.[37]

At the same time it is apparent that in recent years the government has made major strides in attacking the morbidity problem among the poor. Through the Medicaid program the states were offered an excellent incentive to increase the scope of health coverage among those with limited incomes, and, although the criteria vary among the states which have thus far enacted programs, the potential scope of such programs can be observed in the liberal requirements specified in New York State. But even Medicaid tends to benefit those areas of the country that have comparatively good state services, and such programs do not do enough to overcome health problems in many of the most impoverished areas of the United States.[38]

Despite short-run setbacks, it appears evident that when the war in Vietnam ends and abundant funds are once again available for a variety of domestic programs, medical benefits through government support will be increasingly liberalized. Since government's role in providing and organizing health care is really only beginning, it is important that we consider various alternatives for structuring care and attempt to learn what we can from other countries concerning the consequences of different forms of organization. I therefore wish to use the remaining space to consider the relevance of the British experience for developing trends in the United States.

---

[34] D. MECHANIC, *supra* note 17, at 236-70; *see* H. SOMERS & A. SOMERS, *supra* note 6; NAT'L CENTER FOR HEALTH STATISTICS, MEDICAL CARE, HEALTH STATUS, AND FAMILY INCOME (Public Health Service Pub. No. 1000-Ser. 10-No. 9, 1964); Sheps & Drosness, *Prepayment for Medical Care* (pts. 1-3), 264 NEW ENG. J. MED. 390, 444, 494 (1961).

[35] For example, recent studies in Britain show no clear relationship between social status and medical care utilization. The studies available suggest somewhat more utilization among the working class who probably need medical services more. *See, e.g.*, A. CARTWRIGHT, *supra* note 33.

[36] Although health and longevity are related to various aspects of culture and society more than to the availability of medical care, it is important to note that despite the affluence of the American health sector, American adult mortality and infant mortality far exceed many other developed Western nations. *See, e.g.*, NAT'L CENTER FOR HEALTH STATISTICS, INTERNATIONAL COMPARISON OF PERINATAL AND INFANT MORTALITY (Public Health Service Pub. No. 1000-Ser. 3-No. 6, 1967).

[37] The high infant mortality rate in the United States is largely a product of the great excess of deaths among nonwhite infants. *See, e.g.*, NAT'L CENTER FOR HEALTH STATISTICS, INFANT AND PERINATAL MORTALITY IN THE UNITED STATES (Public Health Service Pub. No. 1000-Ser. 3-No. 4, 1965). Also, the excess in nonwhite deaths at all ages, except among the very old where data are particularly unreliable, reflect such discrepancies in access to medical care. *See* D. MECHANIC, *supra* note 17, at 236-70.

[38] The most "liberal" Medicaid programs are available in the following states: California, Connecticut, Massachusetts, Maryland, Minnesota, New Hampshire, New York, Rhode Island, and Wisconsin.

VI

Some Comparisons Between British and American Medicine

The major goals of any medical system are to provide and distribute health services to those who need them and to use the resources, knowledge, and technology available to prevent and alleviate disease, disability, and suffering to the extent possible under prevailing conditions. There are many alternative ways in which these goals may be pursued, and the form that health institutions take is inevitably related to the form of other societal institutions and to the economic, organizational, and value context of which they are a part.

Most medical structures, as in the case of other social institutions, have not been organized to fit a plan of maximal efficiency. Instead, they are "hammered out" in the politics of compromise, responding as well to tradition, societal need, and changing technology. The organization of the English National Health Service illustrates this point since it was clearly part of a long evolution of social services, and it expressed values and embodied traditions that were in no sense new.[39] By the second half of the nineteenth century the poor in England had gained the right to institutionalized care when they were sick. In the Metropolitan Poor Act of 1867[40] it was explicitly acknowledged that it was the obligation of the state to provide hospitals for the poor. The National Health Insurance Act of 1911[41] provided wage earners with a general practitioner service not so different from the one available today. Thus, the formation of the National Health Service in 1948[42] served to extend guarantees of access to care and to organize the nation's hospitals into a national scheme, but the Service itself was of an old and traditional cloth, embodying many of the irrationalities and organizational absurdities that existed prior to the National Health Service. We, too, are in this position as we forge ahead in developing new programs. For as we compromise with the medical profession and other groups to facilitate the implementation of particular organizational forms, we allow various absurdities to persist which will plague us in the future. I believe that the billing arrangements under the Medicare Act constitute one such example.

Essentially, the English National Health Service was organized in three parts. Hospitals were organized on a regional basis to assure greater rationality, thus improving to some extent the very poor distribution of beds and facilities. General practice was, for the most part, organized separately from the hospital system, very much extending the form of the medical panel as it existed under the National Health Insurance Act of 1911. The general practitioners, slow to accept the inevitability of the new National Health Service and weak in their prestige and bargaining

---

[39] *See* B. ABEL-SMITH, *supra* note 2; H. ECKSTEIN, THE ENGLISH HEALTH SERVICE (1964); R. STEVENS, MEDICAL PRACTICE IN MODERN ENGLAND (1966).

[40] 30 & 31 Vict., c. 6.

[41] 1 & 2 Geo. 5, c. 55.

[42] 9 & 10 Geo. 6, c. 81.

position, found themselves with little power but to grumble as the government pushed through a "deal" with the more prestigeful hospital doctors—a deal that won their support and cooperation.[43] Previous to 1948 many general practitioners took on work in hospitals that could not support a full-time hospital doctor, but the new organization of hospital regions allowed assignment of consultants to these institutions, thus more completely disenfranchising the general practitioner from hospital work. Moreover, the salaried hospital doctors were no longer in any sense beholden to the general practitioner for private referrals, and this perhaps has led to an attitude that more readily allows expression of the status distinction between the general practitioner and the hospital consultant—a distinction that has become in recent years more pronounced than ever before with the growing technological sophistication of specialized medical work. Although it was anticipated that the conditions of general practice would be improved through the establishment of general practice centers supplied with ample diagnostic facilities and ancillary help, neither the practitioners themselves nor successive governments were particularly enthusiastic about the idea. The doctors coveted their independence, distrusted both the central and local governments, and were wary about working under the gaze of their medical colleagues. The government, preoccupied with other problems of some magnitude, was probably reluctant to expend the substantial sums necessary to improve the conditions of general practice.

Although conditions in Great Britain and the United States are not comparable, I believe that American doctors have an important lesson to learn from the British experience. British general practitioners have done so poorly in part because they have taken a negativistic and unconstructive stance in opposing inevitable social changes. Had they taken a more constructive view toward social conditions, they might have done much not only to enhance medical practice but to elevate their own position within the structure of the National Health Service. Organized medicine in the United States has also been characterized by stubborn and unconstructive responses to government attempts to attack pressing social problems in the medical field. Although the American Medical Association is no doubt successful in delaying and deflecting programs of change in the short run, they may have a lesser role in structuring future solutions. For example, instead of fighting government subsidy of medical students, thus having a detrimental impact on the quality and range of manpower attracted to the medical profession, the American Medical Association could play an impressive role in insuring that government fellowships would not infringe on the choices made by the student and the integrity of medical practice. Indeed, as the image of the American Medical Association becomes more tainted, its ability to provide leadership among informed and respected medical men

---

[43] *See generally* H. ECKSTEIN, PRESSURE GROUP POLITICS: THE CASE OF THE BRITISH MEDICAL ASSOCIATION (1960), for a brilliant analysis of the bargaining relationships between the British Medical Association and the Ministry of Health.

is undermined. I have little doubt that leading medical figures will to a larger extent participate in ad hoc policy-making groups outside the committee sphere of organized medicine itself.

In one major sense, the situation of general practice in England and Wales portrays in vivid form a dilemma increasingly characteristic of the United States and other Western countries—that is, the dilemma concerning the organization of general practice services within the over-all structure of medical practice. As medical practice becomes more specialized and more dependent on laboratory aids and technical diagnostic approaches, there has been growing concern in defining the relevance and appropriateness of the general practitioner in the over-all scheme of services. In the United States the noticeable departure of doctors from the general practice role poses the important issue of whether or not vast effort should be devoted to reviving or restructuring such services. In England it is believed that the general practitioner has a unique role in dealing with the social and psychological problems of patients as well as serving as a "first line of defence in times of illness, disability, and distress."[44] However, such definitions of the role are rarely accompanied by an explanation of how such a stance might be effectively communicated to the doctor except in the grossest generalities. Since medical education in Britain is extremely conservative and based predominantly on hospital practice, the average doctor does not always assimilate such socially benevolent views.[45] He, too, frequently identifies with the values of the medical school, which places greatest emphasis on the diagnosis and treatment of less common disorders and not on those most frequently seen in general practice. Even more important, however, is the fact that the stance the doctor takes toward his patients is determined as much by the conditions under which he practices as it is by his own motives and values. To the extent that the doctor is faced by a large panel of patients and an exceedingly heavy work load, it becomes difficult for him to practice in a manner which gives high priority to psychological and social needs of the patient.[46] The average general practitioner is far too busy to provide a high standard of social medicine and emotional sustenance.

We are now in a situation in the United States where we are being urged to restimulate general practice and to institute comprehensive medicine at the same time that we are encouraged to meet growing medical demands by increasing the doctor's productivity. But the social changes required to increase the doctor's productivity are contrary to the gains we anticipate would result from a revitalized general practice. To the extent that the doctor's time is organized to provide a maximum of technical services in a particular period of time, it becomes difficult indeed to enhance those aspects of the doctor's role that nourish emotional and social health.

---

[44] BRITISH MINISTRY OF HEALTH, THE FIELD OF WORK OF THE FAMILY DOCTOR (GILLIE REPORT) 9 (1963).

[45] See T. McKEOWN, MEDICINE IN MODERN SOCIETY (1965).

[46] See Mechanic, *Doctors in Revolt: The Crisis in the British National Health Service*, in ENGLISH SOCIETY (I. Weinberg ed. 1968) (forthcoming).

In fact, there is no excuse for failing to do everything possible to increase substantially the production of physicians. Vast subsidies should be provided for medical schools that expand their production of doctors, and the government ought completely to subsidize the direct and indirect costs of medical education for students who are willing to agree to practice for some period after their training in areas officially designated as "medically needy." Such a program would not only help alleviate the difficult financial state of medical schools but would also draw doctors from a wider range of talent irrespective of economic background. It would also provide some incentive for helping to redistribute in a more equitable way the nation's medical manpower.

The question of general practice also brings out in sharp focus some of the economic issues underlying health care, although they take a somewhat different form in the United States and Great Britain. Although the impression is often given in both countries that patients receive the best medical care that money can buy, the kind and quality of medical care depend very largely on the funds invested in health care and health resources. In spite of the fact that the National Health Service tries to make access to medical care more equitable, its presence does not insure the availability of a high standard of care to the average patient. The typical doctor sees far too many patients to assess their problems carefully, and he devotes far too little time to each patient. In a study of a random sample of general practitioners in England and Wales,[47] more than half of the doctors studied reported that under present conditions of organization it was not reasonable to expect general practitioners to provide a high standard of medical care or to practice good social or preventive care. More than two-fifths of the doctors felt it was not even realistic to expect the general practitioner to adequately screen out patients with serious physical disorders, to keep informed of new knowledge in medicine, or to provide a high quality doctor-patient relationship. Although we do not have comparable data relevant to medical practice in North America, there are indications that the situation is not much better.[48] To the extent that medical practice affects mortality and morbidity—and this may be a dubious assumption—there is little basis for assuming American superiority.[49]

Economic issues affect medicine in other ways as well. Because such high eco-

---

[47] D. Mechanic, General Practice in England and Wales: A Report on a Survey of a National Sample of General Practitioners (mimeo., Department of Sociology, University of Wisconsin, 1968). *See generally* Mechanic, *General Practice in England and Wales*, 6 MED. CARE (1968) (forthcoming).

[48] *See* K. CLUTE, THE GENERAL PRACTITIONER, STUDY OF MEDICAL EDUCATION AND PRACTICE IN ONTARIO AND NOVA SCOTIA (1963); Peterson et al., *An Analytic Study of North Carolina General Practice 1953-1954*, J. MEDICAL ED., Dec. 1956, pt. 2, at 1. *See generally* COLUMBIA UNIVERSITY SCHOOL OF PUBLIC HEALTH AND ADMINISTRATIVE MEDICINE, THE QUANTITY, QUALITY, AND COSTS OF MEDICAL AND HOSPITAL CARE SECURED BY A SAMPLE OF TEAMSTER FAMILIES IN THE NEW YORK AREA (1960), for a picture of the quality of work of general practitioners in hospitals.

[49] *See* Peterson et al., *What is Value for Money in Medical Care?*, [1967] 1 THE LANCET 771; Moriyama & Guralnick, *Occupational and Social Class Differences in Mortality*, in MILBANK MEMORIAL FUND, TRENDS AND DIFFERENTIALS IN MORTALITY 61 (1956); references cited notes 36 & 37 *supra*.

nomic valuation is placed on the doctor's technical services, certain aspects of medicine which may still be desirable become relatively uneconomical. Doctors are increasingly unwilling to make house calls because of the loss of time and money intrinsic to such inefficient forms of practice; patients as well would be unwilling to pay the cost of such house calls as measured against a comparable value received in office practice for a given time unit. The unwillingness to make house calls is highly developed in the United States where doctors, for the most part, work on a fee-for-service basis; but the proportion of the doctor's time spent in home care is decreasing in developed medical systems throughout the world.

Finally, it is important to consider the relevance of general practice to modern technical medical care. The general practitioner is a doctor of first contact. Ideally, he is sufficiently trained, technically speaking, to deal with most of the common disease conditions and to recognize those less common situations which require specialized attention. Moreover, he is a kind of medical ombudsman in that he is expected to make assessments of the quality of specialized services available, to channel his patients into those routes most likely to offer a high quality of care, and to survey and, if necessary, intervene in the medical care provided to his patients so that their interests are best served. He is an educator in that his role is partially concerned with instructing the patient in health care, advising him on general medical problems, and encouraging his understanding and cooperation in treatment. Also it is assumed that he is sufficiently conversant with the personal and social history of the patient so that he can provide a meaningful kind of emotional sustenance and can consider social and personal factors in managing the patient and his illness in an optimal manner. Finally, it is assumed that taking into account the social and psychological dimensions of medical care enhances treatment decisions in that social facts and attitudes affect the course of illness and the range of disability.

It is reasonable to inquire as to what structural and organizational factors would allow such a role to be implemented and what social features would interfere with its success. Obviously the doctor must be reasonably competent in a technical sense, and conditions must be conducive to allowing him to maintain and upgrade his skills. Also he must be in a position to assess realistically the qualifications of specialists in the community and the quality of care they are able to provide. Moreover, he must have real alternative choices among such specialists, and this assumes access to a large specialist pool. Furthermore, he must be in a position to provide continuing care to his patients and be sufficiently aware of their histories and needs to instruct and advise them intelligently. It is also assumed that his relationship with the patient is a continuing one and that his practice is characterized by a relatively low degree of mobility. Finally, it is assumed that he is sufficiently in contact with other doctors providing care to his patients so that he can bring important facts concerning their health and personal histories to these doctors' attention and, in general, can look out for his patients' interests when they are placed within particular referral routes. Using these structural prerequisites, it is instructive to evaluate the role of general practitioners as they most commonly function in Britain and the United States.

England is an interesting country to assess since practitioners and officials frequently express pride in their ability to resist the trend toward specialization and impersonal medicine. The average general practitioner there is as well trained as his American counterpart, although the scope of his responsibility for caring for patients is much more limited because of his exclusion from hospital practice. He practices, for the most part, in isolation from other doctors who can scrutinize his practice and can help correct his mistakes, and he usually does not experience situations where medical problems are intensively discussed and skills sharpened. Moreover, his busy practice, largely devoted to common and uncomplicated medical problems, provides little incentive to maintain and develop new skills in dealing with less common disease entities. Although efforts are made to encourage continued postgraduate involvement, the doctor's investment in continuing education is less than ideal. Although the general practitioner may know specialists by reputation, because he has little place in the hospital he rarely has a personal opportunity to scrutinize the quality of the consultants' work, and even if he did he would have little power to affect the hospital situation. Finally, unless he is located in a major medical center such as London, he may have few real alternatives for referral, and his major role may involve scheduling an appointment for the patient or arranging for a hospital bed. Frequently patients are referred to the hospital without designating a consultant at all.

The continuity of general care in Britain is very much disrupted because the doctor has no place or responsibility in his patient's care once the patient is sent to the hospital. Sometimes the hospital report on the patient is so late that the doctor is not in a position to follow up treatment when the patient returns to him. Moreover, the separation of the general practitioner from hospital care usually means that his knowledge of the patient will not be used at a time when it might be most relevant. Furthermore, the general practitioner has no controls or sanctions to exercise in relation to the hospital or the consultant if he feels his patient is not receiving optimal care. Even if his contribution were valued by the hospital, his own feeling of lack of welcome and his lower prestige relative to the consultant make him reticent to interfere in hospital work. In short, despite the high ideals with which general practice is often described within the National Health Service, the location of general practice within the structure of care does much to negate the possibilities of the general practitioner's role.

General practice in Britain, however, has some assets more obviously lacking in general practice in the United States. British populations are less geographically mobile, and individual practices are more likely to be organized so that they correspond with neighborhood and family patterns. Moreover, the typical British general practitioner seems to know his community and patients better than does his American counterpart, and he spends much more time visiting their homes. He appears to have a better appreciation of the social problems existing in the community and how these problems impinge on the life and health difficulties of his patient. Indeed, the British general practitioner seems more concerned with the social aspects of medicine, although the organization of general practice does much to interfere with the success of a social viewpoint.

The role of the American general practitioner is more difficult to describe since it is less patterned and more variable. The American situation provides opportunities for both better and poorer general care than is available in Great Britain in that it provides the general practitioner a greater chance to use his influence to encourage and stimulate a high level of medical care, but it also provides greater incentive to exploit the patient for economic gain and greater need to protect himself from competition with other community practitioners.

Although the typical American practitioner is no better trained than his English counterpart, he undertakes a wider variety of work because of his access to the hospital. Although this increases the risk of errors in the management of a serious disease, it also provides incentives for the doctor to maintain his skills, and it encourages greater contact with other doctors. Moreover, in such situations the doctor's work is more visible to his colleagues since much of his activity takes place in the more open atmosphere of the hospital where others obtain some opportunity to observe how he manages his cases. However, because of the economic structure of general practice in America, there is greater incentive for a doctor to keep his patients and treat them himself than to refer them to outside practitioners. The American doctor is frequently faced with the threat of losing his referred patients not only because of the competitiveness of private practice, but also because of patients' increasing sophistication concerning the qualifications of doctors. If the doctor is in group practice, he can protect himself by restricting referrals within the group, but this severely restricts the range of care he can provide his patients. In other situations he may seek to avoid loss of his patients by referring patients to specialists outside his immediate locality. The convenience factor is thus likely to bring the patient back to his original doctor. In short, it is reasonable to believe that doctors will develop solutions to protect themselves and their practices which may not be conducive to the highest level of care. Therefore it is necessary to encourage organizational forms which are conducive to practicing a high level of care in the patients' best interests.

In contrast to his English counterpart, the American general practitioner has a better opportunity to assess the competence of his colleagues since he may come into closer contact with them through hospital work and consultations. But the extent of his awareness can be very much exaggerated, and it is often based on hearsay rather than on a serious opportunity to evaluate colleagues' work. Since the American specialist, however, is dependent on general practitioner referrals to a large extent, he is more susceptible to the general practitioner's influence. Thus, in this respect, the American general practitioner is in a much stronger position to play the role of a medical ombudsman and to influence the specialist in directions conducive to his patients' well-being.

The same conditions and scope of flexibility that provide the American general practitioner with an opportunity to promote the interests of the patient also promote a variety of abuses. The incentive to maximize income and, therefore, to retain one's patients encourages the doctor—perhaps not consciously—to undertake work beyond his capacity, and it may bring about unnecessary and harmful medical procedures.[50] Moreover, the referral system itself encourages trading relationships, some regarded as clearly unethical such as fee splitting, others more ambiguous from an ethical point of view but probably not conducive to a high level of medical care. With the studies available, it is impossible to ascertain to what extent the greater flexibility of referral in the United States serves to maximize patients' care as opposed to benefiting the doctor; the optimal interests of the patient and his doctor are not always compatible, however.

In contrast to the British general practitioner, the American doctor is less likely to have his patient population concentrated in one small area, and his patients are more likely to be geographically mobile. Thus the costs of home care are greater, and it is more difficult for the doctor to know his patient and his family situation well. Also, like the British general practitioner, his work load under present conditions of demand is sufficiently large to make it difficult to provide the time and attention necessary to deal with emotional and psychosocial problems of patients.

VII

Some Final Notes on Medical Practice in the Future

Although it is possible to construct ideal models of what medical care should be, the types of medical care programs that will evolve in the future will be of the same cloth that presently exists. Despite the rhetoric and enunciation of high ideals, we should be aware that medicine will accommodate to the community forces that affect it, and the community will have little impact on the over-all structure of medical services unless it can modify the community conditions, resources, and demands that compel medical adaptations. Ultimately, the condition of medical practice will depend on who controls the organization and structure of medical work, and this is the basic key to the growing confrontations between government and the medical profession.

The deficiencies obvious in medical practice in the United States and Great Britain have led many informed observers in both countries to suggest solutions that are

---

[50] *See* Roemer, *supra* note 5; Columbia University School of Public Health and Administrative Medicine, *supra* note 48.

strikingly similar; indeed, these suggestions seem to take what appears to work best in both systems and combine their advantages. The concept of health centers—bringing together large numbers of doctors in association with supporting specialties and ancillary workers to provide medical care for defined geographic groups—offers opportunities to improve not only the technical quality of medical care, coordination of services, and the level of emotional and social care, but also tremendous incentives for medical education, supervision and control over quality of services, and more economical use of medical resources. Although the National Health Service in Britain was designed on the assumption that such health centers would become widespread, it is only recently that the government is making a serious effort to encourage such organization.

In a recent article in the *New England Journal of Medicine*,[51] Russel Lee endorses the practicality of community health center organization in the United States. These health centers, as he visualizes them, are to be staffed by group-practice clinics and supported by prepayment plans in which consumers have a voice. He sees the health center integrated with the hospital, extended-care facilities, convalescent homes and nursing homes, and facilities for the long-term care of the mentally ill. He believes that such health centers should be organized around populations of approximately 150,000 people and units of approximately 750 beds. He further notes:[52]

> The people should "belong" to the center as they belong to a church. They should be organized as a consumer co-operative group, should bargain with the group practice clinic to obtain their care on a capitation prepaid basis and should support the operation of the center by a fixed monthly fee.

Such solutions to the problems of medical care are more easily voiced than accomplished. But with medical care in a state of crisis and medical thinking in a state of ferment, and with vast federal and state funds flowing into the medical care area, there is a great opportunity for constructive government action that provides the incentives for the restructuring of medical care so that the distribution of services are more equitable, the delivery of services is more effective, and the organization of medical care is geared more closely to the medical and social needs of the population. We must constantly be aware that the various facets of the medical care area—the financing of medicine, medical education, building of hospitals, development of new specialties, and so forth—are intertwined in a complicated net, and that decisions made in any sphere have consequences throughout the entire medical structure. We must attempt to use the growing government influence in medical care not only to increase the scope and quality of medical care, but also to insure that new medical structures provide a range of choice and a scope of action that facilitate serving man not only as a biological entity but also as a person.

---

[51] Lee, *Provision of Health Services*, 277 NEW ENG. J. MED. 682 (1967).
[52] *Id.* at 685.

INNOVATIONS AND EXPERIMENTS IN USES OF HEALTH MANPOWER—THE EFFECT OF LICENSURE LAWS*

EDWARD H. FORGOTSON[†] AND JOHN L. COOK[‡]

INTRODUCTION

Present trends indicate that growth in the output of personal health services will exceed the growth in population.[1] At the same time, the relative and absolute physician shortage will, in all probability, continue to deteriorate.[2] These apparently contradictory predictions are evidence of fundamental problems confronting personal health care delivery systems.

To understand this paradox it is necessary to examine the nature and distribution of available personal health care. Such an examination reveals that there is a national crisis in the provision of medical care, characterized by spiraling costs, inadequacies in services rendered to the disadvantaged, and widespread discontent with the restricted availability of professional health services despite greater numbers of health workers and more medical facilities per capita than ever before.[3]

In part, these shortages and higher costs may be traced to a lack of skilled health personnel.[4] But they also reflect to an important degree the extraordinarily inefficient manner in which existing health manpower resources are currently used.[5] Organizational changes must be made in the health care delivery system. Until such changes are accomplished, health care will cost more than it should, and it will not be possible to estimate with accuracy the need for additional health manpower in the future.[6] As medicine develops new methods of treatment requiring specialized skills, innovations in functions for existing health personnel must be authorized, and

---

* This article is based in part on a study prepared for the National Advisory Commission on Health Manpower by E. Forgotson, R. Roemer & R. Newman, Legal Regulation of Health Personnel in the United States, Sept. 1967 (mimeo.), to be published in 2 NAT'L ADVISORY COMM'N ON HEALTH MANPOWER, REPORT OF THE NATIONAL ADVISORY COMMISSION ON HEALTH MANPOWER (forthcoming). See also Forgotson, Roemer & Newman, *Licensure of Physicians*, 1967 WASH. U.L.Q. 249 (1967); Forgotson, Roemer & Newman, *Innovations in the Organization of Health Services: Inhibiting vs. Permissive Regulation, id.* at 400; Leff, *Medical Devices and Paramedical Personnel: A Preliminary Context for Emerging Problems, id.* at 332.

† B.A. 1953, University of Texas; M.D. 1957, Washington University; LL.B. 1960, University of Texas; LL.M. 1963, University of Michigan. Associate Professor of Preventive Medicine and Associate Professor of Public Health, University of California, Los Angeles. Member of the California and Texas bars.

‡ Class of 1968, Law School, University of California, Los Angeles.

[1] 1 NAT'L ADVISORY COMM'N ON HEALTH MANPOWER, REPORT OF THE NATIONAL ADVISORY COMMISSION ON HEALTH MANPOWER 6-23 (1967) [hereinafter cited as HEALTH MANPOWER REPORT].
[2] *Id.*
[3] *Id.* at 7.
[4] *Id.* at 6.
[5] *Id.*; NAT'L COMM'N ON COMMUNITY HEALTH SERVICES, HEALTH IS A COMMUNITY AFFAIR 77-100, 211-15 (1966).
[6] *See* HEALTH MANPOWER REPORT 6.

new kinds of auxiliary personnel must be created. The National Advisory Commission on Health Manpower recommended in November 1967 that the federal government give high priority to the support under university direction of experimental programs which would train and utilize new categories of health professionals.[7]

Current professional and occupational licensure laws pose major impediments to the expansion of the functions of existing categories of health personnel and even to the implementation of experiments to develop new ways of employing such manpower or to create new categories of health workers. For these reasons, this discussion will focus particularly on these laws, placing special emphasis on those legal standards defining the allocation of tasks among members of the health service industry.

I

OFFICIAL LICENSURE LAWS

The principal professed objective of licensure laws[7a] is the promotion of high quality personal health care through the regulation of inputs of the health care delivery system.[8] These laws restrict the personnel, facilities, medications, and equipment that may be employed in the health service industry on the assumption that high quality outputs can be obtained by regulating inputs. Whether the regulatory system should be redesigned to focus more on outputs—as malpractice law now does and as a process of continuing supervision might someday do—is a problem that is beyond the scope of this discussion. Nevertheless, such a redesign may someday be appropriate, and the concept and its feasibility should be the subject of continuing research.

State licensure of individuals in the health professions and occupations, setting minimum qualifications and performance standards for entry into or retention in the profession or occupation, is the basic but by no means the sole legal control over the quality of health services and the allocation of patient care tasks among members of the health service industry. The courts also exercise quality and task allocation control through the exercise of jurisdiction in malpractice suits, actions for declaratory judgments, and criminal proceedings for illegal practice.[9] State and federal governments control quality through licensure of hospitals and other health

---

[7] *Id.* at 31.
[7a] Licensing laws may also reflect the licensed profession's desire to restrict entry into its ranks as a means of limiting competition. See pp. 748-50 *infra* for a discussion of this aspect of medical practice acts in the context of an assessment of prospects for professional support of the reforms recommended in this article.
[8] The word *system* is used as a convenient term to describe the health services industry and is not meant to imply the existence of an organized planned undertaking.
[9] *E.g.,* Crees v. California State Bd. of Medical Examiners, 213 Cal. App. 2d 195, 28 Cal. Rptr. 621 (1963) (criminal prosecution); Mitchell v. Louisiana State Bd. of Optometry Examiners, 128 So. 2d 825 (La. Ct. App. 1961) (declaratory judgment); Barber v. Reinking, 68 Wash. 2d 139, 411 P.2d 861 (1966) (malpractice); CAL. BUS. & PROF. CODE §§ 2141, 2141.5 (West Supp. 1967).

facilities and through financing of health programs requiring providers of care to meet certain individual or institutional standards. Professional and other nongovernmental organizations exert quality controls through accreditation of hospitals, certification of medical and dental specialties, and approval of training programs. Within hospitals, moreover, there are professional controls imposed by medical staff organizations, such as those governing hospital staff appointments and those regulating surgery and medical audits.

Nongovernmental standards are essential to promote high and constantly improving standards of excellence for patient care. Occupational licensing is and must probably remain merely a mechanism for the enforcement of minimum standards. At present, nongovernmental regulation is more important in assuring high quality care because it generally specifies higher standards than official licensure. In addition, nongovernmental regulation directly or indirectly affects more factors relevant to the delivery of medical care than do licensure laws, by virtue of its control over activities not regulated by licensure, such as qualification to practice a medical or dental specialty or the number of consultants required where hospitalized patients are not progressing satisfactorily. Finally, many nongovernmental regulatory systems have been given official status by incorporation into licensure provisions.[10]

Official occupational licensure will be the principal subject of this analysis because it almost exclusively controls the allocation of tasks and responsibilities among members of the health manpower matrix;[11] it is therefore also most relevant to experimental programs which would train and utilize new categories of health professionals. Moreover, such laws tend to be less flexible than nongovernmental standards in responding to changes in the social, economic, and technological context of the delivery of medical care.

A. Description

State licensure statutes enacted under the police power to legislate for public health, welfare, and safety are designed to protect the public from incompetent, unethical, and unscientific practitioners.[12] To this end, the statutes define the functions that each occupational group is authorized to perform and specify the requirements of character, education, and training that licensed practitioners must meet. Entrance into practice is further regulated by statutory provisions for approval of educational institutions and examination of licensure candidates. In controlling the continuing eligibility of licensees to practice, the legislatures provide grounds and procedures for renewal, suspension, revocation, and reinstatement of licenses. To enforce these

---

[10] For example, the statutes of several states specifically require graduation from a medical school approved by the American Medical Association or the Association of American Medical Colleges.
[11] See generally E. Forgotson, R. Roemer & R. Newman, Legal Regulation of Health Personnel in the United States, Sept. 1967, ch. 2 (mimeo.) [hereinafter cited as Regulation of Health Personnel].
[12] See Dent v. West Virginia, 129 U.S. 114 (1889).

standards, the statutes establish licensing agencies with administrative, adjudicative, and rule-making powers.

An analysis of occupational licensure laws of the fifty states and the District of Columbia reveals significant problems affecting all health professions and occupations. The licensure process regulates physicians, osteopaths, chiropractors, professional and practical or vocational nurses, professional nurse-midwives, physical therapists, optometrists, podiatrists, dentists, and dental hygienists in all jurisdictions in the United States. Some jurisdictions license psychologists, dispensing opticians, x-ray technologists, and medical technologists.[13] Occupational therapists and dental assistants are not licensed in any jurisdiction. Hitherto unrecognized categories of health manpower, such as the "physician's assistants" now being educated at the Duke University School of Medicine,[14] are of course not licensed in any jurisdiction.

Since the original enactment of most occupational licensure acts in substantially their present form shortly after the beginning of the twentieth century, vast social and scientific changes have taken place.[15] Even though the substrate upon which licensure laws must act has changed, creating new problems and increased demand for health services, there have been no fundamental changes in licensure laws with respect to the allocation of health service tasks and responsibilities among the various members of the health service industry. The changing character of personal health care has brought into being a number of new categories of ancillary health personnel, some of which did not exist as recently as ten years ago.[16] In spite of these developments, laws regulating the practice of medicine primarily recognize only the physician with twelve to fourteen years' of education and training after high school and the professional nurse who may have had as little as two years of formal education after high school.[17] There is a similar problem in the practice of dentistry in which the professional dentist and the dentist hygienist, who has marked restrictions on her activities, are the only two legally recognized manpower categories. These inadequate classifications of health manpower have resulted in inefficient use of other highly trained personnel.

Some understanding of the nature and number of ways in which licensure statutes

---

[13] *E.g.*, CAL. BUS. & PROF. CODE §§ 2900-2984 (West 1962, Supp. 1967) (psychologists); *id.* §§ 2250-2558 (registered dispensing opticians); *id.* §§ 1200-1322 (clinical laboratory technology).

[14] The Duke program is discussed in Stead, *At Duke: A New Approach to the Doctor Shortage*, RESIDENT PHYSICIAN, Feb. 1967, at 84; Stead, *Conserving Costly Talents—Providing Physicians' New Assistants*, 198 J.A.M.A. 1108 (1966).

[15] *See generally* H.E. SIGERIST, *The History of Medical Licensure*, in HENRY E. SIGERIST ON THE SOCIOLOGY OF MEDICINE 308, 316-18 (M. Roemer ed. 1960).

[16] HEALTH MANPOWER REPORT 31; The Allied Health Professions Personnel Training Act of 1966, Pub. L. No. 89-751, 80 Stat. 1222 (codified in scattered sections of 12, 42 U.S.C.), has greatly stimulated the growth of new categories of ancillary health personnel. Interview with William Parson of the Division of Allied Health Manpower, Bureau of Health Manpower, United States Public Health Service, Jan. 15, 1968.

[17] *See* HEALTH MANPOWER REPORT 31.

influence allocation of health service tasks and functions among members of the health service industry may be obtained by inspection of the history and evolution of present licensure statutes. Licensure of health personnel was virtually nonexistent until 1881; previously anyone was entitled to practice any profession or engage in any business because of the influence of the tenet of unimpeachable freedom of contract.[18] Until that time, the only meaningful professional standards were those established by the professions themselves. After 1881, the professional standards were partially incorporated into state licensure laws as minimal governmental standards. These early licensure laws, which were in many cases permissive, merely protected titles and left to the public the task of determining the distinction between licensed and unlicensed medical practitioners. In general, there has been an orderly progression from voluntary nongovernmental standards to permissive licensure and eventually to mandatory governmental licensure, which requires minimal qualifications as a condition of entering or remaining in practice.

The institution of medical manpower licensure began with licensure of medical practitioners to protect the public from incompetent, untrained, unethical, and commercial practitioners.[19] To this end, licensure of medical practitioners was eventually made mandatory, which necessitated statutory definition of the practice of medicine from which unlicensed persons were excluded. These statutory definitions universally defined the practice of medicine in such broad terms that all personal health service functions were encompassed. Subsequent to the enactment of the medical practice acts, other categories of health manpower sought recognition through licensure. Legal recognition of these new categories of manpower through licensure made necessary the carving out of limited exceptions to the broad medical practice acts. The scope of these exceptions was limited to those tasks and duties specifically defined by law.[20] Under the present licensure system, the physician has an unlimited license, while other licensed health personnel have limited licenses to perform tasks which had previously been within the exclusive province of the physician. Personal health care services not specifically recognized by other licensure laws as appropriately rendered by allied and auxiliary health personnel can be rendered only by the physician.

The history of licensure also reveals that enactment of the present occupational licensure statutes was based on considerations not necessarily related to optimal allocations of responsibilities among the allied or auxiliary health professions and occupations or to different productive delivery of health and medical care to the entire population as a "civil right" of the people. Optimal allocation of health resources and expanded accessibility of health and medical care are now recognized as proper

---

[18] *See generally* L. Friedman, *Freedom of Contract and Occupational Licensing 1890-1910: A Legal and Social Study*, 53 CALIF. L. REV. 487 (1965).

[19] *See* H.E. SIGERIST, *supra* note 15, at 317.

[20] *E.g.*, CAL. BUS. & PROF. CODE § 2141 (West Supp. 1967).

subjects of governmental concern.[21] A design for optimal allocation should be developed by viewing the health service professions and occupations as a matrix in which duties and responsibilities should be allocated on the basis of actual capabilities for performing specific tasks, measured by education, training, and experience, and demonstrated capacity rather than by possession of a categorical title.

New allocations of roles in the health care industry and experiments to determine which innovations are safe and effective are beset with serious legal difficulties. Present occupational licensure laws tend to preserve the status quo, discouraging new allocations of responsibilities within the health manpower matrix and inhibiting experiments to test the safety and effectiveness of new manpower uses. While this is probably the most significant problem that occupational licensure laws present relative to new programs designed to advance achievement of our national health goals, there are other significant problems as well. These other problems include (1) whether present licensure laws provide even adequate minimum standards and (2) the effect of these laws on innovations in the education of physicians and other health personnel.

B. Adequacy of Minimum Standards

1. *Educational Obsolescence*

In providing minimum standards, regulatory programs must contain realistic provisions to minimize activities which can endanger the public. Licensure laws evolved at a time when the amount of knowledge concerning delivery of personal health care was clearly finite. These laws were enacted before the technological and information explosion which began in the late 1930s and consequently did not, as a general rule, recognize that development of new information would render a person's initial qualifications to practice obsolete unless they were upgraded periodically by a program of continuing education. The laws regulating medicine, dentistry, professional and practical nursing, and physical therapy have no requirements aimed at preventing skills from becoming outdated. Aside from dealing with serious incompetence manifested by something such as gross malpractice warranting license revocation, the licensure process does little or nothing to guard against educational obsolescence. In twelve states osteopaths are required to pursue yearly continuing education programs approved by their state osteopathic associations, but those courses need not be designed to instruct the osteopaths in the latest advances in all of the clinical specialties or basic sciences.[22] Nevertheless, these twelve provisions could be an important first step in the development of legal requirements

---

[21] *See* Heart Disease, Cancer, and Stroke Amendments of 1965, Pub. L. No. 89-239, 79 Stat. 926. *See generally* NAT'L COMM'N ON COMMUNITY HEALTH SERVICES, HEALTH IS A COMMUNITY AFFAIR (1966).

[22] These states are Arizona, Florida, Maine, Michigan, Nevada, New Mexico, North Dakota, Ohio, Oklahoma, Tennessee, Vermont, and West Virginia. In these states attendance at the annual educational program conducted by the state osteopathic association, or its equivalent, satisfies the requirement of continuing, refresher education. Regulation of Health Personnel, ch. 1, at 50.

that can begin to cope realistically with the serious problem of educational obsolescence.

The report of the National Advisory Commission on Health Manpower recommended in November 1967 that either (1) satisfactory completion of periodic programs of continuing medical education or (2) passage of a periodic examination by those not completing such educational programs be made a mandatory condition of renewal of licenses by all physicians graduating from medical school after the time of enactment of such requirements.[23] Implementation of this recommendation would require official approval of the duration and content of the periodic educational programs and of the length, contents, emphasis, and administration of the periodic examinations. Nevertheless, this is a significant recommendation which could lead to overcoming a serious deficiency of present licensure laws.

2. *Hospital Staff Privileges*

It must be noted that it is a nongovernmental process not involving certification or accreditation that probably is the mechanism which most effectively insures the adequacy of the services rendered by personnel, particularly physicians, in hospitals. This process is the granting and maintaining of staff privileges for physicians.

Hospital staff privileges are nongovernmental and do not involve systematic nationwide standards. The standards generally are applied on an institution-by-institution basis, and governmental process becomes involved only in adjudications relating to procedural matters in granting and maintaining staff privileges and denials of equal protection of the law where racial or religious discrimination is alleged.[24] The staff privilege regulatory process affects daily operations of health personnel, involves peer group evaluation of performance of physicians, and can deal with such questions as (1) ordinary incompetence in the exercise of skills, (2) lack of specialized skills, (3) diminution of skills as a result of age, debilitation, drug addiction, or alcoholism, and (4) educational obsolescence. Since it does not involve invocation of quasi-penal provisions such as those presented by cases involving alleged violations of licensure laws,[25] supervision of practices can be more flexible, and procedural standards of proof of improper practices need not be as stringent. Such subprocesses as utilization review, tissue committee review, medical audit,

---

[23] HEALTH MANPOWER REPORT 40-42. The anticompetitive nature of a provision exempting persons already licensed is as clear as the fact that such a provision eliminates the class of physicians most in need of an educational "refresher." Such a "grandfather clause," while seriously subversive of the goals sought to be attained, probably will be necessary to gain for the measure the support of the regulated professions. This appeared to the author to be the major reason for the limitation to newly licensed physicians. The author observed one session of the Commission when this came up.

[24] See Hamilton County Hosp. v. Andrews, 227 Ind. 217, 84 N.E.2d 469 (1949); Levin v. Sinai Hosp. of Baltimore City, 186 Md. 174, 46 A.2d 298 (1946), for the general rule. See Simkins v. Moses H. Cone Memorial Hosp., 323 F.2d 959 (4th Cir. 1963), *cert. denied,* 376 U.S. 938 (1964), for the rule of the courts in cases involving illegal racial discrimination.

[25] *See* Shively v. Stewart, 65 Cal. 2d 514, 421 P.2d 65, 55 Cal. Rptr. 217 (1966), in which the analogy of the criminal law to cases involving potential revocation of licensure was stated.

and professional activity surveys can be incorporated into the over-all process of supervision of staff privileges, and considerable peer group control and professionalism is possible. Since the hospital is an integral element in the health care delivery system and effective medical or surgical practice is not possible without hospital privileges, the importance of this process cannot be understated.

However, the system of staff privileges regulates only physicians directly, though it affects other personnel indirectly by regulating how physicians relate to them in hospital operations. Furthermore, it does not regulate nonhospital-related activities of physicians or other personnel unless they affect hospital operations. And while the system operates in most voluntary nonprofit and public or tax-supported hospitals, it may not provide the same protections in proprietary hospitals. Finally, the staff privilege system does not prevent physicians denied such privileges from practicing at a low level of competence and ethics and perhaps adversely to the health and safety of a significant percentage of the population. Thus, important as they are, staff privileges do not solve the major problems presented by licensure laws.

3. *Cultism*

Licensure laws regulating the practice of medicine clearly have failed in one most important respect, namely, the control of cultism and unscientific schools of practice. Chiropractic, by far the most important category of cultist healers, has grown to include over 35,000 practitioners and is licensed in all states except Louisiana and Mississippi, having been legalized in New York in 1963 and Massachusetts in 1966.[26] It has been clearly demonstrated that chiropractic lacks a scientific basis. Faculty members of chiropractic "colleges" have been demonstrated to be clearly without sufficient education and other qualifications to teach scientific medicine.[27] The states have attempted to control this unscientific school by regulating it with official licensure laws coupled with basic science examinations.[28] Licensure and basic science examinations have not, in fact, controlled chiropractic, which contends that it can and should treat all diseases, and have not upgraded the scientific content of chiropractic education and practice, as evidenced by the quality of chiropractic college faculties and the unscientific claims of practicing chiropractors.[29] Licensing can never give an unscientific system a scientific basis, but it can give it a cloak of legal respectability.

C. Obstacles to Innovations in Education and Training

Professional licensure laws can constrain innovations in education of members of the health professions and occupations. A highly significant question is whether

---
[26] For a review of the licensure statutes, see Regulation of Health Personnel, ch. 1, at 58-62.
[27] AMA Dep't of Investigation, *Educational Background of Chiropractic School Faculties*, 197 J.A.M.A. 999 (1966).
[28] *See* Regulation of Health Personnel, ch. 1, at 61.
[29] ANDERSON REPORT, ISSUES CONFRONTING THE DELEGATES AND MEMBERS OF THE AMERICAN CHIROPRACTIC ASSOCIATION AS THEY SEEK TO SOLVE THE PROBLEMS OF CHIROPRACTIC EDUCATION 8-10 (1964); AMERICAN MEDICAL ASSOCIATION, CHIROPRACTIC: THE UNSCIENTIFIC CULT 5 (1966).

current medical licensure laws, which in many jurisdictions specify course and curricular requirements, unduly hamper medical education and training.[30] An educational curriculum which because of rigid legal restrictions cannot be made more responsive to new technology, scientific progress, the information explosion, and changing patterns of medical care, is not serving the public's best interests.

In the case of medicine, many specific statutory curricular requirements were prescribed in the pre-Flexner era to give physicians some exposure to certain preclinical and clinical subjects. Most specific requirements, however, were the product of implementation of the recommendations of the Flexner report and were designed to close down or improve inadequate medical schools, diploma mills, and commercialized educational programs. However, those problems have long since been resolved, and other problems, such as requirements for curricular innovation in subjects ranging from medical genetics to community medicine, have arisen. Meanwhile, the statutes have been neither modified substantively nor interpreted with the flexibility needed to respond to changing requirements.[31]

Similarly, the statutory requirement for licensure of physicians in over thirty jurisdictions specifying the internship as a separate entity rather than as part of a program of graduate medical education can operate as a barrier to innovations in graduate medical education and to more effective coordination of undergraduate and graduate medical education.[32] This has been pointed out in the report of the Commission on the Graduate Education of Physicians.[33]

II

INNOVATIONS IN USES OF MANPOWER

Innovations in uses of health manpower and experimental programs to train and utilize new categories of health professionals require new allocations of patient care tasks among members of the health professions and occupations and a regulatory program to permit experiments to demonstrate the safety and effectiveness of new kinds of health workers and of new uses for existing kinds of health manpower.

A. New Allocations of Patient Care Tasks

1. *Expansion of Tasks Performed by Present Categories of Allied and Auxiliary Manpower*

Expansion of the tasks performed by present nonphysician manpower categories requires legal authorization by legislative, administrative, or judicial action. In view of past experience, legislative expansions would appear to be unlikely because of

---

[30] *See generally* Regulation of Health Personnel, ch. 1, at 20-21. *See also* address by Ruhe, Federation of State Medical Boards of the United States, in Chicago, Ill., Feb. 11, 1967.
[31] Regulation of Health Personnel, ch. 1, at 21-22.
[32] *See generally id.* at 23-26.
[33] CITIZENS COMM'N ON GRADUATE MEDICAL EDUCATION, THE GRADUATE EDUCATION OF PHYSICIANS 61-63 (1966). For further elaboration of the problems of graduate medical education, see L. COGGESHALL, PLANNING FOR MEDICAL PROGRESS THROUGH EDUCATION (1965).

reluctance to expand tasks performed by present categories until there has been antecedent demonstration of the safety and effectiveness of the new allocation practice by the profession or occupation. However, such antecedent demonstration is curbed by the threat of civil and criminal sanctions for exceeding the statutory scope of practice.[34] Consequently, innovations in uses of present categories of health manpower must be sanctioned by expansive judicial and administrative interpretation of existing licensure laws. The difficulties encountered in achieving such expansions through interpretation can be illustrated by taking a typical "model" statutory definition of professional nursing and speculating on the judicial responses to the scope-of-nursing-practice problems presented by such a statutory definition.

Definitions of the practice of professional nursing address themselves to the two basic types of services that can be rendered by professional nurses—nursing duties which must be performed under orders of a physician and those which the nurse can perform without supervision of a physician. Most nursing practice acts provide in substance that (1) under no circumstances can a nurse diagnose or prescribe therapeutic measures; (2) under orders of a doctor, a nurse can "administer medication and treatments"; and (3) a nurse can independently supervise and teach other personnel, observe care given to and counsel the ill, maintain health, and prevent illness if limitations (1) and (2) are observed. The definition most commonly used provides as follows:[35]

> The term "practice of professional nursing" means the performance, for compensation, of any acts in the observation, care and counsel of the ill, injured or infirm or in the maintenance of health or prevention of illness of others, or in the supervision and teaching of other personnel, or the administration of medications and treatments as prescribed by a licensed physician or a licensed dentist; requiring substantial specialized judgment and skill and based on knowledge and application of the principles of biological, physical and social science. The foregoing shall not be deemed to include acts of diagnosis or prescription of therapeutic or corrective measures.

The most difficult problems concern those activities that lie between the traditional practices of nursing and medicine. For example, do the medical and nursing practice acts permit specially trained nurses, working under standing orders from a physician, to administer cardiopulmonary resuscitation by means of a Pacemaker machine to patients suffering from cardiac arrests? Good patient care may require that this function be performed by nurses and others in many instances, but legal authority for this practice has not been defined clearly.

Resolution of such problems requires an analysis of the purposes and meaning

---

[34] *See* cases cited note 9 *infra*.

[35] The quoted definition has been adopted as a "model definition" by the American Nurses Association. It has been adopted into the laws of Alabama, Alaska, Colorado, Delaware, Hawaii, Idaho, Illinois, Kansas, Kentucky, Montana, New Hampshire, North Dakota, South Carolina (regulation), Utah, and Washington. Variations of the model definition exist in Arizona, Florida, Maine, Nevada, North Carolina, and Oregon.

of the phrase "administration of medications and treatments" and also the phrase "the foregoing shall not be deemed to include acts of diagnosis or prescription of therapeutic or corrective measures." These phrases often give little help in resolving an interpretative problem, such as that concerning the use of a Pacemaker machine by a professional nurse. It is apparent that literal interpretation can produce results which impede innovations in health services and which are not required by considerations of patient safety. For instance, the latter phrase is too restrictive since it is clear that professional nurses can prescribe and do apply certain therapeutic or corrective measures, such as rendition of first-aid and minor treatments in occupational and industrial medical programs. The purpose of this attempted limitation on the scope of nursing practice is to distinguish nursing from medical practice by excising from nursing practice certain types of *acts*. However, it fails to point to the real distinction between a nurse and a physician—namely, the nature of the medical judgments that each is capable of making.[36]

The difficulty with the present statutory definitions is that they attempt to resolve difficult scope-of-practice issues through the use of vague and ambiguous classifications without establishing guidelines by which the public, the courts, administrative agencies, and the professions themselves can determine scope-of-practice issues not specifically resolved by statute.[37] Without further statutory definitions and standards, such terminology is subject to a variety of inconsistent administrative and judicial interpretations. Even within individual states, considerable judicial and administrative interpretation will be necessary to establish with reasonable certainty the content of the criteria. On the other hand, of course, legislative semantic precision is not necessarily desirable because of the inflexibility it could produce.

The primary attempts by the courts to clarify scope-of-practice problems on a case-by-case basis have not been satisfactory. Scope-of-practice issues can come before the courts in the form of malpractice suits, actions for declaratory judgments, and criminal prosecutions for illegal practice.[38] In general, the decisions in such actions have been based on rigid and narrow construction of the statutes rather than upon broad policy considerations involving optimal allocation of tasks among health workers and expanded accessibility of medical care.[39] Moreover, the decisions tend to turn on very narrow points, such as definition of prevailing custom and usage.[40]

Strict construction of these statutes can, of course, be justified on the policy premise that mandatory licensure is designed to protect the public from persons not

---

[36] *See* Hershey, *Scope of Nursing Practice*, 66 AM. J. NURSING 117 (1966).
[37] Committee on Industrial Nursing of the Council on Industrial Health, *The Legal Scope of Industrial Nursing Practice*, 169 J.A.M.A. 1072 (1959).
[38] *See* cases cited note 9 *supra*.
[39] *See, e.g.*, Magit v. Board of Medical Examiners, 57 Cal. 2d 74, 366 P.2d 816, 17 Cal. Rptr. 488 (1961); People v. Whittaker, Civil No. 35307, Justice Court of Redding Judicial District (Shasta County, Cal., Dec. 1966); Barber v. Reinking, 68 Wash. 2d 139, 411 P.2d 861 (1966).
[40] *See, e.g.*, People v. Whittaker, Civil No. 35307, Justice Court of Redding Judicial District (Shasta County, Cal., Dec. 1966).

meeting appropriate standards of ethics, education, and training.[41] Accordingly, it can be argued that the performance of medical functions by nonphysicians should be permitted only when expressly authorized by statutory exceptions. Under this approach, responsibility for developing legal rules and standards regarding delegation of medical tasks is left to the legislature rather than to the courts or administrative agencies or to supervising physicians.[42] While failing to provide needed flexibility and the opportunity to apply a broad public interest standard, such an approach by the courts is understandable and may be even proper inasmuch as the courts lack the necessary experience to make qualified judgments on the broader questions.[43]

The extent to which various licensing agencies deal with scope-of-practice issues is not known, but some tentative conclusions on the administrative approach to scope-of-practice problems can be drawn from a review of the licensure statutes, administrative regulations, and cases.[44] Administrative agencies have seldom used their power to "promulgate rules and regulations"[45] to clarify scope-of-practice problems.[46] Although this hesitancy to encourage more flexible and efficient uses of health manpower through administrative rules is probably based on the perceived original purposes of licensure statutes, administrative agencies should reconsider their position in view of changed policies and needs of the public. The present procedures for authorization of innovations in uses of health manpower have thus produced a significant responsibility gap. This gap is characterized on the one hand by legislative inaction until innovations have been adopted into regular medical practice and on the other hand by judicial and administrative deference to existing legislation. Certainly the greatest criticism should be directed at the administrative agencies, which have failed to recognize the problem and their power to deal with it.

Because of the many variables, both medical and legal, involved in the propriety of delegations, it is difficult to resolve the issue through statutory standards and the accumulation of case law criteria. Ideally, the problem warrants a tripartite solution: first, broad statutory provisions in which the legislature strikes a balance between policies of public protection and manpower use; second, formulation of specific but flexible administrative regulations by a specialized administrative agency applying new broad policies to health service delivery practices; and third, an adjudicative process in which the administrative agency primarily and the courts

---

[41] *See* Indiana State Bd. of Dental Examiners v. Davis, 69 Ind. App. 109, 121 N.E. 142 (1918).

[42] "The history of legislation discloses that in this, as in many other states, there has been developed gradually a policy to commit to boards of experts the question of what persons are qualified and competent and should be permitted to practice in professions and engage in callings that bear directly upon the public health." *Id.* at 128, 121 N.E. at 148.

[43] *Id.* at 128-31, 121 N.E. at 148-49.

[44] *See generally* Regulation of Health Personnel, ch. 2.

[45] *See, e.g.,* CAL. BUS. & PROF. CODE § 2119 (West 1962); IND. STAT. ANN. § 63-907 (1961).

[46] The administrative regulations typically fail to elaborate upon the statutory scope of practice definitions. *See, e.g.,* Cal. Ad. Reg., tit. 16, ch. 14 (1966); 4 Burns Ind. Ad. Rules & Reg., tit. 63, ch. 9 (1967).

secondarily may construe and enforce the statutes and regulations.[47] Early consideration of such a solution is necessitated by the real possibility that, until the issue of delegation is clarified, new and desirable uses of present categories of health manpower may be inhibited by legal uncertainties.

2. *Creation of New Categories of Health Manpower*

In addition to expansion of the scope of present categories of health manpower, optimal allocation of health services requires creation of new categories of health manpower. Merely expanding the scope of present categories is insufficient because in medicine, for example, present legally defined categories of nonphysician manpower are not broad enough to encompass the many medical care tasks which are evolving as new technologies and processes are incorporated into preventive, curative, and rehabilitative services.

Present licensure statutes make no provision for the orderly and systematic creation of new categories of health manpower. Consequently, recognition and widespread use of new categories of manpower will normally be enacted only if such a category of personnel exists and seeks licensure. Obviously, such categories are unlikely to develop without legal recognition because of fear of criminal or civil penalties for engaging in illegal practice.

Legal barriers to the creation of new categories of health manpower through custom and usage arise because the practice of medicine encompasses all health service functions.[48] Consequently, rendition of health care without a medical license violates the medical practice acts unless such services are performed pursuant to the limited license of an allied or auxiliary occupation or profession. Thus, where unlicensed personnel, even working under the direct supervision and control of a licensed physician, are used to perform new functions, the medical practice acts are violated, and enforcement of the licensure statutes could result in any or all the following: disciplinary action against and possible revocation of the licenses of those physicians utilizing such personnel;[49] revocation or suspension of the licenses of any physicians assisting or abetting such utilization;[50] criminal (both misdemeanor and felony) prosecution of personnel rendering the services;[51] criminal (felony) conspiracy prosecution of persons involved in planning the utilization of such services;[52] and injunctive relief restraining further activities in violation of the licensure laws. Needless to say, the threat of such consequences, or even of proceedings seek-

---

[47] If the administrative agencies were structured to properly protect the public interest, consideration should be given to limiting judicial review to due process questions.
[48] Regulation of Health Personnel, ch. 1, at 2.
[49] *E.g.*, Newhouse v. Board of Osteopathic Examiners, 159 Cal. App. 2d 728, 324 P.2d 687 (1958) (supension of license for thirty days); *see* Magit v. Board of Medical Examiners, 57 Cal. 2d 74, 366 P.2d 816, 17 Cal. Rptr. 488 (1961) (revocation of license by Board of Medical Examiners set aside as abuse of discretion).
[50] *E.g.*, CAL. BUS. & PROF. CODE §§ 2361, 2372 (West Supp. 1967); § 2392 (West 1962).
[51] *E.g.*, CAL. BUS. & PROF. CODE §§ 2141, 2141.5 (West Supp. 1967).
[52] *E.g.*, People v. Marsh, 58 Cal. 2d 732, 376 P.2d 300, 26 Cal. Rptr. 300 (1962).

ing to impose them, constitutes a great obstacle to the creation of new categories of health manpower.

The recent California case of *People v. Whittaker*[53] illustrates some of the legal problems of using new categories of health manpower. The case involved a neurosurgeon's use in brain surgery of a trained surgical assistant as an "extra pair of hands." The assistant operated a cranial drill and Giegle saw positioned by the surgeon to bore holes and excise skull flaps during operations. The jury found the assistant guilty of practicing medicine without a license and the surgeon guilty of aiding and abetting an unlicensed person to practice medicine.

The situation is further complicated by a recent decision of the Supreme Court of the State of Washington. In *Barber v. Reinking*,[54] the plaintiff brought an action against a physician and his practical nurse to recover for injury caused by the negligence of the nurse in administering a hypodermic injection. Since the state licensure statute provided that such an injection could be administered only by a licensed professional nurse, the court held that the practical nurse would be liable if she did not have the knowledge and skill possessed by a licensed registered nurse. Her failure to be so licensed raised an inference, which the jury was allowed to consider, that she did not possess this required degree of knowledge and skill. Additionally, evidence that it was the custom and practice in the community for practical nurses to administer such injections was held inadmissible. This case departs from prior decisions holding that evidence of violation of a licensure statute is irrelevant and has no direct bearing upon the skill or care of the defendant.[55] Although the physician's liability in *Barber* was presumably based on *respondeat superior*, the decision increases the possibility of a successful malpractice claim based on the negligent delegation of authority and thus provides an added deterrent to the use of trained but unlicensed health personnel.

B. Experiments to Demonstrate the Safety and Effectiveness of New Manpower Uses

1. *Removing the Legal Impediments*

Clearly, there are substantial legal barriers to experimental programs to develop, train, and use new categories of health manpower. The present legal climate fails to encourage experimentation in the uses of manpower largely because interpretations of licensure standards have neglected broad policy considerations. Such current problems in the delivery of medical care as manpower shortages, the spiraling costs of care, the gap between the kinds of care that *can* be given and the kinds that actually *are* given, and the distribution of care to urban ghetto dwellers and the rural

---

[53] Civil No. 35307, Justice Court of Redding Judicial District (Shasta County, Cal., Dec. 1966).
[54] 68 Wash. 2d 139, 411 P.2d 861 (1966).
[55] *See* Brown v. Shyne, 242 N.Y. 176, 151 N.E. 197 (1926); Gregory, *Breach of Criminal Licensing Statutes in Civil Litigation*, 36 CORNELL L.Q. 622 (1951).

poor have not entered into the making and administration of licensure laws. Furthermore, innovations and experiments are subject to the risks of penal and quasipenal sanctions as well as malpractice civil liability involving large sums of money, and even if there were a basis for confidence that sanctions and damage judgments could be avoided by lengthy litigation, the cost and strains of such litigation is a mammoth deterrent to engaging in such innovations in the first place.

The existing inhibitions against innovations in patterns of delivery of personal health and medical care, in tasks performed by health and medical personnel, and in kinds of health and medical personnel used are not the result of deliberate and planned legislative action. They developed during the evolution of the present occupational licensing statutes when other policy considerations, namely protection of the public against unethical and incompetent practitioners and commercial deception by providers of medical care, were predominant. Removal of these inhibitions is necessary in the light of the conclusion of the President's National Advisory Commission on Health Manpower that the present crisis in the provision of medical care cannot be averted or effectively ameliorated without substantial innovations in the patterns of delivery of health care, even if massive increases in the number of health personnel could be achieved.[56]

Any changes in present licensure laws should balance the public's need for protection from commercial abuses and from research that is scientifically or ethically improper against the need for innovations in the delivery of personal medical care. Commercialized efforts at shortcutting personnel standards would probably continue to be deemed objectionable under the same principles that underlie existing licensure laws, and even where the commercial motive is absent, regulation may be required to guide the pace and direction of innovation and to protect the public against uncontrolled efforts. Even with legislation authorizing new manpower uses on an experimental basis, programs implementing that authorization would continue to be subject to the legal controls applicable to clinical investigation generally; most importantly, this means that the patient's informed consent must be obtained before he is employed as an experimental subject.[57] That clinical investigation is involved seems clear, since manpower experiments are nothing less than the introduction into the medical care process of a new input the value and effectiveness of which have not been demonstrated and which presents potential risks to the health and safety of the patient. Additional legal controls over such experiments may be deemed essential or desirable.

What may be needed is a regulatory program that does the following things:

(1) permits experimental programs by universities and other qualified institutions and individuals for the purpose of developing and demonstrating the

---
[56] HEALTH MANPOWER REPORT 2.
[57] *See generally* Fletcher, *Human Experimentation: Ethics in the Consent Situation*, in this symposium, p. 620; Stason, *The Role of Law in Medical Progress, id.*, pp. 563, 580-95.

safety and effectiveness of new categories of and new uses for existing categories of health manpower;

(2) regulates such programs so that patients will be protected against irresponsible and dangerous experiments and so that hazards to patient safety which develop during the course of such experimental programs can be controlled; and

(3) permits the translation of those innovations that have been demonstrated to be safe and effective into regular patterns of medical care.

Such a program of regulation could be created only by legislation.

A federal program, if it were feasible, would be the most expeditious means of reform. However, political realism makes this course seem unpromising at this time. Moreover, a serious question exists as to whether the federal government's interest in the provision of medical care, growing out of its commitment to the Medicare program, is sufficient to support constitutionally the encroachment on state police powers that would be entailed. Nevertheless, such a law, perhaps restricted to authorizing activities at hospitals participating in Medicare, might pre-empt state legislation, thereby permitting experimentation, training, and employment of federally licensed persons in states where licensure acts would otherwise prove an obstacle. A general sort of precedent for the type of regulation that might be adopted can be found in the Kefauver-Harris amendments to the Food, Drug, and Cosmetic Act in 1962, which govern drug experiments with human subjects.[58]

The Kefauver-Harris amendments illustrate that the public can benefit from the fruits of experimentation and still be protected from uncontrolled and harmful research.[59] Before a drug manufacturer can clinically test a new drug in patients, it must first justify testing the drug on humans and obtain authorization from the Food and Drug Administration. Among other things, the sponsor of the test must (1) demonstrate that adequate animal, chemical, and other tests indicate clinical tests on humans can be initiated with reasonable safety; (2) demonstrate that adequate provision has been made for protection of the public on such matters as selection of qualified investigators, supervision of all patients, and obtaining of the consent of all subjects; and (3) maintain detailed records including the names and addresses of all subjects. The length of the investigational period is limited, and the FDA has the power to terminate the investigation or require it to be modified if there is evidence that the drug is unsafe. Only when the sponsor can produce substantial evidence that the drug is safe and effective is authority to distribute the drug commercially granted by the FDA.[60] While substantial dissimilarities exist

---

[58] Pub. L. No. 87-781, 76 Stat. 780 (1962).

[59] For a more detailed discussion of the Kefauver-Harris amendments, see Rankin, *Progress on Investigational Drugs*, 19 FOOD DRUG COSM. L.J. 237 (1964); Comment, *The Drug Amendments of 1962*, 38 N.Y.U.L. REV. 1082 (1963).

[60] 21 U.S.C. § 355 (1964).

between drug experimentation and experimentation with new manpower uses, adaptation from this system of regulation could prove both desirable and feasible.

State legislation is a more promising goal than federal intervention in an area that in its major aspects is traditionally one of state concern. If one or a few states would amend their licensure laws to permit controlled experimentation in manpower uses, progress could at least begin. Demonstrable success might then lead to further amendments to licensing laws to regularize the employment of new categories of personnel or to broaden the functions of established categories. Work should now begin on a uniform or model health manpower act which could be presented to the states for legislative consideration, as will soon be done in the area of gifts of human tissues for transplantation purposes.[61]

If states choose to regulate experimentation with manpower uses, the federal program for regulating drug experiments might prove to be a useful model. Alternatively, a more modest program might be established to provide something like the following:

(1) that experimentation and training involving unauthorized uses of health manpower might be conducted in university hospitals if a comprehensive plan of the experiment or training program was submitted to and approved by an appropriate hospital committee and filed with the state licensing authority. Particular conditions might be imposed, such as requirements for physician supervision and for written consent from all patients whose care was delegated to nonphysicians as part of the program.

(2) that new functions for existing categories of medical personnel could be created by the state licensing authority upon a showing that experimental results and medical manpower requirements warranted a finding that such action was in the public interest.

(3) that persons trained in such training programs could be licensed on an ad hoc basis, to perform only those functions enumerated in the license, upon certification of competence by the hospital and a showing that experimental results and medical manpower requirements warranted a finding that such action was in the public interest.

This hypothetical program is merely one example of how the issue might be handled, and its exposition here reflects no conclusion that this is the preferable approach. Such a conclusion must await further study and a careful evaluation of the degree of risk that attends programs of the sort that must be created. The author's current involvement in a study of this kind leads him to expect that a recommended legislative solution can soon be devised.[62]

---

[61] Stason, *The Role of Law in Medical Progress*, in this symposium, pp. 563, 571-72.
[62] See references cited note 14 *supra*.

2. Designing the Research

While legal reform is essential to wide-scale employment of new categories of health personnel and to the expansion of the functions of the existing categories, the first objective must be legal authorization of necessary research. Experimentation must be allowed to supply the lacking performance and operational data upon which new legal standards can be based. The medical profession must be prepared to meet this need for experimental data, and thought must now be given to the technical and ethical facets of the experiments to be performed.

The technical facets of manpower experiments will involve planning and designing the program in the way most likely to amplify the quantity and quality of physician-directed medical care. Perhaps the major challenge is the selection of the particular innovations to be attempted. This can be done through the use of pre-experimental models and simulations so that the innovations' cost and potential value can be determined. Criteria for evaluating the performance of individuals and classes of individuals must be developed, and methods for measuring or otherwise determining safety and effectiveness must be incorporated in the research plan. Medical knowledge must be drawn on to establish the necessary scope of the training of specialists for particular tasks, and methods of instilling limited technical capacity and understanding in persons lacking substantial technical training will be essential.

The ethical facets of such experiments must also be considered. These relate to protecting the health, safety, and welfare of the patient from irresponsible, dangerous, and unnecessary experiments. Such problems as the patient's informed consent and the physician's supervisory responsibility must be faced in the context of the legal and ethical considerations applicable to human experimentation generally. Attention must also be given to the difficult problem of striking a balance between patient safety and the potential social value of the innovations being attempted. Whether or not a regulatory framework enforcing these various requirements is developed, the physician's responsibility for adherence to high standards in dealing with these matters will be the same.

III

POLITICAL PROSPECTS: CAN ANTICOMPETITIVE LICENSING LAWS BE LIBERALIZED?

It has been contended that "[l]icensure is the key to the control that the medical profession can exercise over the number of members."[63] If current licensing is, in fact, valued by the medical profession as an anticompetitive device, attainment of the legislative revisions discussed above, which ultimately will amplify the quantity and reduce the cost of physician-directed medical care, may be virtually impossible.

---

[63] Milton Freedman, untitled lecture at Wabash College, summer 1959, quoted in Moore, *The Purpose of Licensing*, 4 J. LAW & ECON. 93 (1961).

This raises two key questions: First, are current licensure laws really laws against competition? Second, even if they were originally intended to limit competition, does it necessarily follow that revisions to expand the delivery of care will be vigorously opposed by the regulated professions and therefore politically unfeasible?

There is considerable controversy over whether licensure laws regulating the practice of the health professions and occupations were designed primarily to thwart new entry and competition or to protect the public interest. Evidence accumulated by a survey-study published in 1961, which analyzed regulated occupations and requirements for entry into them, indicated generally that the concept that society knows best what is good for the individual rather than profit-preserving, monopolistic motives prompted enactment of current licensure laws.[64] However, this study also noted that some particular regulations in the over-all laws, such as those restricting geographic mobility or limiting practice to U.S. citizens or residents of the licensing jurisdiction, clearly show anticompetitive motives.[65] The study concluded that while legislatures seem to license those occupations the regulation of which is most in the public interest, in doing so they usually establish particular regulations which benefit practitioners by restricting competition.[66]

Another analysis of this issue has concluded that economic (anticompetitive) motivations govern licensure of the health professions and occupations.[67] Based on a review of the history of licensure laws, this study noted that licensure laws gained a firm foothold in the United States between 1890 and 1910 as a legitimate exercise of the police power to protect the public health and safety and with the full support of many of the same forces which vigorously opposed social legislation to regulate child labor and the working conditions of women and children.[68] The U.S. Supreme Court, which in 1889 had held that restriction of the right to practice medicine was a legitimate exercise of the power to protect the public health and safety against the dangers of professional incompetence,[69] ruled in 1905 that state regulation of hours and working conditions in bakeshops designed to protect the health of workers was an unconstitutional restriction of freedom of contract.[70]

---

[64] Moore, *supra* note 63, at 93.

[65] For a discussion of citizenship requirements, see Fisher & Nathanson, *Citizenship Requirements in Professional and Occupational Licensing in Illinois*, 45 CHI. B. RECORD 391 (1964). Note, for example, that Hawaii, presumably as a protection against an influx of established professionals attracted by the climate, requires residence in the state for one year and does not endorse the licenses of any other states. HAWAII REV. LAWS § 64-3(b) (Supp. 1965).

[66] Moore, *supra* note 63.

[67] L. Friedman, *supra* note 18, at 505.

[68] *Id.* at 487.

[69] Dent v. West Virginia, 129 U.S. 114 (1889).

[70] Lochner v. New York, 198 U.S. 45 (1905). Professor Lawrence Friedman contends that if a worker had the constitutional and God-given right to contract to work eleven hours per day in a bakery or to be paid in kind instead of cash, he should have had a similar right to contract with an unlicensed physician. L. Friedman, *supra* note 18, at 489.

Even though it can be concluded that current licensure laws have clear-cut anticompetitive purposes and features, it does not follow that all statutory revisions that will amplify the supply and quality of physician-directed medical care will have to overcome the vigorous, economically motivated opposition of the power structure of the regulated health and medical occupations and professions. The demand for the services of the health industry far exceeds the current supply, and it is growing more rapidly than the supply in spite of large public-sector expenditures to increase manpower and other facilities. Therefore, practitioners are not apt to feel threatened by legislative revisions of the type proposed, and anticompetitive motivations should not have much real economic and political force. Furthermore, all economic studies tend to show that as the efficiency and productivity of the health professions are increased, either through technological innovations or increased use of ancillary personnel, the incomes of the professions tend to rise accordingly. Consequently, threats of economic competition will probably have minimal real significance in legislative revisions or current licensure standards to promote manpower innovations and to expand the productivity of the personal health care delivery system. Educational efforts within the licensed professions can effectively assuage whatever apprehensions are found to exist.

Summary

Shortages of all skilled health personnel, both physicians and others, new scientific and technological developments, and new methods of organizing health services have made the question of new uses for allied health personnel the critical issue to be resolved if our supply of health manpower is to be used effectively and productively. Analysis of licensure laws regulating health personnel and administrative and judicial enforcement procedures and attitudes indicate that present legal regulation of health manpower restricts optimal allocation of tasks among members of the medical manpower matrix and operates as a barrier to experiments to train and utilize new categories of health professionals. The many and complex factors involved in expanding the functions of allied personnel warrant a revised legal approach perhaps utilizing broad statutory standards, the expertise of an administrative body, and judicial supervision. Primary consideration must be given to the creation of a regulatory scheme to facilitate experimental programs to train and utilize new categories of health professionals and to translate experimental findings into patterns of regular medical care. To this end, state legislatures must remove the barriers to experimental programs designed to supply the necessary data and knowledge to introduce new categories of health professionals into the personal health service industry.